TOWARD the CONQUEST of CANCER

TOWARD the CONQUEST of CANCER

by Edward J. Beattie, Jr., M.D.

Memorial Sloan-Kettering Cancer Center

with Stuart D. Cowan

A HERBERT MICHELMAN BOOK

CROWN PUBLISHERS, INC.
NEW YORK

Inquiries should be addressed to Crown Publishers, Inc., One Park Avenue, New York, New York 10016

Printed in the United States of America

Published simultaneously in Canada by General Publishing Company Limited

Library of Congress Cataloging in Publication Data

Beattie, Edward J
  Toward the conquest of cancer.

  "A Herbert Michelman book."
  Bibliography: p.
  Includes index.
  1. Cancer—Prevention. I. Cowan, Stuart D., joint author. II. Title. [DNLM: 1. Neoplasms—Popular works. QZ201 B369t]
RC268.B42   1980   616.99′4   80-14462
ISBN: 0-517-541882

10 9 8 7 6 5 4 3 2 1

First edition

DEDICATED
WITH LOVE AND ADMIRATION
TO
PAULINE HORN COWAN
1918–1974

*She fought a gallant fight against the only
enemy she ever knew. May this book give her
death meaning by helping others to live.*

Contents

Preface

AS A PHYSICIAN AND SURGEON who has cared for cancer patients for thirty-five years, I—like my colleagues—am distressed by the unreasoning fear of the disease, the reluctance to discuss it openly, and the clouds of untruths that hover over the word *cancer*.

Fear and ignorance can lead to delay in seeking diagnosis and treatment, delay that may mean the difference between living or dying. One of the most powerful weapons against cancer is an informed public—and that is the objective of this book:

• To demystify cancer and encourage people to regard it as simply another disease—like heart disease—to which mankind is heir, and to talk about it openly.

• To correct the inaccurate information that appears in print and on radio and television and alarms people unnecessarily.

• To show how a surprising number of cancers can be prevented, perhaps as many as 40 or 50 percent.

• To demonstrate that, when detected early and treated properly, about 50 percent of all cancers can be cured (the cure rates for some cancers are in the 80 to 90 percent range); to replace fear and pessimism with hope and optimism.

• To reduce the unnecessary cancer deaths, which are estimated at over 130,000 a year in the United States alone.

• To inform you how to obtain the best of medical care should you, a loved one, or a friend come down with cancer (the quality of medical care varies from doctor to doctor and hospital to hospital).

• To take you into Memorial Sloan-Kettering Cancer Center, New York, to see how physicians diagnose and treat one of the most serious—and preventable—forms of cancer.

Or, stated less precisely, to tell the truth about cancer in order to prevent the disease whenever possible, increase cure rates, and lessen grief and suffering. A side benefit: *preventing* illness is the single most effective way to reduce soaring health care costs, which take money from the pocket of every taxpayer.

I realize that cancer is not the world's most popular subject for a book no matter how vital the information may be to the 50 million of us in the United States who are healthy today but who will—one future day—contract cancer. But the potential for, quite literally, saving thousands of precious lives, and the looks of surprise and relief on the faces of those restored to health, have encouraged me to press on with this project.

Many people helped in many ways in the preparation of this book and I am indebted to them for their advice, assistance, and encouragement.

At Memorial Sloan-Kettering Cancer Center: Kathleen M. Foley, M.D.; Robert A. Good, Ph.D., M.D.; Raymond W. Houde, M.D.; John S. Laughlin, Ph.D.; David Schottenfeld, M.D.; C. Chester Stock, Ph.D.; and Lewis Thomas, M.D.

Ernst L. Wynder, M.D., and Daniel G. Miller, M.D., furnished data on the causes and prevention of cancer and provided valuable ideas and suggestions.

Special thanks go to the *Medical Tribune* for permission to use the material in Chapter 12, and to the individuals whose statements appear in that chapter.

Arthur Holleb, M.D., Adele Paroni, and Edwin Silverberg of the American Cancer Society provided major assistance and graciously granted permission to reprint from ACS literature.

I am most grateful to Frederick Carl Lane, M.D., and Mr. B. E. Spruill for their permission to reprint the letter that appears at the end of Chapter 15.

Willis Kingsley Wing and Herbert Michelman were generous with their counsel and support.

As in every work of this sort, countless individuals helped it see the light of day. At Memorial Sloan-Kettering Cancer Center: Miriam Adams, Rhanda Estrellado, Dina Mastoras, and Tamara Zenck. Others who contributed in many ways: Samm Sinclair Baker, Louise Bradley, Mary Frederick, Jean Hall, Edith Hoy, and James Rahman. Our thanks and appreciation to each of them.

Stuart Cowan and I became friends forty-five years ago as

Princeton freshmen. That friendship was renewed and strengthened when his wife, Pauline, came down with a serious lung cancer. Tragically, Pauline died a year and a half later. As Stu and I talked about cancer, the gestation of this book began. Since he is a writer, a natural team developed with my talking and Stu collecting data and writing. Without his work, persistence, and intelligence, this book never would have been written.

Edward J. Beattie, Jr., M.D.

New York, N.Y.
May 15, 1980

Acknowledgments

Grateful acknowledgment is made to the following for their assistance in furnishing information and/or permission to reprint previously published material:

American Board of Medical Specialties; American Cancer Society; American College of Surgeons; American Dental Association; American Health Foundation; American Heart Association; American Lung Association.

Edward M. Brecher and the Editors of Consumer Reports: *Licit & Illicit Drugs,* Little, Brown & Co.; © 1972 by Consumers Union of the United States, Inc.; quotation from Chapter 24.

Canadian Cancer Society.

Center News and *Clinical Bulletin,* Memorial Sloan-Kettering Cancer Center, New York, N.Y.

Connecticut Hospice, Inc., for permission to reprint Hospice Goals from the publication *Frequently Asked Questions About Hospice,* New Haven, Conn., 1978.

Georgetown University, Public Services Laboratory.

Joint Commission on Accreditation of Hospitals.

Ann Landers, Field Newspaper Syndicate, *The Daily Item,* Port Chester, N.Y., for permission to reprint the column in Chapter 13.

National Hospice Organization; Preventive Medicine Institute/Strang Clinic; The Tobacco Institute.

Schick Centers for Control of Smoking; Seventh-day Adventists (Five-day Plan); SmokEnders.

U.S. Department of Agriculture; U.S. Department of Energy; U.S. Department of Health, Education and Welfare (Bureau of Radiological Health; Food and Drug Administration; National Cancer Institute; Office on Smoking and Health; Public Health Service).

The Unhappy Truth About
the Cancer We Give Ourselves

IN NOVEMBER 1977 A LOVELY 48-YEAR-OLD WOMAN, a devoted wife and the mother of three attractive children, was referred to Memorial Hospital by her physician for diagnosis. Her persistent cough had become more violent and the spells lasted longer. But she looked well, felt well, and had experienced no pain or weight loss.

"I simply can't believe there is anything wrong with me," she said at our first appointment. She held her husband's hand tightly.

Four days of diagnostic tests were inconclusive, which is sometimes the case, but we suspected cancer of her right lung. The chest X rays showed a vague white shadow in her upper and middle lobes—but shadows in chest X rays can be caused by a number of conditions other than cancer.

Thoracic surgery is indicated to arrive at a positive diagnosis in about 15 to 20 percent of these cases and to remove the malignant (life-threatening) lesion if our suspicions are correct.

After a frank discussion of the problem and her alternatives, the patient and her husband agreed that surgery was the wisest course.

As Margaret Young* lay relaxed and asleep on the operating table a day later, I examined her wide-open chest, pried apart by the rib spreader.

The three lobes of her right lung, nestled together, expanded and contracted rhythmically as the anesthesia machine breathed for her, sighing as its pleated black bellows rose and fell. Her pinkish lobes were sprinkled with black streaks and splotches.

My first assistant patted the area dry with a white gauze sponge, soon stained red, and suctioned her chest cavity.

Then I saw the tumor—the grasping, grayish tentacles twisting their way through the tissue of her middle and upper lobes.

---

*Not her real name. All patients' names are fictitious.

Fourteen minutes after small bites of the formless foreign growth were shot by pneumatic tube to the Pathology Department for evaluation, a metallic voice echoed from the intercom loudspeaker on the green wall of the operating room.

"Dr. Beattie, Room 6. On Mrs. Margaret Young, patient number 48-77-43. We received specimens identified as tissue from the right upper and middle lobes. On frozen section, we see large cell undifferentiated carcinoma."

Lung cancer.

I swallowed hard.

Knowing that cancer of the respiratory system is increasing at an alarming rate—and is a major death threat to hundreds of thousands of men and women—never has the same impact as facing a person suffering from lung cancer. Statistics numb the mind, but one sick patient shocks it into focus.

Mrs. Young should have had 25 to 30 years of life ahead of her, but now the chances were slim that she would live many of those years. Only 12 percent of female lung cancer patients are alive five years after diagnosis.

A week after her operation she told me about her little blonde granddaughter and the joyous times they had together. "I love little girls. I hope I can live to see Susan grow up."

"I hope so too," I said softly. "We'll do everything that medicine can do."

Her husband leaned over her bed and kissed her.

Lung cancer has claimed more than its share of the world's good people: the courageous woman who cared more about cheering up the patients on our fifteenth floor than the fact that she was dying . . . the internationally famous physician whose research brought relief to victims of Parkinsonism . . . the young general whose experience and judgment were lost to his country . . . the beautiful, deeply religious woman who on Easter morning sat up in bed, eyes closed, hands cupped for communion as our hospital chaplain read the service; her husband beside her, eyes dimmed with tears, pinching his thigh until it bled.

Lung cancer is no respecter of person: among its victims were Nat "King" Cole, King Edward VI, Walt Disney, Betty Grable, Edward R. Murrow, Boris Pasternak, Robert A. Taft, Franchot Tone, Robert Taylor, Chet Huntley, and too many more—rich and poor, known and unknown.

Cancer Is Not a Disease of Modern Man

Cancer is a complex family of diseases with more than 100 different types classified according to cellular variations as viewed under a microscope. Some types grow slowly, others rapidly.

Cancer strikes men, women, and children of all ages and races in every country in the world. Fossils tell us that ancient man and the prehistoric creatures that once roamed the earth also contracted cancer, so it is not a disease of modern civilization as we are often told. Fish, birds, and animals develop cancer, and some plants, such as the tomato plant, produce cancerlike growths.

Certain cancers are triggered by external environmental influences, whereas others are "blind accidents" born of biochemical breakdown within our bodies, perhaps aided by a weakened immune defense system, which allows the rioting cells to gain a foothold.

Although we do not yet understand the basic disease mechanism of cancer, we can prevent a surprising number of malignant neoplasms—perhaps 40 or 50 percent or more—and encouraging progress has been made in curing cancers that are detected early and treated properly. Cure rates for some forms of cancer are in the 80 to 90 percent range. Cancer is far from an automatic sentence of death.

Every living creature possesses a built-in biological clock that controls the complex aging process and fixes the length of life for each species. Butterflies live 7 months, mice 2 years, birds 2 to 5 years. Dogs and cats live 12 to 18 years and tortoises 150 years. Man is allotted the biblical three score years and ten, although if he remained free of disease man would live into his nineties before wearing out naturally. Lulled by life, we are prone to forget that we are all mortal and that eventually we all must die.

Cancer is closely related to the aging process and is largely a disease of the older years, although it is the number one killer of women between ages 30 and 54, and the number two killer (after accidents) of children 3 to 14.

Cancer is intimately linked to the innermost secrets of life itself, and when the cause and cure of the disease are discovered, they will inevitably be intertwined with the aging process. The minute molecular world of cells is an obscure concept to grasp, and scientists often cannot see the breathtaking world in which they work: *one million human cells make a clump the size of the head of a pin.*

The event of human reproduction, accepted so casually, is as close to a miracle as most of us are likely to get. Each female ovum houses 23 chromosomes, and each male sperm carries 23 chromosomes. The sperm and the egg unite to create one human cell with 46 chromosomes, one-half of the genetic code contributed by the mother and one-half by the father. From this single microscopic cell evolve the precursor cells that divide and grow into the enormous number and variety of cells in the human body—all triggered and instructed by that *single original cell* with its genetic code of 46 chromosomes. This code, in effect, issues billions of instructions to the undifferentiated cells: "You go to the liver," "You build an eye," "You become a leg bone"—until 300 trillion cells have evolved into one living human being.

As the baby takes shape within the womb, the growth and division of cells is astonishingly rapid—but organized and controlled with incredible precision. The cells assigned to create the liver stop dividing the instant that organ is formed. The order to "stop" is obeyed without question.

In cancer, the cells do not stop dividing and growing but continue unplanned, disorganized division, piling up on one another, shoving their way into healthy organs, and creating a mass of excess tissue— a tumor—which causes death if it overwhelms a vital function. If the tumor is not detected early, microscopic cells may break away from the primary tumor and be carried by blood or lymph to distant parts of the body where they seed new malignant growths; this spreading is termed metastasis and is the worst characteristic of cancer. Early malignant tumors that have not invaded adjacent tissue or metastasized are almost 100 percent curable.

Not all cancers are solid tumors. Leukemia is cancer of the blood-forming tissues, such as bone marrow. Lymphomas affect the lymphatic system—the body's disease-fighting network.

When science discovers what triggers the loss of cell control, a cure for cancer will not be far behind. In the meantime, the best one can do is to keep a cool head in the midst of the hysteria and misinformation about cancer and its causes which bombard us. It is the fashion to criticize everything from cancer treatment to food additives with little reference to the facts, and this sort of thing alarms the public needlessly.

Example: The nitrite and nitrate used to preserve meat and prevent deadly botulism cause cancer, we are told, and must be banned. What we are not told is that nitrites and nitrates occur naturally in grains, vegetables, and dairy products, and it is not known whether the nitrosamines they may form cause cancer in man. Or, that human saliva is a rich source of nitrite and that we swallow more nitrite in a day than we could get from cured meats in a month. Or, that the incidence of stomach cancer has dropped sharply—and the stomach is the first place food additives end up, so that by rights stomach cancer should be going through the roof—but instead it has decreased 80 percent in the past 50 years.

Example: Some self-styled nutritionists preach that BHA and BHT—preservatives added to cereals and baked products—are dangerous and cause cancer and other disease. Scientific studies show precisely the opposite: BHA and BHT protect us by blocking the action of cancer-causing chemicals; however, they may have other undesirable effects, and better substitutes are available.

Food-borne carcinogens (cancer-causing agents) exist in small quantities in some parts of the world, but evaluation is extremely difficult because symptoms seldom appear at the doses ingested, and cancer takes many years to develop and occurs only in a small percentage of those exposed. On the other hand, what we eat, and do not eat, plays an important, indirect role in causing, and preventing, cancer.

Cancer Is Not Increasing—With One Tragic Exception

One reads, hears on the radio, and sees on television that the incidence of cancer in the United States is "soaring," "epidemic," and "increasing at an alarming rate." It's enough to keep a person awake nights—except for one thing:

These statements are not true.

The fact is that if it were not for cancer of the lung, the age-adjusted cancer death rates are leveling off and in some cases declining. The major increase in lung cancer among both men and women obscures the progress in other cancers. Lung cancer is the number one cancer that we give ourselves, and every year it kills nearly twice as many people as the next type of cancer (more than 100,000 deaths predicted for 1980).

• Stomach cancer has dropped sharply in the past 50 years for unknown reasons.

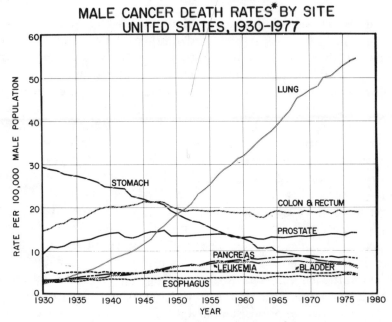

MALE CANCER DEATH RATES* BY SITE
UNITED STATES, 1930-1977

* Rate for the male population standardized for age on the 1940 U.S. population
Sources of Data: National Vital Statistics Division and
Bureau of the Census, United States.

• Deaths from cancer of the uterus have decreased more than 70 percent in the past 40 years due to early diagnosis by the Pap test and to improved treatment.

• Cancers of the rectum and esophagus have decreased substantially.

• Cancer of the bladder has decreased in women but increased slightly in men. Lesions of the colon, prostate, and pancreas have increased slightly in men.

• Overall cancer deaths among women have decreased between 1950 and 1977, 9 percent for whites and 7 percent for blacks.

The careless statistics that purport to show that cancer is increasing are wrong:

1. They fail to take into consideration the substantial increase in overall U.S. population.

2. They do not take into account the vastly greater number of older people alive today; in earlier days people died younger of pneumonia, scarlet fever, diphtheria, tuberculosis, poliomyelitis, and other diseases that medicine has conquered.

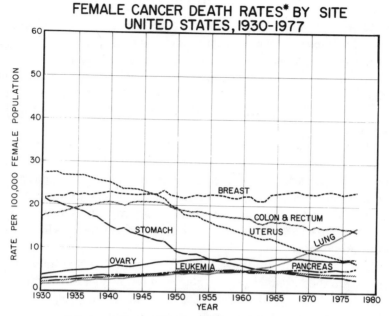

**FEMALE CANCER DEATH RATES* BY SITE
UNITED STATES, 1930-1977**

RATE PER 100,000 FEMALE POPULATION

YEAR

BREAST

COLON & RECTUM

STOMACH

UTERUS

LUNG

OVARY

LEUKEMIA

PANCREAS

* Rate for the female population standardized for age on the 1940 U.S. population
Sources of Data: National Vital Statistics Division and
Bureau of the Census, United States.

3. They do not recognize that cancer is more prevalent in older people than in younger people, that cancer is more accurately diagnosed and reported than it used to be, and that improved treatment means that more ex-cancer patients are living longer.

In order to make valid comparisons of the incidence of a disease between different groups, the rates of occurrence must be "age-adjusted." This technique takes the population groups being compared—such as those of 1900 and 1970—and adjusts them so that each group contains the same number of people in the various age brackets. The incidence of a disease is usually expressed as the number of cases per 100,000 of population.

As the illustrations show, the one malignant neoplasm that is increasing every year is cancer of the respiratory system—the two bronchi and the lungs. At least 80 percent of these cancers are caused by smoking cigarettes over a period of from 15 to 30 years and could be prevented by not smoking. While 30 million Americans have stopped smoking in the past 25 years, 54 million men, women, and children continue to smoke (39 percent of the men, 29 percent of the women, and an alarming number of children imitating their parents).

If present smoking trends continue, 10 times more Americans will die of lung cancer in the next 70 years than died in all the U.S. wars fought from the American Revolution through Vietnam.

And this shocking figure of more than 7 million deaths does not include the deaths from cancers of the mouth, throat, vocal cords, bladder, pancreas, and kidney to which cigarette smoking is a major contributing cause.

Neither does this figure include the even greater number of premature deaths from heart and circulatory diseases that result from cigarette smoking. Nor does it include the spontaneous abortions, premature births, stillborn babies, and the infant deaths shortly after birth attributed to the nicotine, carbon monoxide, and other chemicals absorbed by the fetuses of mothers who smoke during pregnancy.

All told, cigarette smoking kills 325,000 men and women every year—a number about equal to the population of Miami, Florida.

The economic cost of smoking is estimated at $18 billion a year in medical bills (private and government), disability payments, lost production, and lost taxes.

Unfortunately, the cure rate of respiratory cancers is among the lowest of all forms of the disease because lung and bronchial lesions are "clinically silent" and cause no signs or symptoms until a late, dangerous stage at which point it is usually too late to save the patient. About half of all lung cancer patients cannot be helped by surgery because when diagnosed they have advanced tumors that have already metastasized (spread).

It is conservatively estimated that today 200,000 men and women in the United States are walking about their daily lives, unaware that malignant tumors are growing silently in their bronchial tubes or lungs.

Tests to detect respiratory cancers earlier in individuals at high risk (heavy cigarette smokers) are discussed in Chapter 10. The cure rates for lung cancers detected early should be 50 to 80 percent compared to today's dismal rate of about 10 percent.

Lung cancer deaths among women have increased 400 percent in the last 30 years and are still rising as their past smoking habits catch up with them. If the trend continues, by the early 1980s lung cancer will replace breast cancer as the number one cancer killer of women in the United States. Men still have the questionable honor of leading the field in respiratory system cancer, but women are gaining on them. As the U.S. Surgeon General's last report stated, "Women who smoke like men die like men who smoke."

Many Cancers Can Be Prevented

Dr. Ernst L. Wynder, president of the American Health Foundation, wrote in a professional paper, "[We should] remind ourselves of the old lesson of history—that nearly all of the great triumphs of medicine have come not from therapy, but from prevention. . . . Prevention of disease, and specifically environmental cancers, may be possible long before the mechanisms of their induction are understood."

After observing that milkmaids who contracted cowpox never got smallpox, Dr. Edward Jenner in 1796 inoculated an eight-year-old boy with cowpox that immunized him against smallpox and led to the conquest of this scourge. . . . Raging against his colleagues, Dr. Ignaz Semmelweis eventually convinced physicians that antisepsis would prevent the dreaded childbed fever that killed thousands of young mothers. . . . And in 1949 John Enders at Harvard isolated the poliomyelitis viruses that led to vaccines against this fearsome childhood crippler.

A great many cancers are caused by tobacco, diet, ionizing radiation, drugs, chemicals, alcohol, and administered hormones. Relatively easy changes in life-style and dietary habits, steering clear of known hazards, and simple examinations will prevent 40 to 50 percent of all cancers, perhaps more. *Mormons and Seventh-day Adventists who practice some of these measures average 35 percent less cancer than the general U.S. population.* Chapters 8–11 and Reference Information I are devoted to the causes and prevention of cancer where this is possible with our present knowledge.

If 40 percent of the estimated 785,000 new cases of cancer in 1980 were prevented, 314,000 fewer people would have come down with the disease.

I find it impossible to understand why there is such concern about the possibility of saccharin causing cancer and relative apathy about cigarette smoking, which causes more cancers than saccharin ever could—if, indeed, saccharin causes lesions in man. (Since the above was written, three recent studies confirmed that saccharin does not cause cancer in man.) Such are the mysteries of the human mind.

As far as the devastation wrought by cigarettes is concerned, there are bright spots on the horizon:

- The 30 million Americans who have stopped smoking.

- The laws and regulations that restrict smoking in public places.

- The *New York Times* put this lead on a smoking story:

"WARNING: Smoking is hazardous to your social standing." Increasingly, hostesses say, "Yes, I do mind if you smoke."

Many Cancers Can Be Cured

Most people know little about cancer except that it is the most feared of diseases. They hesitate to talk about it openly, and they believe it is an automatic sentence of death—*which it is not*. The outlook for cancer reminds me of Mark Twain's answer when asked his opinion of Richard Wagner's music: "It's probably better than it sounds."

The world does not look upon cancer as just another disease like "heart trouble"—yet the chances of being cured of cancer are often better than those of surviving heart disease: nearly half of all those who suffer acute coronary attacks die immediately or within 30 days.

Today, 50 percent of all cancer cases could be cured if the disease were detected early enough and attacked promptly with the most effective medical treatment. And the cure rates for a number of early Stage I cancers are even higher:

Breast Cancer	80 percent
Colon-rectum cancer	70 percent
Cervical cancer	95 percent
Skin cancer	99 percent
Melanoma	80 percent
Hodgkin's disease	90 percent
Childhood leukemia	90 percent in remission in three years; expect to cure more than 50 percent

You sometimes hear the term *stage* used in connection with cancer; stage refers to the status of the tumor at time of diagnosis.

Stage I—early, localized tumor; *in situ* (in one place); no regional involvement (spread or metastasis).

Stage II—tumor has invaded underlying tissue but is still localized.

Stage III—cancer cells have metastasized (spread) to regional lymph nodes; termed "regional involvement."

Stage IV—malignant cells have spread throughout the body; advanced cancer.

More than 3 million Americans are alive today who once had cancer, and every year they are joined by another 250,000 men, women, and children cured of the disease; these figures do not include the approximately 440,000 people cured of common skin cancer and cancer *in situ* of the cervix each year. Every year about 60,000 more people are cured of cancer than in the 1950s.

If a cure is not possible, then in a number of cases there is a good chance of long-term remission with an acceptable quality of life that reduces cancer to a livable chronic disease, like diabetes or some types of heart disease.

Unfortunately, none of this is true where lung and bronchial cancers are concerned. Early detection is very difficult and the cure rate of all respiratory system cancers in the United States is a discouraging 9 percent.

When a woman enters Memorial Hospital with a breast tumor the size of a golf ball that she has known about for 20 months, or when a man is admitted with a palpable mass in his lower abdomen and a year of rectal bleeding—those are the cases that generate grim statistics.

Cure—"To Heal, Make Well, Restore to Health"

In cancer, a cure is successful treatment in which the disease is eradicated and the patient restored to health. In addition, a precautionary period—usually five years—is added from the date treatment ceases to be sure there is no evidence of disease (N.E.D.) during this time; microscopic cells sometimes linger behind in the bloodstream or lymphatic system and cause a recurrence. The length of the precautionary period is set by the physician and may be as short as one year (skin cancer) or as long as ten years (breast cancer). Once a person passes this milestone, he is considered cured since his chance of dying from a recurrence of that cancer is statistically small. As a matter of good health care, every former cancer patient should have a physical examination annually for the rest of his life.

Although lung and bronchial cancers are among the most stubborn to cure, they are the easiest to prevent since at least 80 percent can be prevented by not smoking cigarettes. But even with the barrages fired against smoking in the past 25 years, 54 million Americans continue to smoke. The latest facts are disturbing, to say the least:

• 100,000 children age 12 and under smoke, it is estimated in the U.S. Surgeon General's report, *Smoking and Health,* issued in January 1979.

• An estimated 6 million girls and boys, ages 13 to 19, smoke cigarettes.

• Teenage girls and young women are smoking more; the percentage of girls 12 to 14 who smoke has increased 800 percent since 1968.

• Pregnant women who smoke are more likely to experience labor complications and bear children with physical and mental defects.

• As success in business is achieved, men smoke less but women smoke more.

• In the past 30 years, deaths among women from lung cancer have increased 400 percent, and are still rising.

What has gone wrong?

Is there something at work that has been underestimated?

The answer, almost certainly, is yes.

Cigarette Smoking Is Drug Addiction

Research among cigarette smokers in 1975 by the U.S. Public Health Service disclosed that 82 percent believe that smoking frequently causes disease and death and that two out of three are concerned about the effects of smoking on their health. The majority of smokers would like to quit, and nine out of ten have either tried to quit or would if there were an easy way to do it.*

If this is true, why then do 54 million Americans place their lives on the line by continuing to smoke?

The answer is not a mystery, although not widely acknowledged: *The nicotine in cigarettes is a major addictive drug, as addictive, some believe, as heroin and morphine.*

"Kicking" an addictive drug habit is not easy, and smokers deserve understanding, assistance, and moral support from family, friends, and physicians—not social scorn or "the stigma of second-class citizens." It is not true that people who continue to smoke are weak-willed or lack strength of character. They are simply hooked on a powerful, pernicious drug. Nicotine is far more addictive than alcohol or barbiturates.

That nicotine is addictive has been known for years, but the fact has never received the attention and publicity it deserves. Most smokers are unwilling to admit addiction; "I'm not addicted," they say. "I can quit anytime!" But they cannot. Teenage smokers do not know that smoking is a true drug addiction that will be very difficult to break later on; many say they plan to quit "in four or five years," but by that time they are hooked.

"Cigarette smoking is true addiction," according to Dr. Vincent P. Dole of Rockefeller University, a leading authority on drug addiction. "The confirmed smoker acts under a compulsion which is quite comparable to that of the heroin user." The level of nicotine—an alkaloid poison—in the brain is a crucial element in this addiction; smoking a pack and a half a day gives the brain a shot of nicotine every 30 minutes of every waking hour.

When heavy smokers (two packs a day) quit, most of them suffer withdrawal symptoms that vary from moderate to severe and may include one or more of the following: nervousness, irritability, drowsiness, difficulty in concentrating, anxiety, fatigue, constipation or diarrhea, dizziness, sweating, palpitations, insomnia, and tremor. Light smokers (half a pack a day) and moderate smokers (a pack a day) have light to moderate addiction and can stop without undue

---

*This research also showed that men with college educations, white-collar jobs, and high income levels are less likely to smoke than high school graduates, blue-collar workers, and men with low incomes. Women who work are more apt to smoke than housewives. Teenagers who smoke are often poorer students than nonsmokers.

withdrawal problems *if* they make a firm decision to quit.

There is evidence that users become tolerant to nicotine and that withdrawal, in some instances, leads to antisocial behavior—both characteristics of genuine drug addiction.

All this explains a phenomenon that shocks doctors when they first encounter it: the lung cancer patient who, after removal of a lung, can't wait to light his first cigarette; the patient whose cancerous larynx (voice box) was removed, smoking cigarettes through his stoma (the hole in his throat); the dying emphysema patient, gasping for breath, who alternates between smoking and breathing oxygen.

Hard to believe?

It happens all the time.

Tests show that a smoker smokes to obtain the drug nicotine. *Lancet*, the English medical journal, reported that when smokers received nicotine by injection, their craving for cigarettes dropped and they smoked less or not at all. A Swedish study and University of Michigan Medical School research confirmed this finding.

Perhaps the most tragic case is that of Dr. Sigmund Freud, who smoked 20 cigars a day and suffered from severe nicotine addiction. This distinguished physician tried to stop smoking but without success.

Sores which did not heal developed on his palate and jaw and the psychoanalyst underwent 33 operations for cancer of the mouth and jaw. In his closing years, Freud had an artificial jaw and relentless pain; often he could not speak, chew, or swallow. Sigmund Freud died of cancer in 1939, an addicted smoker to the end.

Eric Sevareid, formerly of CBS, with his gift of straight talk, hit the heart of the problem when he said, "Confirmed smokers know even better than nonsmokers that it's a rotten habit, dirty, dangerous, expensive; it makes one feel good only for the moment and lousy all the other moments; but for millions, it's an addiction they can't break without a prolonged agony they can't face. . . . Smokers would probably prefer pity to scorn; it could be the beginning of wisdom in this matter."

Psychological Dependence

Cigarette smoking is a complex behavioral phenomenon which involves psychological dependence as well as varying degrees of addiction to nicotine. Dr. Daniel Horn, former director of the

National Clearinghouse for Smoking and Health, who developed the helpful booklet *Smoker's Self-testing Kit*, identifies six "feeling-states" which give smokers insight as to why they smoke. These are stimulation, handling, relaxation, tension reduction, craving, and habit.

Despite physiological and psychological dependence, anyone can break the smoking habit *provided* his or her motivation is sufficiently strong. Interestingly, the two most often cited reasons for quitting are (1) "mastery of my own life" and (2) "disease prevention" and "setting a good example for my children," which tied for second place.

One of my surgeon friends who broke a two-pack-a-day habit told me, "My motivation wasn't only that cigarettes undermine your health, but I was setting a rotten example for my children and my patients. How could I tell them not to smoke if I smoked? Besides, I hated being a slave to a dirty, expensive habit and a tool of the cigarette companies—I wanted to damn well control my own life."

The Effects of Smoking Are Reversible

The precancerous changes that occur in many smokers start to reverse themselves the day that a smoker quits, and after 10 to 15 years ex-smokers enjoy the same life expectancy as nonsmokers of the same age group. The other benefits are immediate: no coughing and wheezing, healthier cardiovascular system, less shortness of breath, better stamina, food tastes better, breath is not offensive, reduced fire hazard, and so on.

So when a smoker says, "There's no point in my quitting now— the damage is done," *that simply is not true.* A number of physicians believe that giving up cigarettes is related directly to intelligence, that is, the more intelligent a person is, the more apt he or she is to be a nonsmoker. Dr. Ernst Wynder believes that "within 20 years, lung cancer will principally be a disease of the low-income, less-educated population."

A "Safe" Cigarette?

A safe cigarette that would not damage the cardiovascular system or cause lung cancer is obviously the ideal solution—provided smokers would buy it. The problem, however, is incredibly complex and it is doubtful whether such a cigarette can ever be developed, despite the efforts of the tobacco industry and the U.S. government.

A nonnicotine cigarette failed miserably in England a few years ago when smokers refused to buy it, presumably because it did not satisfy their need for nicotine. Nicotine and carbon monoxide are the chief villains in heart and blood vessel disease.

It may someday be possible to remove the cancer-causing agents (carcinogens) from cigarette smoke and leave the nicotine, which would result in a "half-safe" cigarette. This is a formidable task since there are more than 1,200 components in cigarette smoke. The smoke is composed of 12 gases hazardous to health, including carbon monoxide, nitrogen oxide, and hydrogen cyanide; particulate matter that is inhaled, most of which remains in the lungs and bronchi; and tar composed of hundreds of chemicals some of which are carcinogens and cocarcinogens (agents that combine with other substances to produce a carcinogen).

On the positive side, smokers who switch to low-tar, low-nicotine, filter cigarettes reduce their health risks although these cigarettes are by no means safe. Among those who smoked cigarettes with the lowest tar and nicotine ratings, deaths from heart disease dropped 14 percent and from lung cancer 26 percent, according to an American Cancer Society study. In 30 years the tar content of the average cigarette has been reduced 50 percent and contains fewer carcinogens; more than half the cigarette brands now contain 15 mg. of tar or less.

Studies of lung tissue taken at autopsy showed that filter cigarettes with reduced tar and nicotine cause markedly fewer precancerous cell changes than regular cigarettes; this research was conducted by the Veterans Administration Medical Center, East Orange, New Jersey, and the American Cancer Society.

One area that bears watching in less harmful cigarettes relates to the flavor additives used to improve taste. "You need to be careful that these additives are harmless," says Dr. Ernst Wynder. "We are continually monitoring this and other developments that relate to the less harmful cigarette."

Is It Safe to Smoke Marijuana?

"With all the bad news about cigarettes, at least I can smoke pot and enjoy it," one veteran smoker told me with a sigh of relief. Apparently, a number of smokers believe that marijuana is harmless compared to cigarettes.

I am sorry to bear bad tidings, but there is every indication that smoking marijuana may be more harmful than presently believed and could be a greater health hazard than cigarettes. The truth is that we know almost nothing about the long-term effects because insufficient time has elapsed since studies were initiated, and the studies to date are conflicting in their conclusions. But the preliminary findings are disturbing:

• The principal drug in marijuana is fat-soluble and remains in the body for days before being metabolized; regular smoking causes a buildup in body organs.

• Marijuana increases the heart rate and weakens the heart's contractions, which can be dangerous to people with certain heart problems.

• Marijuana may contribute to stillbirths, miscarriages, and birth defects by creating breaks in the chromosome chain that carries genetic information; the evidence is not conclusive.

• Chronic use is reported to decrease the level of the male sex hormone testosterone.

• The drug can cause psychological dependence in some people.

On the positive side, in some cases marijuana relieves the nausea caused by cancer chemotherapy and reduces the pressure of vitreous fluid in the eye in glaucoma.

Clearly, additional research on the effects of smoking marijuana is urgently needed.

"Tell Me What It's Like to Have Lung Cancer"

Since in 1980 lung and bronchial cancer will cause the premature deaths of more than 100,000 men and women in the United States, preventing this disease offers an unparalleled opportunity to save precious lives. That is why the story that follows deals with this pervasive threat to the health, happiness, and financial resources of so many families.

Two years ago an attractive Massachusetts woman was telling me her troubles in quitting a two-pack-a-day habit after 24 years of smoking.

Suddenly she said, "I have an idea, Dr. Beattie. Why don't you tell me what it's like to be sick with lung cancer?

"Tell me how a person feels . . . the symptoms . . . how you diagnose lung cancer . . . and how you treat it.

"Perhaps *that* will help me to stop smoking!"

I followed this intelligent woman's suggestion—and it did help her to stop smoking. And that, in turn, led to the story of Austin Raymond and his fight against lung cancer.

Mr. Raymond's dramatic tale is that of patients treated at Memorial Sloan-Kettering Cancer Center, New York, during the past four years. Actual names could have been used, but in the interest of a broader, more vivid portrayal I have used a composite personality. The feelings, anxieties, and experiences of various patients have been combined in the story of Austin Raymond, the journalist who finds himself facing one of the personal crossroads that everyone encounters during his lifetime.

For the first time, you will see a patient referred to a cancer center, learn the problems of diagnosis, and be in the operating room as a chest operation is performed.

Austin Raymond's history will interest those who wish to know more about the medical world, its triumphs and its failures, but should be of particular significance—and perhaps assistance—to cigarette smokers. Removing the mystery from the diagnosis and treatment of the most threatening cancer in the world may help people realize what is at stake and, once again, become masters of their lives.

A word about the hospital you are about to enter.

Founded in 1884 as the New York Cancer Hospital, the first institution to specialize in the treatment of cancer, Memorial Sloan-Kettering Cancer Center is the largest private, nonprofit institution in the world devoted to cancer treatment, research, and education. Occupying 10 buildings in New York City, its staff totals 5,000, including 300 attending physicians, 220 physicians-in-training, 700 nurses, 750 technicians, and 850 volunteers.

The Sloan-Kettering Institute, the research division, has 96 laboratories working to develop improved means of preventing, detecting, diagnosing, and treating cancer. Promising laboratory developments are brought promptly to bedside.

Memorial Hospital physicians pioneered new techniques in surgery, radiation therapy, chemotherapy, and immunotherapy, and established the first facility devoted to the treatment of childhood cancer. A separate outpatient building handles nearly 135,000 outpatient visits a year. People come from all over the world seeking the latest in diagnosis and treatment.

I know of no better way to catch the spirit of Memorial Hospital than by quoting from a talk by Dr. Lewis Thomas, president of Memorial Sloan-Kettering:

"There are, among our responsibilities here, no trivial problems. The hospital has 565 beds, and faces each morning 565 issues of life or death. The Outpatient Department is always crowded with patients whose very survival is at stake. The scientific mission of the Institute is itself a question of life or death. The business of the Center is as serious a business as the human mind can imagine."

Now, join my colleagues and me as we fight to save the life of a 51-year-old man. In the next chapter, Mr. Raymond's family doctor explains his diagnosis and refers his patient to Memorial Hospital; I meet Mr. and Mrs. Raymond, conduct a preliminary examination, and arrange to admit Austin Raymond for diagnosis.

AUSTIN RAYMOND'S STORY

2

Tuesday, June 3.
Presenting Symptom and Sign: Change in
Cough; Shadow in Chest X ray

WHEN I RETURNED TO MY OFFICE from the operating room at 2:15
P.M., there was an urgent note to telephone Dr. Roy Haight, a
physician in Pennsylvania whom I knew at Presbyterian St. Luke's
Hospital in Chicago 17 years ago. I asked my secretary to return the
call, leaned back in my chair, and rubbed by eyes. Over the hum of
the air conditioning I heard the distant rumble of summer thunder.

My phone buzzed. "Roy? I'm sorry I was in the O.R. [operating
room] when you called. It's been a long time—how are you?"

After catching up on the years and mutual friends, this physician
said, "Ted, I have a patient who's a personal friend whom I'd like
you to see. You may have heard of him—Austin Raymond. He's an
ex-newspaperman who has traveled the world and now writes
magazine articles and books.

"Austin's a smoker, between one and two packs a day for many
years. About seven months ago his morning cough became worse—
he coughed longer and brought up more sputum. He went to his
druggist for cough medicine, which he took for about a month.
When that didn't help he tried to cut down on his smoking, without
much success. He switched to a brand with lower tar and nicotine
but his severe coughing continued."

Dr. Haight paused. "It was his wife, bless her, who persuaded him
to see me. She couldn't stand his hacking any longer and she was
worried. When I saw him, Austin had been on a grueling work
schedule, was exhausted and running a low-grade fever with sputum
now slightly purulent. I prescribed elixir of terpin hydrate with
codeine for his cough, and one gram of tetracycline per day because
I suspected a bronchial infection in addition to his chronic smoker's
bronchitis.

"I told him he needed a chest X ray but he delayed it until he returned from a trip to San Francisco. The treatment helped, but when he returned from the Coast and had his X ray, he was still complaining about his cough.

"His chest X ray, P.A. [posterior-anterior] and lateral, disclosed a shadow in the upper lobe of his right lung. Because of that, and his continuing low-grade fever, I wasn't certain whether he had a persistent pneumonia or whether he might have an underlying tumor as well.

"I did a gram stain in the office, saw gram-positive cocci, started him on two grams of ampicillin, and sent cultures to the laboratory. That helped, but a week later, after a violent coughing episode, he spit up blood-streaked sputum. That scared the hell out of him."

"It usually does," I said. "Have you diagnosed any specific respiratory infection?"

"No. The routine cultures were nonspecific and it looks as if the culture for tuberculosis will be negative. I have the feeling that Austin's problem may be serious. It could be a peculiar infection from his overseas trips, but it could also be lung cancer. After all, Austin's been a heavy cigarette smoker for over thirty years. Frankly, I'm worried. If it's a malignant lesion it may already be late in the game. I'd like your people to give him a thorough workup. What we need is an accurate diagnosis, and fast."

"Right. We'll be glad to see him, of course. Have Mr. Raymond come to the third floor of Memorial Hospital's outpatient building, 425 East 67th Street, at 1:30 P.M. this Thursday. I'll see him there. When he arrives, please have him check in with my appointments secretary on the third floor."

"Thanks. I'll have him bring his X rays and medical history."

"Good. We'll want to take a new chest series before I see him, as you know. You'll receive a copy of our medical report on Mr. Raymond, and I'll be in touch with you later, Roy."

Thursday, June 5

Our modern Alfred Jacobsen Outpatient Building teems with activity Monday through Friday, 52 weeks a year. In the comfortable waiting areas you might see a businessman reading the *Wall Street Journal*, a tiny black child in a wheelchair, a beautiful woman dressed like a *Vogue* model doing needlepoint, a frail elderly man walking with the help of his wife, and a husky young man with no hair who looks like a pro football tackle.

Memorial Hospital is devoted to the care of people who may have cancer, who have cancer, and who have been cured of cancer and return for periodic checkups. Since we also care for related diseases, about 30 percent of our surgical patients do not have cancer but some other disease that we treat, such as benign tumors, gallstones, stomach ulcers, and blood vessel disease.

One of our staff put it well when she said in a speech, "Patients come to Memorial Hospital from all over the world. Some are referred by physicians, many come on their own initiative. They arrive by bus, subway, limousine, cab, and plane. They walk in from the street with concerned families, or they come alone. They are of all ages, races, and from every social and economic background."

Our greatest satisfaction is to have a patient referred to us who is diagnosed as having a serious spreading cancer, and then through our diagnostic procedures, with the aid of our skilled pathologists, to find either that the patient does not have cancer at all, or that he has a new, curable cancer—not metastasis (spreading) from earlier disease. Being able to give optimistic news like that to a patient and his family is the most enjoyable moment in the life of a cancer doctor, and fortunately it happens not infrequently.

A great many patients can be treated effectively on an outpatient basis, which saves the trouble and expense of hospital admission and allows them to live at home with their families. Many hold regular jobs. Our patients visit the outpatient building for chemotherapy and immunotherapy treatments, for minor surgery, and for checkups following treatment. In 1979 there were about 135,000 outpatient visits and 15,300 inpatient admissions.

It is here that our staff doctors see patients who are referred to us for diagnosis, consultation, and possible admission, and this is where I first met Austin Raymond, the journalist, and his wife.

That morning, with assisting surgeons, I had performed a pneumonectomy (removal of a lung) on a 68-year-old woman with adenocarcinoma of the right lung. The operation lasted four and a half hours.

After soup and a sandwich, I walked to the third floor of the outpatient building and saw my first patient, Kathy Palmer, a pretty 29-year-old wife and mother from whose upper back we had removed a desmoid tumor (a slow-growing connective tissue tumor)

18 months ago. Kathy was in for her regular three-month checkup; there was no evidence of tumor recurrence and Kathy had gained 11 pounds, an achievement which pleased me but distressed her ("I'll have to let out all my clothes!").

"Mr. and Mrs. Raymond are in Room 3," my secretary said. "He's been to X ray and seen the nurse." She handed me our two X rays and the form that recorded his height, weight, pulse, temperature, respiration, and blood pressure.

Austin Raymond was a tall, thin man with a craggy face, a shock of rumpled black hair, and a broad, ready smile. He reminded me of Edward R. Murrow. His attractive blonde wife wore a black pantsuit with a silver-colored zipper down the front of her high-necked jacket. We shook hands and sat down. The cheerfully decorated examining room contained a small desk and three chairs; behind the orange and yellow sliding curtain was an examining table and related equipment.

"Dr. Haight asked me to give you these X rays and records, Dr. Beattie," Austin Raymond said, handing me a sealed manila envelope.

"Thank you." I tore it open, put the X rays aside, and skimmed the contents; I would study it later. "Mr. Raymond, before we look at the X rays, let me ask you some questions." I picked up a yellow pad and unclipped a pen from my white coat.

"By the way, how is your cough now?" I asked.

"I still have the damn thing. It hasn't gotten any better in spite of the cough medicine and the antibiotics."

"How do you feel? Any complaints other than your cough?"

"I'm a little tired from working hard but I feel pretty good. I have no pain, no weight loss, and my appetite is normal. I'm worried, naturally, about this damn cough and the shadow in my chest X ray that Dr. Haight showed me. What Barbara and I are really worried about is the possibility of lung cancer." He looked at his wife.

"I understand. But I'm sure Dr. Haight told you that shadows in lung X rays can be caused by a number of different things such as pneumonia, tuberculosis, old scar tissue, foreign bodies, partial lung collapse, fluid in the lung, infection and a tumor. Sometimes even mineral oil or oily nose drops end up in the bottom of the right lung and cause confusion and alarm. What we have to do is determine the true cause and then treat it."

I paused and read from his medical history. "I see that eight years ago at a physical examination your chest X ray showed what they termed 'fibrous tissue' in the right upper lobe. That's not too unusual."

"Yes. The doctor said it probably resulted from an old infection and was a natural thickening of the lung."

What they told him was correct as far as it went. Scar tissue in a lung may result from infection, empyemas (abscesses), fistulas (abnormal drainage channels), and tuberculosis. Anyone with scars or fibrosis (excess tissue) in a lung needs accurate diagnosis to be positive that it is a scar and not cancer; a scar should be monitored for life by chest X ray to be sure that it does not develop into a "scar cancer." I am afraid that some doctors and patients do not take old lung scars seriously enough, with the result that a scar cancer can be missed for years and grow to an advanced stage before it is detected. This was something to bear in mind in Mr. Raymond's case.

"Mr. Raymond, how long have you smoked cigarettes and how much do you smoke?" I asked.

"Oh, about thirty years, more or less. I guess I smoke two packs a day, sometimes more."

I made a note on my yellow pad.

"How old are you?"

"Fifty-one."

"Do you have headaches often? Dizzy spells?"

"No."

"How is your hearing?"

"Good, as far as I know."

"Any ear noises? Ringing in the ears?"

"Once in a while I hear a ringing in one ear but it subsides quickly."

"How is your vision? Any problems?"

"I started to wear glasses for reading when I was forty-five, but otherwise my eyesight is okay."

"Any sinus trouble, nosebleeds, or nasal obstruction?"

"No."

"Have you noticed any sores in your mouth?"

"Only an occasional cold sore."

"How about swelling in your face or arms?"

"I haven't noticed any."

"Do you ever have trouble swallowing?"

"No."

"Have you ever noticed a wheeze in your chest when you breathe? Are you ever short of breath?"

"Yes, I wheeze from time to time—doesn't every smoker? But it hasn't bothered me. I'm short of breath more than I used to be, but I attributed it to aging—I remember what Corey Ford wrote about growing older, that the stairs get steeper and the martinis stronger." Raymond laughed. (I wrote "Some S.O.B." on my pad; in transcribing my notes later my new secretary said, "I thought Mr. Raymond was a very nice man, not an S.O.B." I explained that S.O.B. meant shortness of breath.)

"Yes, growing older is a widespread affliction," I said. "Did you read what Bennett Cerf said to the friend who had greeted him by remarking 'You look great but you're not getting any younger'? Cerf replied, 'Do you know anyone who is?'"

We laughed.

"Dr. Beattie, how serious is shortness of breath? Is it a symptom of lung cancer?"

"It's always an important symptom that calls for investigation. People first notice shortness of breath on extra exertion, such as walking up a flight of stairs. Yes, it may be symptomatic of a heart or lung problem."

"Well, I guess you'd have to say I'm a little short of breath at times."

"Mr. Raymond, please let me see your fingers."

He stretched out his hands, palms down, and I examined the ends of his fingers and his fingernails. There were no signs of dysfunction or abnormal formation; for some peculiar reason, "clubbing" of the finger ends sometimes occurs in cases of lung cancer, possibly because the tumor stimulates the central nervous system, which causes excessive circulation to the ends of the fingers.

"Do you have any arthritis?"

"Not that I know of, but I've had low back pain off and on for a few years. In fact, it has bothered me more than usual in the past months." I noted this on my pad.

"Do you ever experience bone pain?"

"No, unless you count the bursitis I get occasionally in my right shoulder. It bothers me particularly when I play tennis—reaching high to serve stirs it up. God, bursitis can be painful."

"It surely can. . . . How about pain in your arms? Any tingling sensations?"

"No, except when I sleep in a peculiar position and apparently press on a nerve. My arm sometimes goes to sleep and tingles when it wakes up."

"That's nothing to worry about. . . . Mr. Raymond, how is your work going? Any changes in your work habits? Any change in your ability to concentrate?"

"I haven't noticed any change. Oh, I get frustrated like every writer. I do seem to tire more easily, and this cough is a goddamn nuisance. I tried to cut down on my smoking, but it made me so nervous that I couldn't keep it up. . . . Dr. Beattie, may I ask you a question?"

"Of course."

"Is spitting up bloody sputum a symptom of lung cancer?"

"It can be, but it usually is not. If the tumor is in the bronchus, which is very vascular—has an ample blood supply—then the sputum may be bloody. But massive bleeding does not usually occur in lung cancer. Blood in the sputum requires an explanation but in most cases it is not symptomatic of a malignant lung lesion."

"God, I'm glad to hear that," Raymond said. "What about my lack of chest pain—is that a hopeful sign?"

"That's difficult to answer precisely. There are no sensory nerves in the lungs and the majority of lung cancers at the time of diagnosis cause no pain. If the tumor has spread from the lung to the pleura—the lining of the chest—to the mediastinum in the middle of the chest wall, or to the diaphragm, then there is pain because these parts of the body contain sensory nerves. So when a lung cancer produces pain it usually means that the tumor is invading something that feels pain. Pain is obviously not a good sign."

"What about this change in my coughing, could that be a symptom of lung cancer?"

"I'm afraid it can be. In fact, a change in cough habit is the most common symptom in more than 80 percent of lung cancer cases. Of course, a change in cough may have other causes. However, it's a major symptom which needs accurate diagnosis. There are several different types and stages of lung cancer, and some forms do not cause coughing."

Austin Raymond and his wife exchanged anxious glances.

"Mr. Raymond, I'd like to listen to your chest sounds—we'll do a complete history and physical in the hospital. Please step behind the curtain and strip to your shorts."

In a physical examination, the first thing we do is make a general assessment of the patient's health to see if he seems acutely sick, weak and pale, chronically ill, or whether he appears active and responsive but understandably concerned about his condition. Alertness and color of skin are major clues. We look for obvious signs of weight loss. In a lung case, such as Austin Raymond, we are especially interested in skin color—whether the patient is cyanotic (blue-tinged), has trouble breathing, and is breathing rapidly—all signs of pulmonary dysfunction.

Mr. Raymond was not cyanotic although he was pale and tired.

"Have you noticed any hoarseness?" I asked.

"Occasionally, Dr. Beattie, but it was probably due to a cold at the time."

Persistent hoarseness can be a major presenting symptom of cancer in the left lung because the nerve to the left vocal cord descends to the middle of the left chest before returning to the vocal cord. We inspect the vocal cords with a mirror in the mouth and a head lamp to observe whether the cords move properly when the patient says "ahhhh" and "eeeee."

Mr. Raymond's vocal cords were normal, which I expected since the shadow was in his right lung.

With Mr. Raymond sitting on the examining table, and then lying down, I listened with a stethoscope to his breath sounds on both sides of his chest, and observed rib movement. If there is fluid in the chest, it blanks out the transmission of breath sounds. If a lung is collapsed, breath sounds are absent. I asked him to talk while I listened to his chest vibrations, known as fremitus. With pneumonia in a lung, the transmission of vibrations is increased. If there is air or fluid in the chest, then fremitus is absent.

One of the key signs we listen for are indications of obstruction in air flow. Wheezes may mean a narrowing of the trachea or bronchus, and if there is fluid in a lung you hear rales, which are the bubbling noises air makes as it passes through fluid. Rales are of various types; for example, in heart failure with fluid in a lung, there are fine rales at the bottom of the lung. In bronchial asthma, the rales are high-pitched and squeaky.

Mr. Raymond's chest sounds were normal except for some diminution of breath sounds in the area of the upper lobe of his right lung.

I observed his heart rhythm and listened for heart murmurs while feeling his pulse. We sometimes measure blood pressure in both arms and both legs since certain diseases interfere with circulation. A tumor, benign or malignant, can obstruct the veins that drain the head and arms, and we make sure that these veins are not distended by a so-called vena cava obstruction with resultant facial swelling. Distended veins and facial swelling may be manifestations of lung cancer.

I found nothing abnormal in my preliminary examination of his cardiac function.

"That's all for now, Mr. Raymond," I said. "You may get dressed. Next week we'll give you a complete examination."

I took the two X rays, clipped them side by side on the view box, and snapped on the light.

"Here's the upper lobe of your right lung," I said, outlining it with my pen. "This whitish area is what we have to investigate. Some of it is old scarring, but some of it is new.

"The right lung has three lobes, upper, middle, and lower, and provides 55 percent of the body's breathing capacity. The left lung has only two lobes, upper and lower." I drew a sketch on the pad illustrating this since it was not clear on the X rays.

"The right main bronchus comes down like this from your trachea—your windpipe—and divides into the three lobar bronchi which go to each lobe of your right lung. Inside each lobe, each bronchus divides into smaller branches to the segments and subsegments of the lobes.

"If the problem is a malignant tumor—and it may not be—we may have to remove one lobe, sometimes two, and less often an entire lung. If you are healthy, you can get along fine minus one lobe and even qualify for the U.S. Air Force. You can live a good, normal life on one healthy lung. Removing a lobe is called a lobectomy and removing a lung is a pneumonectomy. A thoracotomy is any operation into the chest.

"If we operate to make a diagnosis and the tumor is small, depending on its location we usually do a wedge incision in which only the tumor and a small margin of surrounding tissue are removed. The lung is then sewn together while the pathologist examines the tissue. If it is malignant, we would then go ahead with a lobectomy."

"It sounds like one hell of an operation," Raymond said grimly.

"Well, it's a major procedure, but done competently, the mortality rate is low, something under 1 percent in a healthy individual who is a good surgical risk and does not present complications such as cardiovascular disease. Our lung patients are usually out of bed the second or third day and go home after eight to ten days."

"I've read that the cure rate for lung cancer is very low. Is that true?"

"I'm afraid the overall lung cancer statistics are discouraging, but remember that one individual is never a statistic. A person may do a lot better than the statistics, or he may do worse. If you are cured, your cure rate is 100 percent, and if you don't make it, it is zero. Statistics can be misleading, as you know."

"What affects the outcome?"

"Oh, general physical condition, the type of lung cancer, the size and location of the tumor, how early it was diagnosed, the adequacy of medical treatment, the status of the immunological defense system, mental outlook, and so on."

"Well, if it is cancer, I'm a pretty tough old bird," Raymond said with a wry grin. "What's the cure rate for lung cancer?"

"In the United States a small lesion, diagnosed early and with negative lymph nodes, has a cure rate of 60 to 70 percent. Early asymptomatic non-oat-cell lung tumors with negative chest X ray and positive sputum cytology (showing cancer cells), which are found with a special fiberoptic bronchoscope, should have a five-year cure rate of about 90 percent.

"The cure rate of all patients who undergo a lobectomy or pneumonectomy is about 35 percent. If the lymph nodes are negative, the rate increases to 40 to 60 percent. If the nodes are positive in the lobe and negative in the mediastinum, the cure rate is roughly 20 to 40 percent."

"Those percentages are a lot better than I thought," Raymond said.

"Yes, but unfortunately the situation can be worse. If the disease is in the lymph nodes of the lobe and the mediastinum, then the cure rate drops to 5 to 10 percent. If the disease has spread out of the chest, the cure rate is very low. We're searching for ways to improve these figures but it's slow going.

"The overall cure rate for all types of lung carcinoma in the United States, treated and untreated, is about 9 percent, which is grim."

"Those are sure damn lousy odds," Raymond said, turning to his wife. She held his hand tightly.

"What I suggest you do, Mr. Raymond, is check into Memorial

Hospital next Sunday around noontime. Luckily, we have a bed for
you and my secretary will give you the details. Next Monday, we'll
start tests to see what's what. We'll do a bronchoscopy, which lets us
look inside your trachea, your bronchus, some of your small
bronchi, and parts of your lungs. We'll take small tissue samples for
lab analysis."

"I've heard that's a damned uncomfortable examination."

"I don't think it will bother you too much the way we do it. We
do bronchoscopic examinations under light general anesthesia, so
you are asleep and comfortable. Our objective is not to make sword
swallowers out of our patients."

"I'm glad to hear that."

"You will also have a complete history and physical examination,
pulmonary function tests to see how well your lungs work, X rays if
needed, and blood chemistry tests which include studies of kidney,
liver, and endocrine function.

"My secretary will give you a cytology jar to take home today.
Each morning when you awake and cough, please put a sputum
sample into the jar. Bring the jar with you on Sunday. Morning
sputum is the most concentrated and best for our analysis. The jar
contains 100-proof alcohol. If you spill it, just pour in some 100-
proof vodka, it works just as well. Our cytologists will examine the
sputum for malignant cells."

"What's a cytologist?" Raymond asked.

"A physician specially trained in cell identification. They're an
important part of our Pathology Department."

"That's a new one. Tell me, do these fellows ever make mistakes?"

"Every human being makes mistakes once in a while and lab
people are no exception. But the mistakes are very few in number
because we always err on the conservative side, and there are
numerous double checks. If there is the slightest doubt, we obtain a
second or third opinion from other physicians in the department.
Borderline tissue is difficult to classify and the same is true in
interpreting borderline X rays. During an operation if there is any
doubt about whether a frozen tissue section is malignant, we stop
the operation."

I put my notes in the envelope with Mr. Raymond's X rays and
history and stood up. "To get things going, I'd like you to see our
lab people before you leave and get the skin patch tests started.
One patch will be DNCB—dinitrochlorobenzene—which tells us

something about how well your immune system is working—your body's ability to fight off infection and disease. My secretary will tell you where to go.

"And Mr. Raymond, please don't smoke cigarettes from this point on. You have severe chronic bronchitis and your swollen bronchus is like raw beefsteak. It's important to give this irritation and swelling a chance to subside, and to give the tiny air passages in your lungs, which are now swollen shut, a chance to open up and start functioning again. We want to keep your lungs clean and well inflated because of the possibility of surgery."

I shook hands with Mr. and Mrs. Raymond. "I'll see you next Monday. In the meantime, try to worry as little as you can. Even if it is cancer, I think we have a good chance of curing it."

3

Sunday, June 8.
Admission to Memorial Hospital

Monday, June 9.
Diagnostic Procedures

In this chapter, Austin Raymond undergoes a thorough physical evaluation by a house physician. The problems of diagnosing lung cancer are discussed and the elusive clues we seek described. Mr. Raymond's "vital capacity" is measured, we discuss the precancerous changes in cigarette smokers, and a bronchoscopic examination is scheduled. Austin Raymond asks if we will tell him the truth about his condition.

ON SUNDAY, AUSTIN RAYMOND and his wife returned to Memorial Hospital where they were interviewed by an admitting officer who filled out "front sheet data"—name, address, religion, next of kin, insurance coverage if any, and so on. We admit a great many patients on weekends because other patients are discharged just before or during the weekend and beds are usually available. Weekend admitting saves valuable time.

After his interview, Mr. Raymond was given a battery of tests which included blood chemistries, blood counts, an EKG (electrocardiogram), and a urinalysis; chest X rays were omitted since we had filmed his chest three days earlier.

Mr. Raymond was then escorted to the fifteenth floor where the house officer took his medical history and gave him a thorough physical examination using an eight-page form; he also filled out a special form which we use for patients suspected of having a lung tumor. The nurse who admitted Mr. Raymond noted his height and weight (important in specifying drug dosage), took his vital signs, and made a professional nursing evaluation of the patient, writing her observations on the *Nurses' Notes* form.

Sir William Osler (1849–1919), the distinguished Canadian physician, said that the proper practice of medicine consisted of "diagnosis, diagnosis, diagnosis," and I cannot stress too strongly the universality of Osler's observation. Most of the medical mistakes that I see result from incorrect diagnosis.

In an illness with perplexing signs and symptoms and misleading or inconclusive test results, making a correct diagnosis can be exceedingly difficult even for a thorough, experienced physician. ("Signs" are the clues that a doctor seeks, such as an abnormal X ray; "symptoms" are what a patient complains about, such as a change in cough.)

The first step in accurate diagnosis is interviewing the patient with scores of questions and noting his answers no matter how insignificant they may seem. The questions cover a broad area including the five sensing organs, with emphasis on visual signs. Among the questions are these:

- "Have you ever had enlarged lymph nodes in your neck?" (Lymph nodes may become enlarged from disease, but enlarged nodes also may indicate cancer of the blood or lymphatic system.)

- "As a child, did you ever receive X-ray treatment to your chest or neck?" (Such radiation can cause cancer in later years and is no longer used.)

- "In your travels, were you ever exposed to parasites?" (Baffling diseases can result from parasites acquired in foreign countries.)

- "Have you ever had continuing problems with headache that awakens you from sleep, dizziness, or disturbed vision?" (These are important symptoms that require competent investigation.)

- "Have you ever worked in an asbestos factory or in a factory that processed coal tar or its derivatives?" (Asbestos is a carcinogen— cancer-causing agent—as are coal tar products.)

- "Are there fatty foods, or other foods, that you cannot digest?" (Such intolerance is suggestive of gall bladder disease.)

- "Have you noticed any change in bowel habits—continuing constipation, diarrhea, or black, tarry stools?" (These may be symptoms of bowel cancer, which is highly curable if detected early and treated properly.)

- "Do you ever have pains in your calves or feet when walking?" (Heavy smokers frequently have claudication—a limp—due to impaired blood circulation in the legs resulting in pain.)

• "Has anyone in your immediate family had cancer? Are your parents living? If not, what caused their deaths?" (While cancer is not inherited, there is a tendency for it to run in families.)

In the physical examination we start at the head and work down to the feet, searching for obvious and elusive clues. The eyes, for example, may lead to the diagnosis of a tumor in the upper portion of a lung because these lesions result in constriction of the pupil and a drooping eyelid (Horner's syndrome). Some of these people notice a drooping eyelid and see an ophthalmologist when what they actually have is a chest tumor.

When peripheral vision is restricted, it may be a sign of increased intracranial pressure caused by the spread of cancer cells to the brain from a primary tumor somewhere else in the body. By moving a finger, or a light, slowly into the fields of vision we check to be sure that the patient sees normally in all four quadrants.

Lung cancer, because it is the most hormone-producing of all cancers, can cause bizarre symptoms. Some individuals with advanced lung tumors, for example, secrete parathormone, the hormone that controls calcium metabolism. These people come in with hypercalcemia and are distraught and mentally confused because of the high calcium level in their blood; the hypercalcemia usually disappears when the lung tumor is removed. Of the five types of lung cancer, oat-cell carcinoma is the most apt to produce hormones.

Lung cancer may also produce an antidiuretic hormone that retards urine secretion, which in turn causes pulmonary edema (fluid in the lungs) and heart failure. So you can have a patient who presents a classic picture of heart failure when actually he has lung cancer.

If a lung tumor involves the nerve to the diaphragm, it interferes with normal breathing and the patient becomes short of breath. Or, if it involves the lining of the chest, it may produce fluid, so-called malignant pleural effusion; if any volume of fluid accumulates, the lung is compressed and the patient becomes very short of breath.

If the tumor is in the trachea (windpipe), the patient wheezes when he breathes and if it involves the esophagus, swallowing is difficult. Lung tumors may cause headaches, or a stroke, if the malignant cells have migrated to the brain.

Fatigue, general malaise, and anorexia (lack of appetite) usually are not symptoms of early lung cancer but are more apt to indicate infection or possibly metastasis to the liver.

For some strange reason, pulmonary disease can produce a condition known as pulmonary osteoarthropody, which results in "clubbing" of the ends of the fingers and toes, as I mentioned earlier. The ends of the fingers become hot and look like small balls. When the tumor is removed the swelling usually subsides. One of my patients at Presbyterian St. Luke's Hospital in Chicago was a farmer whose chief complaint was that he had difficulty getting on and off his tractor. Diagnosis revealed lung cancer with involvement of the mediastinum (center of the chest) and pulmonary osteoarthropody causing pain in his knees. Some of these people are admitted to orthopedic hospitals with "arthritis" when their problem is actually a malignant lung tumor.

The admitting physician tested Austin Raymond's hearing, looked for nasal obstruction, observed facial nerves, and felt for enlarged lymph nodes in the neck and armpits. He fingered the scalp for bumps and scrutinized the skin for moles; he asked Mr. Raymond whether any moles had changed in size or color recently (skin cancer is almost 100 percent curable, but neglected or treated improperly, it can be a frightful, disfiguring disease and can even cause death).

In exploring the abdomen we look for tenderness, masses, and signs of air and fluid. We palpate the liver to see if it is enlarged or contains hard masses, and in males we feel the testes because a testicular tumor may be the source of a malignant lung lesion. Since Mr. Raymond was in the age group (50 and up) that frequently experiences prostate difficulties, the admitting physician did a rectal examination and felt his prostate gland for nodules and enlargement. The results were negative.

While cigarette smoking inflicts major damage on the lungs, it causes 10 times as much destruction in the heart and blood vessels, and in an examination we seek signs of this damage. Smoking causes arteriosclerosis—inelasticity and thickening of blood vessel walls—which decreases blood flow to the body. This is a serious condition which results in illness and premature death. Arteriosclerosis of the blood vessels to the brain can lead to a stroke, while in the femoral artery supplying blood to the legs it can result in intermittent claudication (pain due to lack of blood supply), dusky, cyanotic toes, and even gangrene. We note whether the patient's feet are discolored as they hang down when he sits on the table.

We assay the state of the blood vessels by reading blood pressure at various places on the body (not only the arm) and by feeling the strength of the pulse in key locations (not only the wrist). An early sign of obstruction in the blood vessels to the legs is a weakened pulse in the femoral artery (which supplies the lower extremities). We feel the pulses in both carotid arteries while listening with a stethoscope, because if a blood vessel is narrowed you hear a "bruit" (a murmur or noise) caused by blood turbulence in a partially obstructed vessel. Bruit in a carotid artery may indicate impending stroke, which can be prevented by repairing the artery surgically; the carotid arteries are the two large arteries on either side of the neck that supply blood to the head and brain.

Mr. Raymond's blood pressure was 148/80 and his pulse was 84, both within normal limits although on the high side, probably because of tension. Normal pulse rates vary from the high 40s and low 50s in superbly conditioned athletes to the 70s and low 80s for most of us.

The first blood pressure figure, 148, is the systolic pressure, which is measured while the heart is contracting, pumping blood out through the arteries. The second figure, 80, is the diastolic pressure, which is measured when the heart is resting between contractions and is the low pressure in the main arteries. While both figures are important, the diastolic pressure is more indicative of potential cardiovascular trouble; in a man of Austin Raymond's age, 51, we like this figure to be 80 or less.

The admitting physician measured Mr. Raymond's blood pressure in both arms, which is good practice since it is possible to have normal blood pressure in one arm and high blood pressure in the other, especially if there is some kind of block in the aorta.

Most patients are surprised when we take the blood pressure in their legs with the cuff placed above the knees, but there is an excellent reason for this. There is a congenital anomaly where a person is born with a block in the aorta between the arms and the legs. These people have high blood pressure in the arms and low blood pressure in the legs and frequently die in their forties of hypertension. This condition, coarctation of the aorta, is surgically correctable if diagnosed correctly and treated properly. For this reason, physicians examining young adults should be alert to high blood pressure in the arms and low blood pressure in the legs, and anyone who has high blood pressure in his arms and has never had the pressure measured in his legs is not being diagnosed properly.

The human nervous system, composed of the three-pound brain, the spinal cord, and the intricate network of nerves that encompass the body, receives internal and external stimuli and coordinates the body's responses. Sensory nerves carry stimuli to the brain while motor nerves carry back the brain's decisions on how to react. The autonomic nervous system controls heart rate, blood pressure, and digestion and, for the most part, is not under conscious control.

We evaluate the central nervous system by testing facial motions, sight, hearing, balance, skin sensation, and pharyngeal motion on swallowing; we also tap tendons and watch for the involuntary response, or jerk, which confirms that a nerve reflex arc—the pathway to the brain and back—is normal. Certain neurological problems are indicated by an increased reflex response, such as when there is pressure on the spinal cord. If peripheral nerves are damaged, the knee jerk and ankle jerk may be absent.

Because Austin Raymond had complained of low back pain, we were particularly interested in his knee and ankle reflex arcs, which seemed normal although somewhat diminished. Lung cancer can cause bizarre neurological changes that are reversible with removal of the tumor. If questionable signs are noted, a complete neurological workup is ordered.

So the signs and symptoms of lung cancer may, quite literally, be almost anything and diagnosis is often difficult. When the physician has pinpointed the abnormalities he puts on his thinking cap, or programs the facts into a computer, and comes up with a list of diseases that the patient might have. He is a medical detective assembling a complex jigsaw puzzle.

Monday, June 9

Early Monday morning I met with the admitting physician, and after studying the X rays and the examination results we agreed on a diagnostic workup. I took the elevator to the fifteenth floor and went to Austin Raymond's semiprivate room, 1521B, to explain what we wanted to do and answer his questions. (My first assistant does this if I am involved in medical or administrative meetings.)

He was sitting in a chair in his bathrobe reading the *New York Times*. I pulled up a chair and sat down. "Mr. Raymond, I'd like to tell you about the tests we want to do to help us nail down a diagnosis. Don't hesitate to ask questions.

"This morning we've scheduled pulmonary function tests to tell us how efficiently your lungs absorb oxygen and expel carbon dioxide. They will also measure your so-called vital capacity.

"After lunch we want to take X rays of your right shoulder and your lumbosacral spine, the low back portion where you've noticed pain. I don't think they'll show anything, but we need to be sure."

"What about the additional X rays—I thought that X-ray radiation caused cancer," Raymond said.

"In excessive amounts, ionizing radiation does cause cancer. We use modern equipment powered by extremely high voltages and the newest X-ray tubes to reduce radiation to the patient by up to 90 percent compared to older equipment. Besides, the value of essential diagnostic X rays far outweighs the small radiation dosage a patient receives. You get more natural radiation in three days living in Denver, Colorado, at a 5,000-foot altitude than you do from one modern chest X ray."

"Well, I'll be damned," Raymond said. "What about the pulmonary function tests—are they painful?"

"No, in fact some people look on them as a sort of game. You breathe through your mouth, with a soft clump on your nose, into tanks and machines and your scores are tabulated. The tests measure the flow of air in and out of your lungs, the air distribution in both lungs, the maximum amount of air you can inhale, residual air after you exhale, and the speed with which you can inhale and exhale after exercise."

"Why do you need to know all that?"

"Because if a person has lung cancer we probably will have to remove one or more lobes and sometimes an entire lung. We need to know how efficiently each lung works and we need data to estimate how much surgery a patient can tolerate.

"Another test uses a radioactive gas, xenon-133. You breathe this odorless gas while six scanning cameras count the radioactive emissions from the alveoli—tiny air sacs—in your lungs. The appearance time and concentration of the xenon-133 in your lungs tells us about your ventilation."

"Sounds complicated," Raymond said.

"It's a sophisticated test that has been used for the past few years. We do a second test with this gas in which we dissolve a small amount in a liquid and inject it into a vein. The cameras record when the isotope reaches your lungs, how much arrives, and where in the lungs its concentration is strongest. This tells us how good the circulation is to your lungs."

"Is that the last test?"

"There's one more," I replied. "It's a measurement of arterial blood gases—the amount of oxygen and carbon dioxide, the acid/base balance, and the oxyhemoglobin saturation in blood taken from an artery."

"Do they take just one blood sample?"

"No, three. The second is after moderate exercise, which alters the concentration of the gases. The third is after breathing pure oxygen and is valuable in patients with severe lung dysfunction."

"You certainly assemble a hell of a lot of information," Raymond said.

"Yes, and sometimes we need it to save a life. If we run into something abnormal we would do a 3-dimensional X-ray movie of the heart and lungs called an angiocardiogram. Chest tumors are sometimes close to the heart, or may even be attached to it, or may be compressing the heart and blood vessels. We need to know in advance if we have to put the patient on the heart-lung machine during surgery."

"How long will these tests take?" Raymond asked.

"Most of the morning."

"If lung efficiency is so damned important, why don't doctors give a vital capacity test when they do an annual physical?"

"Some of them do and all of them should. What's needed is a spirometer—two small tanks, one inside the other, connected to a tube. When you blow into the tube, the inside tank rises and measures the volume of air your lungs can handle—your vital capacity."

"Isn't there a quick check on this?"

"Well, if you can hold your breath for one minute your lungs are in pretty good shape. But people with heart trouble should not attempt this test."

"I don't think I'll try that just now," Raymond said.

"If your lungs aren't doing their job, it affects a number of your body's organs starting with your heart. Cigarette smokers have severely reduced vital capacity from lung damage and this damage, added to the damage to the heart and blood vessels that usually accompanies it, invariably leads to disease and death.

"Smoking causes severe bronchitis and emphysema—scarring of

the lungs—which means the lungs can't transfer enough oxygen into the bloodstream and can't get rid of the waste carbon dioxide fast enough. There are more than 325,000 deaths a year in this country from illness caused by cigarette smoking."

Austin Raymond folded his *New York Times* and placed it in his lap. His mouth was a grim line. "What happens this afternoon? And how soon will you have the test results?"

"Late this afternoon. After lunch you'll attend a class to learn how to breathe and cough properly, which most people don't do. It lasts an hour and is run by our nurses and physical therapists."

"A class? For God's sake, why are coughing and breathing that mysterious?"

"Proper breathing and coughing are vital to a possible candidate for chest surgery. After a lung operation you have less lung tissue, your chest muscles hurt, you lie still, breathe shallowly, don't cough, and retain mucous secretions in your lungs. The most important thing postoperatively is to breathe properly, cough properly, and keep your lungs clear."

I paused and then added, "When you breathe and cough correctly you expand your lungs, keep them flexible, put more oxygen into your bloodstream, and speed the elimination of carbon dioxide. And after surgery this helps to prevent pneumonia and atelectasis— lung collapse. Proper breathing loosens muscles and joints and at bedtime helps you relax and fall asleep."

"Okay, I'll take your word for it," Raymond said. "How does one breathe properly?"

"Put your hand on your midriff and exhale all the air you can. Now take a deep breath and see if your hand rises as you inhale. If it does, your abdominal muscles are helping your diaphragm force out stale air and bring in clean air."

Mr. Raymond tried this several times. "Yes, I feel it now. . . . What about coughing?"

"General anesthesia dries out your respiratory tree, which forms sticky mucous secretions in your lungs. Vigorous coughing expels those muscous plugs. When they cough after surgery, most patients support the incision by holding a pillow under the arm."

"God, I bet that hurts like hell," Raymond said. "Tell me, why do you have this class ahead of time?"

"Because it's easier to teach someone preoperatively than when he has a lot of pain, is on narcotics, and isn't listening," I said. "Coughing does hurt but it hurts less each day and it's essential to a good post-op course."

An orderly pushing a wheelchair entered and I stood up."You're off to the Pulmonary Function Lab now, Mr. Raymond, and I'm due at a meeting. I'll drop around this afternoon to give you the test results and tell you about tomorrow."

At 6:20 P.M. I revisited Austin Raymond, trailed by three residents making rounds with me. He was in a chair by the window, a book open in his lap, breathing into an incentive spirometer through a corrugated tube in his mouth. An amber light atop the small white tank winked on whenever he inhaled enough air to reach a preset volume; the idea is to light the light 10 times an hour, and a counter records how often the light blinks on.

Raymond removed the tube and greeted us with a wave. "You didn't tell me about this dandy little gadget," he said. "I'm doing a little better, but making that damn light go on isn't easy. . . . Those pulmonary function tests were interesting—I had no idea I was in such lousy shape in the breathing department."

"You didn't do as badly as many heavy smokers," I replied, looking at his reports. "The tests gave us good data in the event you require surgery. I'm glad you stopped smoking last week because your chronic bronchitis has subsided a bit even though you probably exhibit the four precancerous changes that many cigarette smokers develop whether or not an active carcinoma follows."

"Precancerous changes? What are they?" Raymond asked.

"Okay. First, let me explain the construction of the lining of your trachea and bronchial tubes—the epithelium.

"On the surface are long, thin, vertical columnar cells and from these cells extend millions of tiny hairs called cilia. These cilia protect the delicate tissue by waving back and forth 50,000 times an hour moving mucus, dirt, smoke particles, and other foreign matter from the lungs and bronchi to the trachea, where they are expelled by coughing, spitting, or swallowing. Under these columnar cells lie the basal cells, which rest on a thin basement membrane.

"In every cigarette smoker a sequence of changes occurs. First, the cleansing motion of the cilia is slowed or stopped so that tar and other smoke products, dust, pollen, and other foreign matter accumulate in your lungs and bronchial tubes. Small air passages become clogged and may disappear. The cilia become paralyzed and fewer in number.

"Second, the number of columnar cells decreases and the remaining cells become flattened and enlarged into what we call a squamous structure. Third, there's an increase in the number of basal cells and a thickening called hyperplasia. Fourth, the nuclei of some of the cells become disordered and in heavy smokers there are numerous lesions consisting of cells with abnormal nuclei and no cilia."

Raymond was silent.

"The result is often a carcinoma *in situ,* that is, a small malignant growth in the epithelial—surface—layer of the trachea or bronchi. When the cells break through the basement membrane, the cancer usually spreads to other parts of the body."

"What does *in situ* mean?" Raymond said.

"That's a cancer located in only one small spot in the body which has not yet invaded adjacent tissue. *In situ* cancers are almost 100 percent curable. The problem is knowing that the lesion is *there,* since at this early, curable stage it sends forth no signs or symptoms."

"How long might a cancer remain *in situ?*"

"It depends on the type of cancer. Some indolent cancers grow slowly and silently for 20 or 30 years before being detected. We call this the latent period."

"My God, I had no idea it could take that long. I thought malignant tumors grew rapidly," Raymond said.

"No, in fact some low-grade malignant cells grow slower than normal cells. That's one reason why there are at least 200,000 cigarette smokers today—men and women—walking around leading normal lives while cancers are growing silently in their tracheas, bronchi, or lungs. It may be years before these tumors are discovered and by that time it will be too late to save most of these people."

Raymond thought for a moment. "And cigarette smoking definitely causes the four precancerous changes you mentioned?"

"Yes, it does. We believe these changes create atypical cells which precede an *in situ* cancer. There's a long chain of events over many years from atypical cell to detectable tumor."

"Why don't all cigarette smokers eventually develop cancer?"

"We don't know," I said. "But we do know that precancerous changes occur in many cigarette smokers and it may be that if they lived long enough all of them would eventually develop cancer. Remember that smoking has an even more deadly effect on the heart and blood vessels and many smokers die of heart disease or emphysema before they develop a lung tumor.

"Another theory is that some people have an enzyme in their blood which protects them, but this is only conjecture." I paused and through the window watched a small red and white helicopter beat its way past the Gothic structure of New York Hospital. "The encouraging thing is that these precancerous changes start to reverse themselves on the day that a person stops smoking cigarettes."

"They do? I'll be damned," Raymond said. "At least that's good news. . . . What's the schedule for tomorrow, Dr. Beattie?"

"We want to examine your trachea, bronchi, and lungs with a bronchoscope. Actually, we use two bronchoscopes; one is a rigid type and the other is a flexible fiberoptic instrument with which we can see around bends."

"I think you said you do bronchoscopic examinations under general anesthesia," Raymond said.

"Yes, we use light general anesthesia to eliminate apprehension and discomfort. The patient is relaxed, we don't have to hurry, and it's easier to do a thorough examination. You'll be medicated in your room to make you drowsy and in the operating room you'll be put to sleep with an intravenous barbiturate. You'll be in the recovery room for a few hours and then back in your room."

"Is the examination entirely visual or do you also take a biopsy?"

"The visual part is important but we also obtain specimens for laboratory analysis by washing, brushing, and taking tiny bites of tissue."

"What are washing and brushing?" Raymond asked.

"In a washing we inject a small amount of saline solution through the bronchoscope into the area and suction it out for examination by our cytologists. A brushing is done by rotating a tiny brush against the tissue to be studied."

"How long does it take to get the reports?"

"Usually 48 hours. The time is needed for cell staining, microscopic classification, checking, and report writing.

"Later this evening you'll be given a hospital form to sign consenting to the anesthesia and the bronchoscopy, but this conversation is your principal 'informed consent.' Do you have any more questions, Mr. Raymond?"

"Is there any danger to this examination and is there an alternative?"

"There's always a small degree of risk to any medical procedure, particularly where anesthesia is involved. But the risk is extremely low, a fraction of 1 percent. Bronchoscopic examination is the next logical diagnostic procedure since we need to know the status of your bronchial tubes. We may want to do a needle aspiration biopsy later, but I'm inclined to doubt it."

"What's that?"

"Under local anesthetic, a hollow needle is inserted through the chest wall into the tumor to collect cell samples. We get a tiny bit of material inside the needle and deposit it on a glass slide which is sent to Pathology."

"That sounds like a hell of an unpleasant procedure," Raymond said.

"Well, it's not a favorite of our patients and we only do it when necessary. A needle biopsy gives us microscopic data but doesn't tell us anything about the condition of your bronchial tree."

"How long does the bronchoscopy take?"

"It depends on what we find. If a tumor is located readily, it takes only 10 to 15 minutes. If we are investigating someone with positive sputum cytology but negative chest X rays—a so-called T_x, or unknown, tumor—then it might take one or two hours. Yours shouldn't take long."

"One last question: if I have cancer will you tell me the truth?"

"Yes, that's our policy. We tell our patients the truth but we don't burden them with a lot of clinical detail. Most people want the truth about what's wrong with them. It makes things easier for everyone in the long run."

"All right, Dr. Beattie, let's go," Raymond said.

"Good. I'll see you in the operating room at 8:15 tomorrow morning."

4

Tuesday, June 10.
Bronchoscopic Examination; Report from
Department of Diagnostic Radiology

Wednesday, June 11.
Bone Scan; Report from Department of
Pathology; Final Diagnosis

---

*With the patient under light general anesthesia, my assistant
and I explore Mr. Raymond's bronchi and lungs using a rigid
bronchoscope and a flexible fiberoptic bronchoscope.
Washings and brush biopsies are sent for evaluation by our
pathologists. On Wednesday the pathology report is received
and I discuss the diagnosis with Mr. Raymond.*

AT 6:30 A.M., HAVING HAD AN EMPTY stomach since midnight,
Austin Raymond was given by intramuscular injection pentobarbital, 100 mg., to induce drowsiness, and atropine, 0.6 mg., to dry
up nasal and throat secretions and suppress vagus nerve reflexes
that otherwise could slow his heartbeat.

In green scrub suit, hood, and mask I met him in Operating
Room 6 shortly after 8 A.M. and walked over to the operating table
where he lay. "Good morning, Mr. Raymond. How do you feel?"

A faint smile flickered on his lips. "Relaxed . . . sleepy . . . and
worried," he said, laboring over each word.

"I don't blame you, but don't worry. You won't feel any
discomfort. I'll see you this afternoon and tell you what we found.
Now the anesthetist is going to put you to sleep with an injection
through that needle in your arm."

Austin Raymond lay on his back on the table, his body draped,
his right arm taped to the arm board, palm up, fingers curled. An
electronic monitor checked his vital signs; a catheter ran to the
needle inserted in a vein in his forearm. Anesthesia was induced
quickly with thiopental and maintained with nitrous oxide and
oxygen which the patient breathed; fluothane gas was supplemental.

This man had an infiltrate in his right upper lobe that could be
pneumonia, or it could be a tumor with some atelectasis (lung
collapse) suggesting the possibility of bronchial obstruction. On the

other hand, consolidation in pneumonia can also produce bronchial obstruction. I thought that he might have a combination of infection and tumor, or all infection, or all tumor. It was by no means certain that he harbored a malignant lung lesion although I suspected that a tumor was involved. I studied his latest X rays on the lighted view box on the green operating wall.

After Mr. Raymond was asleep the nurse anesthetist under the supervision of the anesthesiologist sprayed Xylocaine, a local anesthetic, into his throat and larynx. This topical anesthesia decreases the stimulation that the bronchoscope produces and enables us to keep the patient relaxed and asleep with less general anesthetic.

At Memorial Hospital, we have 15 operating rooms for major surgery. Anesthesia is administered by a nurse anesthetist under the supervision of an anesthesiologist who is a physician. We have 28 nurse anesthetists who are all highly trained individuals skilled in the science of anesthesia. In addition to bearing responsibility for anesthesia, our 16 attending M.D. anesthesiologists are in charge of postoperative care in the recovery room and, in collaboration with the Department of Surgery, our special care and intensive care areas. General anesthesia calls for highly competent people because any time there is manipulation of the airway, risk is never far away.

"The patient is ready, Dr. Beattie," the anesthesiologist said.

The head of the table was lowered and Raymond's head tilted far back. The anesthetist removed the face mask. I slid the Storz ventilating bronchoscope slowly through the patient's mouth and down his throat. This rigid steel bronchoscope, 8 mm. in diameter and 40 cm. (15 inches) long, affords through its lens a clear view of the throat, vocal cords, trachea, and large main-stem bronchi. Through a "side arm" extension from the instrument the anesthetist maintains sleep and ensures good ventilation either by assisting the patient's breathing or by breathing for him.

I examined Mr. Raymond's vocal cords, which were relaxed in an open position and looked like an inverted V; normal vocal cords are pearl white but his were reddened from cigarette smoking. His vocal cords were free of tumor. Sliding the instrument gently through the widest opening in the cords, I studied the walls of his trachea and bronchial tree which were normal although irritated and reddened from smoking. The mucous membranes of heavy smokers are inflamed and bleed easily if you scrape them; smokers have an excess of mucous secretion and their sputum, which is normally whitish, can become yellow or green when infection is present.

With the addition of short "telescopes" to the rigid bronchoscope we can see at angles of 45, 90, and 135 degrees and can study the upper, middle, and lower lobe orifices of the right lung and the upper and lower lobe orifices of the left lung. However, only about 20 percent of lung tumors are visible through a rigid bronchoscope because they are growing in locations inaccessible to the instrument.

I inspected the normal side first to be certain it was free of disease; Austin Raymond's left upper and lower lobe orifices were patent (not blocked or obstructed) with no obvious disease. We injected 10 cc. of saline solution through a side arm in the bronchoscope and suctioned it back up into a collection trap which the circulating nurse labeled "Austin Raymond, #51-72-65, left bronchial washing."

"Phil, everything looks normal so far," I said to the senior surgical resident assisting me. "Take a look before we do the other side." I stood up and stepped aside; the resident sat down on the stool at the head of the operating table.

"Joanie," I said to the circulating nurse, "send those washings marked 'Rush' for cytology and bacteriology." The laboratory would grow cultures from this material to identify any bacteria, tubercle bacilli, or fungus infection; fungus infections can cast shadows in the lung X rays. There is no good way to culture a virus, such as in viral pneumonia, but we can measure the antibodies to a virus in the patient's blood.

The resident looked up. "Things look okay."

I drew the bronchoscope back into the trachea and slid it down the right main stem bronchus. The first thing I saw was the right upper lobe orifice—the lobe with the shadow—but little detail was visible because it goes off at a right angle. I could have used a telescope but since we would use the flexible bronchoscope later, I did not. The middle and lower lobe orifices appeared clear; we took washings which were labeled by the nurse and sent to the laboratory.

Slowly I withdrew the bronchoscope, and when it was out the anesthetist took over the patient, using the face mask.

"Good. Now let's see what the fiberoptic scope shows," I said.

The fiberoptic bronchoscope is a bundle of fine, smooth, flexible glass fibers which conduct light and visual images along their lengths and around corners. A high-powered cold light source illuminates the dark inner spaces of the body, allowing the surgeon to examine, sample, and photograph suspicious tissue. A control at the eyepiece enables the physician to flex and unflex the tip of the instrument so he can guide it.

With the fiberoptic bronchoscope and an expensive $150,000 electronic attachment we can take color motion pictures of the bronchial tree and the lungs, and project on a color television receiver what the examining physician sees. These color pictures, in astonishing anatomical detail, can be videotaped for later study; at Memorial Hospital we are building a library of videotapes for teaching purposes in hospitals and medical schools, a program underwritten in part by the National Cancer Institute.

After ventilating the patient to be sure he was well oxygenated, the anesthetist exposed Mr. Raymond's larynx with a laryngoscope and passed an endotracheal tube—a flexible, hollow plastic tube 9 mm. in diameter—into his upper trachea to maintain a reliable airway; anesthesia was maintained through this tube.

I glanced up at the clock on the O.R. wall. It was 8:50 A.M. The first examination had taken 10 minutes.

After Mr. Raymond breathed through the endotracheal tube for a few minutes, I turned to the anesthetist. "Suzy, are you all set?"

"Yes, Dr. Beattie. The patient's doing well. We're ready."

I looked up at the monitor above the operating table; heart rate, 82; temperature, 37.2° C; EKG, a dancing blue line moving from left to right on the oscilloscope traced Mr. Raymond's heart action; there was an audible beep just before every contraction of his heart. The anesthetist felt the patient's pulse, measured his blood pressure, and watched his color and respiration.

"Okay, let's go."

I inserted a three-way cap in the top of the endotracheal tube and attached the anesthesia machine to one of its side arms. The fiberoptic bronchoscope was on the instrument stand; I picked it up and slid the instrument slowly through the tube and down into the trachea.

When we are searching for a hard-to-find tumor in a patient with positive sputum cytology but negative chest X rays, we must examine every section of the lungs. There are 18 major segments and from 36 to 54 subsegments, depending on whether certain bronchi bifurcate or trifurcate. We examine and take washings and brushings of suspicious areas, which later should tell us the source of the malignant cells. This meticulous procedure can take up to two hours. In Austin Raymond's case we had a good idea where the trouble was and, after a general look at the other lung structures, I concentrated on the upper lobe of his right lung.

Looking through the eyepiece I saw again the bifurcation of the trachea. I flexed the tip of the bronchoscope and guided it into the right upper lobe orifice. This was patent and the three segments of the right upper lobe also appeared normal. Now I could see the anterior, posterior, and apical segments of the bronchi to this lobe.

"I'm in the right upper lobe," I said in a low voice. "The anterior and apical segments are not obstructed. The posterior segment, however, is definitely narrowed. But I don't see any intrinsic tumor."

These small bronchi are cartilagenous, horseshoe-shaped tunnels with the open portion covered by a thin membrane. Inside is a mucous lining which you see up against the eyepiece of the bronchoscope: whitish tissue crisscrossed with fine red blood vessels. The narrowing in the posterior segment could result from a compression outside the bronchus or from a submucosal tumor; I assumed the tumor was submucosal but was not certain.

"This is the suspicious area," I said. "Let's brush and wash it."

I inserted the wire backbone of a tiny brush through the instrument and under direct vision pushed the brush through the obstructed area. After withdrawing the instrument, I smeared the brush on two slides and then shook it in a saline solution. The nurse labeled the jar "Austin Raymond, #51-72-65, rt. upper lobe, posterior seg." The pathologist would centrifuge this specimen down and examine the sediment for tumor cells and stain the smears on the slides.

I removed the brush and reinserted the bronchoscope. "Okay, now let's wash it. The brushing may have liberated tumor cells," I said to the nurse beside me. She inserted the tip of a syringe in the side arm opening and injected 10 cc. of saline solution. Five seconds later we suctioned the secretions out into a collection trap which she labeled. We took three washings.

"That's it," I said, withdrawing the bronchoscope in slow motion.

The anesthetist, paying close attention to what I was doing, stopped the anesthetic and let Mr. Raymond slowly wake up. She maintained breathing support until the patient was breathing strongly on his own and then disconnected the anesthesia machine. Before removing the endotracheal tube, she suctioned out the saliva and retained secretions in Mr. Raymond's mouth, pharynx, and trachea. With assistance, she removed the tube and positioned the patient so that when he awoke any secretions would drain out by gravity rather than be aspirated into his lungs. This position is important because if an unconscious patient vomits while lying on his back, he could aspirate the vomitus and die.

The nurses transferred Mr. Raymond to a stretcher and an orderly wheeled him toward the recovery room. I walked beside him for a short distance and saw his eyes blink open.

"You did fine, Mr. Raymond. It's all over. You're going to the recovery room now. I'll see you this afternoon." I knew he would not remember what I said but that did not matter.

It was 9:30 A.M.

Another diagnostic maneuver we can use is the bronchogram, a special X-ray picture of the bronchial tree done by radiologists in the Department of Diagnostic Radiology. After receiving a mild sedative to dampen apprehension, the patient is positioned behind a three-dimensional fluoroscope. The radiologist anesthetizes the skin over the windpipe above the collarbone and inserts a hollow needle into the windpipe. He injects an anesthetic and then inserts through the needle a fine, radiopaque catheter which he guides into the area we need to examine, watching its progress on the fluoroscope.

The patient is on his side, or in other appropriate position, so that when the radiopaque contrast material is injected it flows by gravity into the suspicious area. As the material flows in, the radiologist records a three-dimensional motion picture which is studied later for any abnormality. This test is particularly useful in occult, or T_x, lung cancers where we find malignant cells but do not know their source. With the information from the bronchogram, we can often rebronchoscope the patient and go directly to the abnormal area.

We saw no point in scheduling a bronchogram for Austin Raymond since we knew that the trouble was in or near his right upper lobe; we try to schedule only essential diagnostic tests to reduce patient discomfort and hold costs down; a protracted series of tests can cost an extra $3,000 and add little to what is already known. I am afraid there is sometimes a tendency to subject a patient to too many tests when accurate diagnosis could be made with fewer examinations, provided the necessary tests were made. In deciding which tests to order, the physician needs a heavy dose of good judgment.

Mr. Raymond dozed in the recovery room for two hours while the nurses monitored his vital signs and observed his recovery from anesthesia. At noon he was returned to room 1521B where his wife waited.

Early that afternoon, I received the report on his shoulder and spine X rays and studied the films on the view box. They were negative, but after discussion with the radiologist we agreed we had to make certain there were no metastases to any of his other bones; malignant cells from a lung carcinoma have a bad habit of spreading to skeletal bones and to the brain. If Mr. Raymond had cancer, and if it had spread, we might not subject him to surgery since the chances of a cure would be very low. Here again, judgment is the crucial ingredient.

There are two ways we conduct a skeletal survey. The first utilizes a series of standard X-ray pictures of the entire body. This has limitations because a tumor must be fairly well advanced before you can see it on a regular X ray. The second method, a radioactive bone scan, is more sophisticated and detects malignant neoplasms earlier than X ray. We decided to do a bone scan.

At 6:30 P.M. I dropped in on Austin Raymond, who was sitting up in bed talking with his attractive wife.

After greeting the Raymonds, I pulled up a chair. "Well, I have some news for you. The X rays of your shoulder and lower spine were negative—the radiologist saw no abnormalities. That's encouraging. In the bronchoscopic examination this morning, I saw no visible tumor in your right upper lobe, but there was a narrowing of the posterior segment of the bronchus to this lobe. However, I could see no evidence of tumor in the bronchus itself. We did washings and brushings of the area and the specimens are in the Pathology Department for analysis."

"When will you have their report?" Raymond asked.

"Probably late tomorrow afternoon. It usually takes 48 hours but they're going to try to speed things up."

"Good. This waiting is hell."

"I know . . . I'll give you the results as soon as I can," I assured him. "Meanwhile, we've scheduled another test for tomorrow and I want to tell you about it.

"It's called a bone scan and its purpose is to make sure nothing is wrong with the skeletal bones. About 10 A.M. you'll get an injection in your arm of radioactive fluorine-18 which is made here in our cyclotron. This isotope is absorbed by the bones and about three hours later is visible to a scanning camera which travels slowly back and forth over your body as you lie on an examining table. With each traverse the camera advances a notch until your entire body has been scanned. The resulting data is analyzed by a computer."

"Is the test painful?" Raymond asked.

"No, the only slight pain is when the doctor gives you the injection. Lying still on the table is boring but there's no pain."

"How long does it take?"

"About an hour."

"How does it indicate if there is metastasis to a bone?"

"Normal bones absorb a certain amount of the radioactive fluorine but a tumor has increased isotope uptake which shows up on the scan as a 'hot spot.' We end up with a little picture of your skeleton about 12 inches high which is studied by an expert in nuclear medicine."

"How accurate is the scan?"

"Quite accurate, although a positive scan doesn't necessarily mean that cancer has spread to the bone. For example, if in the past you broke a bone, the camera would pick up a hot spot where the new calcium formed to heal the break. If there was a previous thoracotomy, we probably would get a positive scan on the side the chest was opened. So this test, like most others, must be interpreted in light of the patient's history.

"If we saw a positive bone scan and could not attribute it to some external event, we would get an X ray of the bone and, if abnormal, would biopsy the bone to see what was causing the hot spot. But a negative scan and a negative skeletal survey by X ray are the best evidence of no bone involvement."

"Let's hope it turns out negative."

"There's an excellent chance that it will, Mr. Raymond." I stood up. "I'll drop in tomorrow afternoon and give you the results."

Wednesday, June 11

My office received the report of Austin Raymond's bone scan at 4 P.M. There was one hot spot in his left leg.

From 2:30 to 4:30 I attended the Thoracic Service teaching conference that we hold every Wednesday afternoon. At these meetings—attended by our thoracic surgeons, at least one radio-therapist, medical oncologist (tumor specialist), chest physician, and pathologist, house staff residents and fellows, medical students, nurses, and visiting physicians—new cases and problem cases are presented. An average of eight to ten patient histories are discussed every week and at times we invite the patient to be present.

At 4:45 P.M. the Department of Pathology telephoned my office with the report on Mr. Raymond's washings and brushings and his sputum cytology. One of my secretaries typed a summary and put it on my desk, noting that the complete report would follow.

Austin Raymond was finishing his dinner as I entered his room accompanied by the senior resident on Thoracic. Mrs. Raymond, in a green suede pantsuit, stood looking out the window. The sunny, pleasant day was fading into evening.

"How was your dinner, Mr. Raymond?" I asked, surveying the empty plates. "I wouldn't say that you had any problem with your appetite."

"No, I don't. It's only my lung. Actually, the meals are quite good. I'm surprised." He pushed his tray away. "What about the results, Dr. Beattie—do you have them?"

"Yes, they arrived a short while ago. Your sputum cytology was negative—that's from the specimen you brought in Sunday. Your bone scan also was negative—except for one hot spot attributable to the leg you broke skiing in New Hampshire. But I'm afraid that Pathology's report on the brushings and washings we took during the bronchoscopy is not so good."

Mrs. Raymond, standing beside the bed, gripped her husband's hand and stared at me with luminous brown eyes.

"What is it?" Raymond asked.

"Our pathologists found the material positive for epidermoid carcinoma."

"That means it's cancer?"

"Yes, it does. Epidermoid carcinoma is a common cancer that we see in people who have been heavy smokers for many years."

"Where is the tumor?"

"In or near the posterior segment of the bronchus to your right upper lobe."

"Is this a positive diagnosis—no room for error?"

"Yes, it is. I watched the nurse label your specimens in the O.R. Our pathologists, cytologists, and their technicians are among the best in the world. Their work is meticulous and carefully double-checked. If there were the slighest doubt, they would not have made this diagnosis. I have every confidence in them—but I also understand your concern."

"What's next? Surgery?"

"That's the preferred treatment. Other treatment modalities may be used later as adjuvant therapy. It depends on what we find."

"What are the alternatives?" Raymond asked.

"Well, you can do nothing, of course, but the tumor will continue to grow until it interferes with the functioning of a vital organ. Radiation is not used for this kind of lung cancer in operable patients, although it's sometimes used to shrink large tumors before surgery. Chemotherapy—the use of powerful drugs—and immunotherapy—the use of drugs and agents to make the body's immune system work harder—are not primary treatment modalities for malignant lung tumors."

"When would you do the operation? And what's it called—a lobectomy?"

"Yes, removal of a lung lobe is a lobectomy. . . . There's no point in wasting time, Mr. Raymond. I'd suggest we do it tomorrow morning—I have you on the schedule tentatively for 8:30 A.M."

"That seems a bit sudden, but then. . . . How long will the operation take?"

"It depends on what we find, but probably three or four hours. We'd start about 8:30 and finish around noon. You'll be in the recovery room overnight and back here the next morning."

"Will you do the operation yourself, Dr. Beattie?"

"I'll be responsible for the surgery but I won't make every cut and tie every knot. There will be an attending surgeon and two other surgeons with me and at times all of us will be busy. This is a teaching hospital, as you know, and we have highly qualified surgical residents with from four to nine years of experience; they will perform parts of the operation under my close supervision. Any complex or difficult procedures, of course, I do myself."

"That's about what I thought. . . . What about the risks?"

"The risk of a lobectomy in a man your age, in relatively good condition, in a good hospital, with good anesthesia and competent surgery, is well under 5 percent. The risk of wound infection is something like 2 percent, but with proper treatment these infections heal up; they're not a fatal complication although we do everything we can to prevent them.

"There's no such thing as a surgical procedure without risk, Mr. Raymond, as I'm sure you know. By the way, one of our problems today is that because of medical TV shows and magazine articles, many patients believe that surgery can work miracles. We do our best, but we're not miracle workers."

"I understand that," Raymond said. "Is there a chance that you might have to remove the entire lung?"

"That's a remote possibility, but the evidence indicates it won't be necessary. We avoid a pneumonectomy whenever possible because it's a much more serious operation; it means the heart has to pump all the blood through one lung instead of two. Most of the people with lung tumors are in their fifties, sixties, seventies and have been lifelong cigarette smokers, so their hearts and lungs are not normal. In this group the risk of a pneumonectomy is 10 to 20 percent. We prefer a radical lobectomy—removal of the diseased lobe and the lymph nodes around the lung and in the mediastinum."

"I've heard a lot about 'informed consent'—do I sign my consent on a piece of paper?"

"Yes, they'll bring around a hospital form this evening for you to sign consenting to the anesthesia and authorizing me and my assistants to perform a lobectomy and, if necessary, a pneumonectomy. But your real informed consent is this and our previous conversations. Which reminds me of one of my surgeon friends who had a state supreme court judge as a patient. As you can imagine, with the malpractice uproar, doctors are leery of operating on judges, lawyers, and their families.

"Since alleged lack of proper informed consent can become a problem, this surgeon said, 'Now, Judge, I am going to give you an informed consent. . . .' He proceeded to tell the judge the cure that might result from the procedure, but at great length and in harrowing detail he explained every disaster that could happen—the risks of general anesthesia, every conceivable surgical crisis that could arise, the medical risks to follow, and on and on.

"The judge grew ashen as the long list lengthened and finally broke in, 'For God's sake doctor, stop! Don't tell me any more. Just do what you have to do."

Mr. Raymond and his wife laughed.

"And there *is* a chance of my being cured of this damn lung cancer?"

"Yes, there is. After surgery, many of our lung patients receive adjuvant therapy—chemotherapy and perhaps immunotherapy— which we believe gives us a still better chance of curing them. We have an aggressive attitude toward lung cancer even though it's one of the worst forms of the disease."

"Well, I'm damned glad you're aggressive," Raymond said. "I'd hate to be in the hands of a passive defeatist. . . . How soon can I go home?"

"Probably by the ninth or tenth day. . . . Let me tell you a little about tomorrow.

"When you wake up, you'll feel as if a horse had kicked you in the side, but you'll be given strong pain medication and should be fairly comfortable. There will be two tubes coming out of your right side to drain air and fluid from your chest."

"How soon can I see my wife?"

"You can see her tomorrow morning before you go down to the operating room, if you wish. I'll see her right after the operation and tell her how things went. On Friday, you can see her as soon as they bring you back to your room."

"How about the postoperative period?" Raymond asked.

"Well, you'll be on a liquid diet almost immediately and solid food by the second or third day. You'll get out of bed the first day but your walking will be limited since the chest tubes are attached to a drainage device. The tubes should be removed by the third or fourth day.

"You'll get a sleeping pill tonight and about six tomorrow morning I'm afraid they'll wake you for more medication."

I hoisted myself up out of the chair and rested my hand on Austin Raymond's forearm. "Visit with your wife now, watch the TV news to see if the world's holding together . . . and relax. I'll see you about 8:15 tomorrow morning."

Glancing out the window I saw the last rays of the sun illuminate the towering dark clouds. Across the East River, smokestacks stained the sky with black smoke.

5

Thursday, June 12.
Operating Room 6; Lobectomy

In a thoracotomy, an operation in which the chest is opened, we never know exactly what we will find. In Austin Raymond's case, frozen section biopsies confirmed our diagnosis. These pages describe the three-and-a-half-hour operation, including how anesthesia is administered and the precise steps in this surgical procedure.

6:15 A.M. AT BREAKFAST IN MY APARTMENT a block from Memorial Hospital, I unfolded the *New York Times* and scanned the front page. The rising sun tinted the early morning sky pink; it was going to be another warm day.

Last evening, the anesthesiologist visited Austin Raymond to study his chart, take an anesthesia history, and explain how the anesthesia would be given for the operation today. Noting Mr. Raymond's height, weight, and history, the physician wrote his orders for preoperative medication.

If the anesthesiologist has the slightest question about a patient being ready for surgery, he can cancel the operation and tell the surgeon to do something else that morning. This has happened more than once.

Later that evening, an orderly trimmed the hair on Austin Raymond's chest and in his right armpit, using electric barber clippers but no shaving cream or razor. Patients are surprised by this, but razor-shaving the operative site increases the risk of wound infection, especially if it is done the night before surgery.

Mr. Raymond was awakened early and encouraged to clean his lungs and bronchial tree by coughing. As before his bronchoscopy, he received pentobarbital, 100 mg., to make him sleepy and lessen apprehension, and atropine, 0.6 mg., the drying agent that is a chemical form of tincture of belladonna.

At 7:30 A.M. the floor nurse took Mr. Raymond's pulse, temperature, respiration, and blood pressure to make sure that there was no change in his condition during the night. Shortly before 8 A.M., a full-length sling was placed under the patient and a mechanical hoist on the wheeled stretcher lifted Mr. Raymond gently onto the carrier. This sling, which transfers the patient to the operating table, back to the stretcher, and to his bed in the recovery room, is safe and comfortable and saves the backs of hospital personnel.

Mr. Raymond was taken down by elevator to Operating Room 6 on the second floor. In the O.R., the nurse anesthetist examined Mr. Raymond's plastic wristband to be sure it had his name, my name, and his hospital serial number. Verification that the right patient has been brought to the right operating room is the first in a long line of infinite details.

I greeted Austin Raymond as he lay on the operating table. "Good morning, Austin. How are you feeling?"

"Pretty damn woozy," he said thickly.

"Good. You'll be asleep in a moment. I'll see you this afternoon in the recovery room."

He closed his eyes and gave a perceptible nod.

Pentothal, 150–200 mg., a fast-acting, short-lived barbiturate administered through an intravenous (I.V.) line, put Mr. Raymond to sleep. Pentothal leaves the brain rapidly, but before it does the patient is hyperventilated with oxygen and gases are administered to maintain anesthesia.

After Mr. Raymond was asleep the anesthesiologist set a hollow needle in the vein in front of his right elbow and through it passed a tiny, flexible catheter up his arm, past his shoulder, and down toward his heart into the superior vena cava. Through this catheter the anesthetist would monitor his central venous pressure (CVP). If blood pressure is expected to be a problem, we insert a needle in an artery to record it continuously. A thermocouple probe monitors esophageal temperature.

The I.V. lines would be used later to drip solutions into the patient's bloodstream to maintain electrolyte balance; they could also be used for blood transfusions, if needed.

Anectine, 80 mg.—a derivative of the poison curare used by South American Indians—was administered to relax Mr. Raymond's muscles, make it easier to operate, and keep the patient quiet on the table. After receiving Anectine the patient's skeletal muscles are paralyzed and he is unable to breathe for himself; his breathing is done for him by the anesthesia machine through an endotracheal tube in his throat. Mr. Raymond was turned onto his left side and a black rubber strap fastened over his thigh as a safety precaution.

The high-pitched beep-beep-beep of the heart monitor was audible in the O.R. with every contraction of Austin Raymond's heart, and the oscilloscope's blue line danced a reassuring parade of narrow vertical lines.

The skillful administration of anesthesia is as vital to the success of a complex surgical procedure as the surgery itself. New, odorless, nonexplosive anesthetic agents such a halothane, fluothane, and halogenated ether have replaced the older explosive gases such as ether, ethylene, and cyclopropane. These newer agents are extremely potent and are given in low concentration combined with nitrous oxide, adequate oxygen, and often one or more narcotics such as morphine or Innovar. Since halogen compounds may adversely affect the liver, they are either not used in the presence of liver disease or used with great care.

The anesthesiologist and anesthetist now began a complicated "cocktail" of nonexplosive anesthetic agents to keep the patient asleep, relaxed, and free of pain. Nitrous oxide, oxygen, and halothane were administered through an endotracheal tube in the windpipe from which corrugated inhalation tubes ran to a pleated cylinder enclosed in glass on the anesthesia machine, which expanded and flattened like an accordion with each breath.

It is vital that everyone in the O.R. and recovery room know at all times what drugs are being administered to the patient; this is why, when the anesthetist puts a drug in an I.V. bottle or syringe, she attaches a label identifying the drug and the dosage. Printed repetitively in large black letters on Scotch tape rolls colored red, green, yellow, and blue are the names Anectine, Atropine, Curare, Demerol, Droperidol, Fentanyl, Innovar, Morphine, Pentothal, and Xylocaine.

Earlier in the surgeons' locker room I had stripped down to my shorts and slipped into the freshly laundered trousers and shirt of a green scrub suit which resembled poorly fitting pajamas. Hood, surgical mask, and shoe coverings of soft, strong blue paper completed the routine of dressing. Women wear either a scrub dress or scrub suit. The hood or cap worn by everyone in the operating room covers the hair. The surgical mask over nose and mouth is an effective bacterial filter but is changed when worn more than three or four hours.

In the operating room are two classes of people and objects, sterile ("clean") and nonsterile ("dirty"), and rigid techniques avoid contaminating clean personnel, objects, and areas. The people who are not sterile are the anesthesiologist, the anesthetist, the circulating nurse (a senior nurse in charge of the O.R.), and any observers, technicians, and orderlies. These individuals keep at least two feet from anyone, and any object, that is sterile.

The sterile personnel are the surgeons and the scrub nurse who hands the instruments to the surgeons. Before they enter the O.R., these people scrub their hands and forearms with a brush, Betadine (an iodine-based detergent), and running hot water for 10 minutes, or 30 to 50 brush strokes on each skin area. After entering the O.R. they don sterile gowns and sterile latex gloves.

If anyone who is sterile brushes against anything that is nonsterile, he puts on a new sterile gown and gloves. Anyone who spots a break in aseptic technique is responsible for calling attention to it.

Austin Raymond's skin from neck to hips was sterilized with Betadine by the circulating nurse, holding gauze swabs in forceps. Ten minutes passed as she painted with the germicide, tinting Mr. Raymond's skin yellow-brown. The scrub nurse covered the patient with gray sterile drapes, leaving exposed only that part of his right chest through which we would make the incision. A blue drape across the table at the patient's neck, supported by upright poles, separated the sterile surgical team, the sterile field, and the sterile instruments from the anesthesia area.

The first assistant surgeon, using a sterile black marking pen, drew a 14-inch curved line on Mr. Raymond's skin along the fifth interspace, between his fifth and sixth ribs, as a guide to the scalpel.

The anesthesiologist, peering over his blue mask, adjusted the flow meters controlling the anesthetic mixture.

The only sounds in the operating room were the chirp of the heart monitor, the rustling of sterile paper packages being opened, and occasional low conversation.

There was no odor of anesthetic gases.

The air was cool.

Overhead, four brilliant surgical lights were focused on Austin Raymond's chest by the circulating nurse; sterile handles on each light permit the surgeons to reposition the lights.

The scrub nurse stood on a low metal stool beside the instrument stand so she could look down into the surgical field. A good scrub nurse knows which instrument is wanted by the stage of the operation. There are also hand signals that save time and enable the surgeon to keep his eyes on what he is doing instead of turning to the scrub nurse:

- Hand extended, palm up—"Give me a hemostat."

- Hand extended, palm down—"Give me a ligature."

- Two fingers moving together and apart—"Scissors."

- Bent index finger and thumb moving together and apart— "Thumb forceps."

- Hand outstretched, turning hand and wrist over rapidly— "Suture."

- Sweeping motion, thumb and index finger together—"Scalpel, please."

In a smoothly functioning surgical team accustomed to working together, when I put my hand out the scrub nurse often gives me the instrument I need without my asking for it—or sometimes I ask for the wrong instrument and she gives me the right one. One of the senior surgeons who taught me was a crotchety old gentleman who once asked for a specific instrument; when the scrub nurse handed it to him he threw it across the operating room and said, "Goddamn it, give me what I need—not what I ask for!" Which simply shows that as a scrub nurse, it's hard to win.

The instrument table, positioned over the bottom half of the operating table, was covered with sterile drapes on which, in neat rows, were scalpels, clamps, scissors, forceps, retractors, needles and sutures, dozens of hemostats, and specialized instruments. More than 1,000 instruments may be used in a complicated operation.

Austin Raymond's chest X rays were clipped to the lighted view box on the green O.R. wall where we would examine them from time to time as we progressed.

"The patient is ready, Dr. Beattie," the anesthetist said, intent on her instruments. The anesthesiologist stood beside her; this morning he would supervise anesthesia in two operating rooms.

The clock above the O.R. door read 8:43 A.M.

I took my place at Austin Raymond's back with the first assistant surgeon on my left and the second and third assistant surgeons facing us across the table. My first assistant was an attending staff surgeon while the other two assistants were residents on the Thoracic Service.

"Scalpel, please."

The scrub nurse placed the scalpel firmly in my outstretched palm.

I pressed the sharp steel blade into the skin and drew it slowly along the curving black pen line. The right periscapular incision began under the right nipple, carried down around the scapula and up along the right side of the spine. A thin red line of blood trailed the knife.

The yellow-painted skin, stretched tight by the patient's position, pulled apart with moderate bleeding; the assistant surgeons, following the scalpel, clamped the bleeding blood vessels with hemostats and patted the incision dry with white gauze sponges, soon stained bright red. Before we removed the hemostats, we ligated (tied) the larger blood vessels to minimize blood loss and coagulated the smaller vessels by touching the hemostats with the electrocautery probe. Hemostasis (stoppage of bleeding) was achieved quickly, leaving the field bloodless.

After the sweeping incision to a depth of half an inch, sterile skin towels were clipped over the edges of the incision to ensure that no bare skin, with its potential bacteria, would be in contact with the wound. These towels remain until the tissue is closed at the end of the operation.

I dropped my scalpel into the basin for used instruments—the razor-sharp blade was dulled by cutting through the skin.

Beneath the skin, yellow globules of fat lay exposed down each side of the incision. Fortunately, Austin Raymond was not obese. There is increased risk of wound infection in obese patients since fat has poor defense mechanisms and surgery is more time-consuming.

"Okay, Frank," I said to my first assistant as he exposed the muscles of the chest wall. There are two large superficial muscles, the trapezius and the latissimus dorsi. Beneath this layer lie the deep muscles, the rhomboids and the serratus anticus.

"Scalpel."

I continued to divide the muscle layers slowly; bleeders were clamped as we advanced. There was no attempt at speed, only careful, concentrated effort. Speed in surgery comes from no delay and no undue hesitation—not from rapid motions.

"Clamp."

"Silk."

"You better use the cautery on that one, Joe." The second assistant touched the hemostat with the probe and coagulated the bleeder.

"That's a big vessel, tie it with silk." The vein was tied off with 3-0 silk.

"Suction."

An assistant put the sucker, which was attached to a long transparent tube, in the bottom of the wound where blood had collected. The blood disappeared up the tube with a slurping sound—like a straw sucking out the last of an ice-cream soda.

"Someone's stepping on the suction!" A surgeon or nurse sometimes steps inadvertently, for a moment, on the long plastic tube snaking its way over the floor from the operating table to the suction bottle.

In every operation an accurate tally of blood loss is written in crayon on a wall chart by the circulating nurse. Blood from the incision is suctioned into a plastic bottle calibrated in cubic centimeters; gauze sponges are weighed and the absorbed blood measured (a one-gram increase equals 1 cc. of blood); blood spilled on the drapes is estimated by the surgeons.

If blood loss is 500 to 1,000 cc. (one or two pints), it is replaced by transfusion during the operation, frequently using plasma rather than whole blood, although whole blood of the patient's type is in the O.R. ready for instant use.

If blood is needed, the anesthetist runs it through a blood-warming coil so that when it enters the patient it is at body temperature. This is not as important if you are transfusing a pint an hour, but if you have a major hemorrhage and must transfuse several pints quickly, the blood must be near body temperature because cold blood can cause the heart to beat irregularly or even stop.

The anesthesiologist and anesthetist watch the patient's central venous pressure and arterial blood pressure in their continuing assessment of how he is withstanding the assault on his body. Everyone watches the color of the blood; if the patient is receiving too little oxygen, blood color changes from bright red to dark red.

The circulating nurse constantly moved around the O.R. checking equipment and bringing in fresh supplies.

We were down to Austin Raymond's chest wall and the fascia, the thin, semitransparent sheath that encloses the ribs and intercostal muscles. The ribs are connected to one another by two muscle bundles; the pleura, inside the muscles and the ribs, lines the thoracic cavity. We planned to enter his chest with an intercostal incision and separate his fifth and sixth ribs with a rib spreader.

I cut through the fascia and, with a curved hemostat, elevated the muscles in one area so an assistant could cut them with scissors.

"Scalpel, please," I said, holding out my left hand. (I am left-handed although I use instruments designed for right-handed surgeons. A grateful patient once gave me a set of left-handed instruments which quickly became mixed in with the hospital's instruments during cleaning and autoclaving [steam-sterilizing]. More than once I heard a colleague mutter, "Where the hell did *these* scissors come from? The damn things won't cut!")

We carried the intercostal incision the full extent of the primary incision and tucked sponges into the wound to soak up blood and compress insignificant bleeders. Blood was well controlled and we worked in a virtually dry field.

Once the thoracic cavity is opened, we use for sponges laparotomy pads with long tails to which metal rings are sewn so they cannot easily be left in a body cavity, or sponges on long clamps for quick wiping.

The silence in the operating room was broken by the chirp of the heart monitor, the click of instruments, and the slurp of suction, punctuated by quiet conversation.

Once, many years ago when I was at Presbyterian St. Luke's Hospital in Chicago, a patient made an unusual request before his surgery. He asked me whether his priest could bless my surgical instruments. I told him, "Yes, of course."

A fellow surgeon who witnessed the somewhat unusual ceremony asked me later whether it did any good.

"I don't know," I told him, "but we surgeons need all the help we can get."

The operation was successful and the ex-patient is enjoying his retirement in Arizona.

There is a widely held, mistaken belief that seconds count in surgery, whereas what does count is care, skill, and judgment.

Dissection is slow and careful. We often wait 10 to 15 minutes for a frozen section biopsy report before going further. The only time when speed is vital is in stopping a hemorrhage or where a patient is so sick that any anesthesia poses a grave danger. With today's improved techniques, time under anesthesia for most patients is no longer the consideration it once was. Great speed, histrionics, and throwing instruments belong to a long-ago era of surgery.

After severing the muscles between Mr. Raymond's fifth and sixth ribs, we saw the pleura, the glistening, partially transparent membrane that lines the chest cavity. I cut the pleura to accommodate the two blades of the rib spreader.

Most patients believe that we cut out a section of rib or remove entire ribs. Actually, we do that only when a patient is severely arthritic or has a brittle chest where using the rib spreader might break ribs, which we try to avoid.

With an intercostal incision we go in through the side of the chest, spread the ribs six to eight inches apart, and work through this opening. This permits us, if necessary, to work on the front, sides, and back of the lung. If we enter the chest from the front, it limits exposure and in cancer surgery you never know in advance what you will find.

The powerful rib spreader consists of two broad, dull, slightly curved blades which are inserted between adjacent ribs. You pry the ribs apart slowly by turning a crank which forces the blades away from one another.

I cranked the handle that forced Austin Raymond's fifth, fourth, and third ribs upward and his sixth, seventh, and eighth ribs downward. When the crank tightened I stopped, waited a minute or so, and then gave it a few more turns.

It took only a few minutes to pry a seven-inch opening in Austin Raymond's right chest.

I glanced up at the orange numbers on the monitor which display pulse rate on a second-by-second basis. The numbers were shifting rapidly: 78, 80, 84, 87, 91—then 86, 80. The variation mirrored the body's responses to the rib spreader.

Now, through the wide opening in Mr. Raymond's chest, we saw the three lobes of his right lung rhythmically expanding and contracting, controlled by the anesthesia machine. Although the three lobes nestled together as one, the fissure lines separating them were visible.

The patient was relaxed in deep sleep, a placid expression on his face—with a gaping gash in his right chest. My mind flashed back to Dr. W.T.G. Morton and his demonstration of anesthesia at the Massachusetts General Hospital in 1846. Anesthesia is truly one of the momentous blessings of man.

The healthy lung of a nonsmoker is pinkish-white in color.

Black spots, some as large as a dime, and black, irregular streaks discolored the lobes of Austin Raymond's right lung. These deposits, typical of heavy cigarette smokers and city dwellers, permeate the spongy, life-sustaining tissue that fills each lobe. Cigarette smoking over a long period of time stains the lungs, scars them severely, and impairs their function.

In a surgical operation, with the patient's head hidden in drapes at the head of the table and his body cloaked to the toes, only the limited operative site is exposed to view. The rest of the body is walled off, remote, which helps the surgeon detach himself from the sick human being and concentrate on the delicate task at hand. During these critical hours the patient is a medical challenge to be conquered, not a specific individual with an anxious family. A surgeon cannot focus his skill and judgment on the problem before him and be worrying about whose husband, wife, or child is lying on the operating table.

That is why a surgeon needs in ample measure, at different times, the antithetical qualities of compassion and detachment—compassion in the trying periods before and after the operation in dealing with the patient and his loved ones, and total detachment during the exacting surgical procedure, which may last three, six, eight hours, or longer. Which is why a surgeon does not operate on members of his own family.

Twenty-one years ago, after a grueling nine-hour operation on a 47-year-old male—a heavy smoker—I remember thumbing through the *Nurses' Notes* in the patient's history as the orderly wheeled the still form of the patient from the O.R. In her neat, round hand the nurse had written: "Husband and father. Pleasant and talkative. Two small children still at home. Very concerned about effects of his illness on wife and family. Tires easily."

I pressed my left hand in its white latex glove, now streaked red, deep in Austin Raymond's chest and gently explored the rubbery lobes of his right lung. I felt behind the lobes to the middle of his chest but did not encounter an obvious tumor or enlarged lymph nodes. His middle and lower lobes appeared uninvolved, but in his right upper lobe I felt a hard mass, two inches in diameter, where the X ray showed it.

Nonmedical people who watch surgical procedures are surprised by how deeply the surgeon thrusts his hands into the body, picking up or moving aside organs such as the lungs, spleen, liver, and intestines, but there is good reason for this. It is the surgeon's responsibility to explore the area thoroughly to make certain that what he thought was there is actually there, and that no new, unexpected problems exist. He does this by visual inspection and by his sense of touch since there are areas which can be explored only by palpation. Thorough exploration is good medical practice and I explain this to my patients.

"Gently palpate the tumor in the right upper lobe," I said to the assisting surgeons. After they withdrew their hands I said, "Okay, let's go."

The hilum or root of the lung contains four main structures—the right main bronchus, the right main pulmonary artery, and the two pulmonary veins that drain the lung.

First, we had to locate the branch bronchus to the right upper lobe, and later the arteries and veins. I felt the trachea, identified the main stem bronchus and its branch to the upper lobe; I palpated the branch to make sure it was normal and that a lobectomy would give adequate surgical margin.

"Thumb forceps and scissors, please."

I snipped the pleura over the hilum to gain access to the bronchus. The bronchus is easy to identify, but locating a nerve 1 mm. in diameter buried in a mass of soft bloody tissue is quite another matter.

I freed up the bronchus with a dissecting sponge by pushing extraneous tissue away from it.

"Mixter clamp." I closed this long curved clamp on the bronchus toward the tumor side.

"Suction the lung and reinflate it," I said to the anesthetist. She applied suction to aspirate accumulated secretions, reattached the anesthesia machine, and inflated the lungs. The right middle and lower lobes inflated well but the upper lobe remained collapsed, confirming that we had clamped the correct bronchus. This is not a problem with the right upper lobe, but with the other lobes it is important, by lung collapse and reinflation, to be certain that the correct bronchus has been identified and clamped.

An assistant retracted the lobe out of my way while another held the sucker ready to aspirate the blood that would run from cutting the bronchus; we don't want blood getting into the open bronchus and down into the lung.

"Fifteen blade, please," I said the the scrub nurse.

With this small scalpel I cut a few millimeters of the upper lobe bronchus, leaving a small stump on the main bronchus so we would have room to sew it; cutting only a few millimeters at a time prevents too large a hole with too big an air leak.

My first assistant was ready with a suture of 3-0 silk on a special atraumatic needle which is used for fine stitches. I closed the hole in the bronchus with my fingers while he got ready to tie the knots; air leaked for only a few seconds.

Quickly, but not too quickly, he tied square knots in the silk suture. In five similar steps I divided the bronchus while he placed the stitches and knotted them securely.

In tying knots we usually use a surgeon's knot, a square knot, but often throw one or two overhand knots (a "granny") because when you pull gently but firmly you tighten these knots. On top of these I throw two square knots as additional ties, which is like wearing a belt and suspenders. Tying knots correctly is vital, which is why residents who are not tying their knots properly hear about it quickly and loudly.

An alternative to sewing is the surgical stapler which inserts stainless steel staples. There are times when it is better to staple and times when it is better to sew, and since Memorial is a teaching hospital we make sure that everyone can do both.

Once the bronchus was cut, we had a better view of the blood vessels to and from the lobe. Working slowly and with great caution, we dissected out the arterial branches. Where this is tricky, and even dangerous, is if there is tumor or infection surrounding these tiny blood vessels. You want the tumor to go with the specimen, not stay with the patient.

I was relieved to see that no tumor was evident in the hilum. We tied off each of the arteries as close to the main pulmonary artery as we could, using ligatures of 3-0 silk reinforced by sutures to be sure that our ties would not slip off.

We next identified and dissected out the veins draining blood from the upper lobe, placing 3-0 silk ties and sutures on each.

With the bronchus, arteries, and veins divided, we thought that only connective tissue, at the hilum, still attached the upper lobe to Austin Raymond's body.

"Okay, let's take the lobe," I said, handing my scalpel to the scrub nurse.

I picked up the collapsed lobe and examined it. The transverse fissure separating the upper and middle lobes was incomplete and lung tissue still connected the upper lobe with parts of the middle and lower lobes.

"We'll have to dissect out the inferior part of this lobe from the other lobes," I said to the three surgeons who were peering into the cavity. Even though we are pretty sure of our anatomy, we would have to proceed with caution going through this lung parenchyma (tissue) so as not to damage the middle and lower lobes, or accidentally cut a major blood vessel.

"Take a big curved clamp and wedge that section," I told the third assistant, pointing to an inferior portion of the lobe.

"Hey, that's a pretty big wedge—can't you take less tissue?"

He backed off and made the wedge smaller.

"That's better.

"I guess we can cut that stuff now. . . . Stand by. . . . Scalpel, please."

I cut the clamped portion of the lobe free.

"Give me a stitch."

My assistants sewed the lung tissue back and forth deep to the clamp. As I handed my needle to the scrub nurse, the hand of one of the surgeons blocked the way.

"Watch out for the needle! Getting stabbed is how surgeons get hepatitis." (Surgical needles are curved like a half-moon and held in long needle holders, which lets us sew in confined areas deep within the body.)

"Duval." With this lung clamp we kept the middle lobe out of the way while we separated it from the upper lobe.

I saw a tiny connection which looked like a blood vessel. "Give me a small clip, please.

"Scissors.

"Stitch.

"Two knots only—it's coming out.

"Watch out for his phrenic nerve!

"Suzy, watch his heart action. You're probably going to have to give him some blood.

"Let me have a small curved, please.

"Clamp.

"Scalpel."

I cut the lobe free.

"Forceps."

I grasped the spongy, blackened lobe with the forceps and lifted it out of Austin Raymond's chest. The bulge created by the tumor was clearly visible. I dropped the dripping mass of life-threatening tissue into a sterile pan.

"May I have a sterile field setup, please."

The circulating nurse covered a small table with a sterile sheet. I sliced open the lobe, removed a wedge of the white, gristly tumor, and placed it in a sterile container. Gray-white tentacles fanned out from the tumor and wound their way through the tissue.

"Send the lobe for frozen section, Joanie," I told the circulating nurse. We wanted confirmation of the diagnosis and the status of the bronchial stump before finishing.

She wrapped and labeled the specimen and dispatched it by pneumatic tube to the "surgical bench" in the Department of Pathology, four floors above and one building away. Here the tissue would be frozen by liquid nitrogen spray at –196° C, sliced, stained, and examined under a microscope by a physician skilled in cell identification. In 10 to 20 minutes he would call his findings to us through the intercom on the O.R. wall. The sterile piece of tumor would be sent to the Immunology Department for tissue culture, deep-freeze storage, possible vaccine production, and cancer research.

Because microscopic cancer cells can migrate throughout the body via the lymphatic system, our next step was to dissect out of Austin Raymond's chest the bean-sized lymph nodes around the trachea, bronchus, and the principal arteries and veins of the lung.

Lymph nodes are filters that trap the cells and bacteria of disease; Austin Raymond's subcarinal nodes were enlarged, either from old infection or from his carcinoma; the other mediastinal lymph nodes seemed normal. The nodes we removed were placed in the compartments of a metal tray marked with their locations and sent to Pathology for analysis.

Removing the subcarinal nodes caused bleeding, which we controlled with small silver clips on the blood vessels. These clips are quick and effective and show up on X-ray film; should a tumor recur, it pushes the clips apart and we can measure its growth.

As we worked next to Austin Raymond's heart, the monitor beeps suddenly became fast and irregular because of irritation to the autonomic nervous system which controls heart action.

While we were waiting for Pathology's reports, I used the time to ask questions of the resident surgeons.

"Bill, show us where the azygos vein is.

"Point to the superior segment of the right lower lobe.

"How many arteries do you see to the middle lobe, Joe?

"Where is the innominate artery [a major branch of the aorta]? Touch it.

"Show me where the phrenic nerve inserts into the diaphragm."

Our question session was interrupted by a metallic voice from the Executone intercom: "Room 6—Dr. Beattie."

"Yes, go ahead."

"On Austin Raymond, patient number 51-72-65. This is an epidermoid carcinoma by previous diagnosis which we have confirmed by frozen section. The bronchial margin is clear of tumor."

"Thank you, Mike."

With Austin Raymond's chest cleared of tumor, I cut the inferior pulmonary ligament that holds the right lung down in the chest so that the middle and lower lobes could rise to fill the vacant space left by the lobe we had removed. The lungs possess amazing elasticity—like a latex balloon—and expand readily if they are healthy.

The intercom clicked on again. "Dr. Beattie, on Austin Raymond. We received a specimen identified as subcarinal lymph nodes. On frozen section, we see hyperplastic nodes, no cancer. The other specimens also are negative."

"Thank you. Always glad to get good news."

With the operation close to completion, the circulating nurse refigured her sponge count to be sure that no gauze pads remained in Austin Raymond's chest. The chest is not closed if the sponge count is wrong.

Our next step was to pour a pitcher of sterile water into the chest cavity.

"Keep the lungs well inflated, please," I said to the anesthetist, who squeezed the black rubber breathing bag on the anesthesia machine with her hand. She stood and peered over the drapes into Mr. Raymond's chest.

Under the clear water I saw the middle and lower lobes swell up like a balloon. The water enables us to detect any leaking from the bronchus or lung and fix it before closing the chest.

"I don't see any blood or air bubbles, fellows, do you?"

"Looks okay," said Frank, the first assistant. The others nodded.

Sterile water also washes out and hemolyzes (kills) any malignant cells that remain behind by causing them to swell and burst.

The water was suctioned out carefully, so as not to wet the drapes since bacteria can move through wet drapes.

After checking that our suture lines were tight, I made two small skin incisions below the main incision, inserted two plastic catheters into Mr. Raymond's chest, and sewed them to his skin. The smaller tube went to the top of his chest to drain any air while the larger tube terminated in the bottom of his chest to drain blood and serum. The catheters dropped down to a Pleur-evac drainage device which lets air and fluid out but has a water-seal to prevent their return; if necessary, we can put suction on these tubes to improve drainage.

Continuous catgut sutures (made from sheep intestine), which the body absorbs, closed the pleura and the intercostal muscles. The large chest muscles and the fascia were joined using 2-0 interrupted silk sutures in two layers; silk is a strong, permanent material. Subcutaneous tissue and skin were closed with 3-0 silk. The chest must be as airtight as possible because if there is a lung leak and the chest is not tightly closed, air can seep into subcutaneous tissue and the patient can swell up like a sick pup.

The assistants placed a sterile gauze dressing over the incision and applied snug adhesive tape to "splint" the incision and support the chest. We leave this bandage on only a day or two because the wound seals itself quickly and adhesive tape is an irritant.

The gray gowns and white latex gloves of the four surgeons, spotless three hours ago, were spotted and streaked with blood.

Austin Raymond was turned gently onto his back and observed to make sure that he was breathing properly without assistance. Accompanied by the anesthetist and a resident surgeon, he was wheeled to the recovery room.

The clock read 12:08 P.M. The lobectomy had taken 3 hours and 25 minutes.

I changed into my street clothes, put on my long white coat, and walked to the reception area on the first floor where Mrs. Raymond waited. She arose as I approached and held out her hands which I took in mine.

"Mrs. Raymond, your husband is fine. We finished 15 minutes ago and he's now in the recovery room."

"Was it cancer, Dr. Beattie?" Her voice was soft and low.

"Yes, as Pathology reported from the bronchoscopic examination, it was epidermoid carcinoma which we confirmed by frozen section during the operation. The cancer seemed confined to the right upper lobe, which we removed. We also took out over 15 lymph nodes from the center of the chest, which seemed normal."

"And Austin's all right?"

"Yes. He withstood the operation well."

"When may I see him?"

"Well, as you know, we don't like to have visitors in the recovery room. Besides, he's groggy and sleepy. You can see him the first thing tomorrow morning in his own room. He'll spend tonight in the recovery room just to be sure that everything remains normal. If anything's the matter, I'll call you right away."

Mrs. Raymond's brown eyes filled with tears which she blinked back.

I put my arm around her shoulders and gave her a hug. "Believe me, I know what a strain this has been, Mrs. Raymond, but please don't worry. I'm sure Austin will make a good recovery."

6

Friday, June 13-Sunday, June 22.
Postoperative Care

As he recovers, Austin Raymond asks a number of questions—about the feelings of doctors and nurses, the problems of postoperative complications, the differences between the various kinds of surgery. As a journalist, Mr. Raymond's reactions to the Playroom Times, *the mimeographed newspaper that our young patients write, are illuminating, as are his feelings about the sights he saw and his thoughts about the future.*

THE ANESTHETIST AND ONE OF THE resident surgeons walked beside Mr. Raymond as he was wheeled to the recovery room, where they made sure that he was waking up properly and breathing well. The endotracheal tube was withdrawn when Raymond was sufficiently conscious with a good cough reflex; the danger is that the patient may vomit and get gastric juice in his airway, which can be fatal.

At 6:30 P.M. I visited Austin Raymond in the recovery room on the second floor. The wide double doors swung back with a whoosh of compressed air as I brushed the aluminum wall panel with my arm.

Raymond was awake but groggy from pain medication; a light, transparent oxygen mask covered his mouth and nose. He raised his left hand in a weak greeting. I nodded at the nurse and she removed the mask for a moment.

I laid my hand on his forearm. "How are you feeling, Austin?"

He managed a weak smile. "Okay," he whispered. He wet his lips with his tongue. "How'd it go?"

"Fine. We got the tumor out. You're in good shape. I'll explain everything when you're feeling better."

Austin nodded and closed his eyes.

The nurse replaced the oxygen mask.

I checked his chart and studied the heart monitor at the head of his bed.

Patients often do not remember these early visits, but I like to see them as soon as possible after the operation. If there is bad news, I skip it and wait until the patient is back in his own room and feeling better. As already mentioned, we are honest with our patients and our rule is not to tell lies.

We do not like to have visitors in the recovery room because it is a congested area with 24 beds, a lot of complicated equipment, and a good deal of activity. While most of the patients are doing well, they look very sick to a visitor, who may become upset or even faint. If someone were desperately ill we would, of course, make an exception or move the patient to the intensive care area where relatives could see him for short periods. It is important for loved ones to know exactly what is going on and to see the patient frequently.

The most dangerous part of an operation is immediately after the surgery and before the patient is fully awake, which is why diligent patient supervision and care in the recovery room and intensive care unit are vital. Good hospitals consider postoperative patient monitoring to be as essential as monitoring during the surgical procedure.

The house staff surgeon wrote a series of postoperative orders for Mr. Raymond which were incorporated into his chart. These orders cover: pain medication; care of the chest tubes; patient position and movement; I.V. fluid maintenance; liquid nourishment; recording of vital signs and urinary output; blood counts; daily portable chest X rays; and blood transfusion, if needed.

During an operation the patient's pulse rate, respiratory rate, and blood pressure are recorded every 5 minutes by the anesthetist. In the recovery room, vital signs are recorded every 15 minutes until they are stable, after which they are measured every hour.

Temperature is taken when the patient arrives in the recovery room to be sure that he is neither running a fever nor that his body temperature is too low (patients often cool off during an operation and are warmed up in the recovery room). Abnormal temperatures are recorded hourly and normal temperatures every four hours. When we have a patient who is hyperpyrexic (has an abnormally high fever), we monitor temperature continuously with a thermocouple in the esophagus or rectum.

Postoperatively, chest operations hurt like the mischief every time you breathe and cough—there is no way you cannot breathe, and if you do not cough you get into serious trouble. So, for a good-sized healthy male like Austin Raymond, the pain medication is morphine sulfate, 10 mg. by intramuscular injection every three to four hours. We want this medication used freely to relieve pain so that when the patient is told to cough, *he will cough*. The complications of thoracic surgery are minimized by coughing; if you lie motionless in bed and do not cough, you get into trouble from retained lung secretions, the lung may fail to expand, pneumonia may set in, and you become sick and may even die. So it is crucial to relieve pain with adequate doses of narcotics, but not so much that they make the patient nonresponsive.

Drainage into the Pleur-evac from the chest catheters is watched for unusual blood accumulation which indicates internal bleeding. Soon after entering the recovery room, a portable chest X ray was taken with Raymond propped up in bed to be sure that his right lung was expanded, his left lung normal, and that there was no accumulation of blood or air in his chest, serious conditions which require prompt action. Portable chest X rays are taken daily until the chest tubes are removed.

Austin Raymond, like most surgical patients, had an I.V. running when he entered the recovery room; since he would not be taking much by mouth for several hours, the resident surgeon wrote, "Continue present I.V.—2.5 percent glucose in half normal salt solution. Follow with 1,000 ml. 5 percent dextrose in distilled water." We keep an I.V. running until the next morning to maintain fluid balance and to treat the patient quickly, if need be. The position order read, "Pt. on side until conscious; turn side to back every hour." We want patients moved around and not in one position too long.

Soon after Austin Raymond was in the recovery room, blood was drawn for a hematocrit and hemoglobin concentration. If a patient has difficulty breathing, we make sure that his airway is clear and his chest X ray normal; if the difficulty persists, we draw an arterial blood sample and measure blood gases. While Austin Raymond experienced no trouble breathing, an oxygen mask with low-dose oxygen and high humidity was used for a few hours to make him more comfortable.

Friday, June 13

At 9:15 A.M. Austin Raymond, wide awake and with stable vital signs, was wheeled from the recovery room to his semiprivate room,

1521B, which he shared with another male patient. Half of our rooms are semiprivate, each with two beds.

He received I.M. (intramuscular) injections of morphine sulfate almost every four hours and was relatively free of pain. The nurses encouraged him to cough every hour and to move around in bed; with their assistance, he sat up twice on the side of his bed the first day. A portable chest X ray was filmed in bed after his lunch of custard, toast, chocolate ice cream, and hot tea; in the recovery room he had been given small sips of water and other liquids. The first day post-op, patients may have liquids and a soft to normal diet depending upon how they feel; the nurses use their own good judgment.

During each day, Austin Raymond was seen three times by a house staff physician and I saw him daily on my rounds between 6 and 7 P.M. When I entered his room late on Friday, his eyes were closed even though the tiny-screen TV set on a movable arm by his bed was tuned to the evening news. Barbara Raymond sat beside his bed, holding his hand.

"How do you feel tonight, Austin?"

His eyes blinked open. "Better—but you were wrong about one thing, doctor."

"What was that?"

"You said when I woke up I'd feel as if a horse had kicked me in the side. It feels more as if an elephant did the kicking."

"I'm sorry—I stand corrected. But the pain medication ought to be keeping you fairly comfortable."

"It is—but I'll probably end up an addict."

"There's no danger of that," I said. "Are you coughing when the nurses and physiotherapy people tell you to?"

"I am, Ted, and it hurts like hell even with the pain medicine."

I went over the operation with the Raymonds and told them that the final Pathology report on the lymph nodes that we dissected out of the chest would be on my desk in four or five days.

Saturday, June 14

By the second day post-op, Austin Raymond's appetite had improved and he was back on a normal diet. The doctors and nurses watched for postoperative complications, but his vital signs stayed within normal limits, his airway remained clear, there was no occult bleeding, and his lungs inflated well. The X rays showed that his right middle and lower lobes had expanded to fill the void left by the removal of his right upper lobe.

The physiotherapy team visited Raymond and started him using the incentive spirometer on the table beside his bed; this is the small white tank with an amber light atop it that winks on when the patient's air input through the connecting tube reaches a preset volume. If the air volume is below par, the light remains dark. This device enables patients to check their vital capacity and improve their lung function.

In the middle of the afternoon, Austin Raymond got out of bed, walked to a chair by the window, and sat down; his wife and a nurse were at his side in case he became dizzy from the pain medication; the nurse carried the jug to which his chest catheters ran. From now on, he would be encouraged to walk increasing distances each day, either carying the chest jug or letting a nurse or his wife carry it.

When I stopped by that evening for a brief visit, Raymond commented on the attention of the house staff physicians, therapists, and nurses.

"I must say I'm surprised. They seem to really care how I feel and what happens to me," he said. "I'm impressed. Especially in a big hospital like this."

"Well, we try, and I'm not sure we always succeed. I remember an amusing incident that happened one day at surgical grand rounds, which we hold at 8 A.M. Wednesdays in the Hoffman Auditorium.

"One of the cases dealt with a 51-year-old woman who had been cured of ovarian cancer. After her doctor presented the medical details, he brought in his patient to talk over the P.A. system from the stage to the assembled doctors and nurses, about 175 people. Mrs. X, a tall, impressive woman with salt-and-pepper hair, wearing a gray pantsuit, talked frankly about her cancer and answered questions from the large audience, which included doctors from other hospitals.

"I was about to thank her for appearing and ask for the next case when she said through the microphone at the podium, 'Dr. Beattie, do you mind if I say something about Memorial Hospital?' I had no idea what was coming but I asked her to go right ahead.

" 'Well, I had six admissions to this hospital and received, I think, the finest medical care in the world. You doctors and nurses were just wonderful to me and my husband and we are most grateful. But I had one problem: on two of my admissions I had a bad cold. Do you think I could get *one* doctor to prescribe anything for my cold? I could not, Dr. Beattie. You wonderful people cured my cancer but no one was interested in my cold!' With that salvo, she walked off the stage waving goodbye, to generous applause.

"I told her we know this is a problem, we're working on it with the house staff, and that while we can cure many cancers, we can't cure the common cold."

Austin Raymond and his wife laughed.

"I think something else that helps us doctors understand how patients feel," I said, "is to keep in mind what a well-known surgeon at the Albert Einstein College of Medicine used to tell entering classes: 'When dealing with patients, you must never forget that but for the grace of God you might be occupying the bed next to his, if not now, then perhaps tomorrow.' "

Sunday, June 15

The hospital is quiet on Sundays except for throngs of visitors wearing everything from Beethoven T-shirts to Brooks Brothers suits.

Certain patients are given permission to spend days at home with their families if their situations warrant. I recall one 73-year-old gentleman facing a pneumonectomy who asked if he could leave the hospital to visit his family and grandchildren. Permission was given since his operation was not until late in the coming week. This white-haired patient checked out with a broad smile, ate a joyous dinner (including two martinis) with his family, and the next day won $159 betting on the ponies at Aqueduct racetrack. On his return, he told his doctor that he felt wonderful; there are many things beyond the scope of medicine.

The Protestant chaplain visited Austin Raymond on Sunday morning and the house staff saw him during the day. On the third, fourth, and fifth days we are particularly watchful for signs of wound infection and urinary tract infection. There were none.

Sunday afternoon, accompanied by his wife, Austin Raymond took walks in the hospital corridor.

I returned from visiting friends in the country late Sunday night and did not see Raymond until the next day.

Monday, June 16

The two chest tubes, which remain in place until all fluid is drained from the chest and there are no air leaks, were removed on the fourth day by a house physician. In a clean lobectomy, the lung is airtight and the fluid drains from the cavity in 48 hours.

We remove the chest catheters by giving the patient pain medicine, removing the sutures holding the tubes to the skin, and withdrawing the tubes; a sterile sponge with adhesive tape pressure is placed over the small openings for a few days. If the lung is leaking air, or there is protracted fluid drainage, the catheters are left in place until this stops.

When I saw Austin Raymond on rounds in the evening he was eating his dinner, sitting up in bed, with the news on the tiny-screen TV.

He turned the TV volume down. "Well," he said, "they took out those damn chest tubes today."

"Good. I hope removing them didn't bother you too much."

"Your staff doctors said I'd barely notice it but they're masters of euphemism," Raymond said. "Did you ever hear Senator Everett Dirksen's story about euphemism? A man was filling out a life insurance application when he came to the question, 'How old was your father when he died, and what was the cause of his death?' The applicant's father had been hanged but he didn't want to write that on the application. After puzzling over the question he wrote, 'My father was 68 when he died. He came to his end while participating in a public function when the platform gave way.' "

I laughed. "That's like Mort Sahl's story of the captain of the *Titanic* announcing to his worried passengers, 'Just be calm. We've stopped to take on ice.' "

"For God's sake, don't make me laugh," Raymond said, wincing. "It hurts like hell."

Tuesday, June 17

In spite of precautions, complications following surgery occur in 5 to 10 percent of healthy individuals. If treated promptly, they usually do not amount to much, but if you fail to recognize them, they may become serious. Our postoperative orders are aimed at preventing complications and the nurses and house staff physicians keep a watchful eye out for danger signs such as elevated temperature.

Besides atelectasis (lung collapse) and pneumonia, another potential complication is phlebitis which can lead to a blood clot traveling to a lung. To prevent phlebitis we use a pulsating boot and keep some patients on anticoagulants. This is why we want patients moving their legs in bed, and out of bed walking around right after an operation instead of lying motionless or sitting around with their leg veins full of stagnant blood in which clots can form. We watch for swelling of the ankles and legs and tenderness in the calves, all signs of trouble.

When I visited Austin Raymond shortly before dinner he was in a cheerful mood. "Do you know what one of your volunteer workers asked me this afternoon, Ted? She asked if I wanted to go to the movies tonight. The *movies*, for God's sake! Another offered me books and told me about classes in jewelry making, music, needlepoint, and block printing. Your doctors don't think I'm cured—but your volunteers do!"

"I'm glad to hear that," I said, examining the lab report which I had received that afternoon. "Austin, I've got your final Pathology report on the tissue we removed. You recall that we took out some 15 lymph nodes from the center of your chest. None of that material contained malignant cells—it was all negative. That's optimistic news because it means the chances that the cancer metastasized are reduced."

"You're telling me the truth?"

"Yes. You know that's our policy."

"What about bad news—do you tell that to your patients, too?" Raymond asked.

"Well, if a person is extremely ill we usually wait a few days but we don't change our policy. We feel that the patient has a right to know his problem, the seriousness of his illness, and his alternatives. I think he should be told the truth in a compassionate, serious, but basically optimistic manner. But I don't think that a patient should be burdened with a lot of clinical detail or depressing figures of average survival time, which may not apply in his case."

"I understand that not all doctors and hospitals follow such a policy," Raymond said.

"That's true, and they're entitled to their views. But in my judgment, failing to tell the truth to a patient and his family erects barriers of suspicion, fear, and mistrust which create a lousy doctor-patient relationship. You can't build trust on a lack of candor and the feeling that something is hidden. Our experience here shows that telling the truth is the wisest and most compassionate way to handle a difficult situation."

"It must be damn tough to give a patient rotten news," Raymond said, leaning back to rest his head on the pillow.

"It is, and that's where the art of being an understanding and compassionate physician shows itself."

"Where do you learn it?"

"If you ever learn it, you learn it by living."

Wednesday, June 18

With his chest catheters removed, Austin Raymond took long walks with his wife in the corridors on his sixth day post-op and made new friends by visiting with other patients.

When I stopped by at 6:45 P.M., he waved and motioned me to the chair at the foot of his bed.

"What did you do today to earn a living, Ted?" he asked.

"A bronchoscopy, a lobectomy, and an argument with the lawyers."

"Sounds impressive. I walked a lot, talked with some friendly nurses, and met more people in my predicament . . ." He paused. "May I ask you about a sensitive subject?"

"Of course."

"Do doctors and nurses ever become accustomed to living with illness and death?"

"No, they don't. I don't think a good doctor or nurse ever loses a sense of compassion for patients. Of course, they can't become emotionally involved with every patient or they couldn't do their work. And for the most part, they can't show their emotions, at least in public. But they care.

"In fact, one of our problems at Memorial Hospital is that our staff sees only our sickest patients—those admitted to the hospital. They seldom see the thousands of people we treat as outpatients who work and live at home, many of whom are cured. And they rarely see cured patients after they're discharged."

"I sensed that," Austin Raymond said softly, "but I wasn't certain."

"Anyone who believes that medical people are insensitive to suffering should be part of a large hospital for a few months. They might see a young nurse in Pediatrics hide in a closet, weeping over the death of a tiny patient. Or a physician so shaken by disappointment and what he sees as his own failure that he snaps at the staff and is not himself."

There was a long silence.

I stood up and examined Raymond's chart. "I'm glad you're feeling better and eating a normal diet, Austin. Be sure to walk as much as you can."

"When do you think Austin can go home?" Barbara Raymond asked; she was with her husband every afternoon and evening and her quiet understanding and supportive relationship was a key factor in his recovery.

"Probably Sunday if everything remains stable."

Thursday, June 19

By the seventh day post-op, most lobectomy patients are in relatively good condition, eating regular meals and receiving oral pain medication such as methadone, Levo-Dromoran, or Percodan instead of morphine sulfate by injection. They still have a good deal of chest pain, which is controlled by the drugs. Austin Raymond had no fever and his chest X rays were normal as were his hemoglobin, white blood cell count, and urinalysis.

At 11 A.M. the house physician on duty removed the interrupted silk sutures from Raymond's red 14-inch incision, causing the patient minor discomfort. The incision was healing well.

"I saw a fascinating sight this afternoon in the X-ray Department," Austin Raymond said when I saw him late in the day. "A group of girls and boys—I would guess they ranged in age from 5 to 15—were waiting their turns. They were in wheelchairs and obviously pretty sick youngsters—but they were smiling and clapping.

"A lovely young woman, she couldn't have been more than 19 or 20, was strumming a guitar and singing softly to the children. She wore a white smock with the Memorial insignia and had long, glistening brown hair. It was the most moving sight I have ever seen. I . . ."

Austin Raymond stopped.

"Yes, I've heard of her. I think she works in X-ray."

After a while Raymond said, "They took out my stitches today. After I saw that sweeping incision I began to think about the risk of infection. How many operations lead to infection?"

"Infection occurs in about 1 or 2 percent of clean operations in spite of preventive techniques. We live in a sea of bacteria and even though the skin is self-cleansing, millions of bacteria thrive on its surface. At least half of all wound infections come from the patient's own bacteria even though we cleanse the skin with a strong germicide."

"I'm curious about the scrubbing at a sink that you surgeons do before an operation—how effective is it?"

"Very effective. When you start, you have about 10 million bacteria from fingertips to elbows. You are considered 'clean' when you are removing less than 250,000 bacteria per minute."

"What kind of bacteria?"

"Two types. Resident, nonpathogenic—nondisease-producing—bacteria are always with us. Transient bacteria are the dangerous ones because they're potentially pathogenic."

"And you protect against them by scrubbing?"

"Yes, and by wearing sterile gowns and gloves. It's also important for surgeons and scrub nurses to avoid getting bad bacteria on their hands by avoiding lacerations and dermatitis, and by wearing gloves or using instruments when they do dressings. They shouldn't change a tire on a dirty city street and they ought to wear gloves when spreading garden fertilizers, and so on."

"Ted, does a surgeon's technique affect the risk of wound infection and postoperative pain?"

"Yes, it does."

"How? What can a surgeon do?"

"Oh, a number of things. Injure as little tissue as possible. Cut cleanly with a sharp knife and a sure hand. Change blades frequently—blades become dull. Don't tie off large sections of tissue—only what's essential.

"Minimize blood loss by cutting cleanly, clamping blood vessels promptly, and ligating large vessels before cutting them. Avoid leaving holes in which clots can form; clots encourage bacterial growth and retard healing. Leave a minimum of necrotic [dead] tissue which is apt to become infected."

"What about the use of antibiotics—doesn't that reduce the risk of infection?" Raymond asked.

"Not necessarily. Using antibiotics for identified bacteria is good technique, but the general use of antibiotics in surgery is poor technique because it kills off protective bacteria and allows pathogenic bacteria to flourish.

"There are only two situations where antibiotics are routinely administered: in heart surgery, and in 'contaminated' or 'dirty' procedures where antibiotics are started several hours before surgery so that there is a level of antibiotics in the bloodstream during the operation."

"What's contaminated and dirty surgery?" Raymond asked.

"Procedures where the risk of infection is high because of the type of operation. A stomach resection and a cleaned-out bowel resection are contaminated operations because bacteria are present. A ruptured appendix or a gunshot wound of the lower abdomen are dirty or septic procedures because pus and feces are present in the operative field."

"What's the percentage of infection in those cases?"

"It depends. Complications and infection occur in about 25 percent of dirty operations but they can usually be managed successfully."

Friday, June 20

We continued to monitor Austin Raymond's condition; on the eighth and ninth days we are particularly concerned with healing as shown by X ray and observation of the incision.

Austin was writing in his green notebook when I dropped by that evening. "I've been jotting down what's happened to me in the past two weeks—which is one hell of a lot. Have you got time to answer a few questions?"

"Sure."

"I understand some operations last eight or nine hours, or even longer. Don't the surgeons become exhausted? Do you take time off to eat?"

"Yes, long procedures are tiring, particularly to the legs, feet, and arms, not to mention the mental fatigue. In a four-to-six-hour operation there's usually no relief. In a long, complicated operation there are four or five skilled surgeons working together so, except during a critical phase, one or two can leave the O.R. for five or ten minutes—although we often skip lunch. They scrub again, of course, before returning.

"Bear in mind, Austin, that surgery today is not a tour de force by the chief surgeon but a sophisticated team effort by highly skilled people. Our resident surgeons are independently good surgeons who are five, six, or seven years out of medical school and extremely competent."

"Is the operating room organization different for major cases?" Raymond asked, writing in his notebook.

"Yes, for a complicated procedure we may have an anesthesiologist, two anesthetists, two senior surgeons and two or three assistant surgeons, two scrub nurses, two circulating nurses, and several technicians."

"What do you do if you get into unexpected, serious trouble during an operation?"

"Well, that doesn't happen very often, as you know. But when it does I take whatever action is required quickly and quietly—such as closing a hole in an artery with my fingers to stop a hemorrhage. If I need another senior surgeon to assist me, I tell the circulating nurse whom to get—fast. He would be someone who works swiftly and skillfully without a lot of conversation.

"I might add that I agree with Mark Twain when he wrote, 'In certain trying times, desperate times, impossible times, profanity furnishes a relief denied even by prayer.' "

Austin Raymond chuckled. "Is there any type of surgeon who's apt to get into trouble?"

"Probably the fellow who tries to do everything himself instead of calling in a specialist when he finds himself facing a problem with which he's had little or no experience. When I find a tumor that has spread into the spinal canal, for instance, I call in a neurosurgeon even though I might be able to deal with it myself. A neurosurgeon spends his life perfecting the delicate techniques that demand special skills and special miniature instruments. . . . The fellow who knows everything and can do everything is a dangerous bird to have beside an operating table. I'm worried by people who are rarely right but never in doubt."

"I know what you mean," Austin Raymond said. "Ted, when you visit an operating room can you tell quickly whether the surgery is going well or badly?"

"Yes, I think every experienced surgeon looks for the same clues.

Is the atmosphere quiet and peaceful? Is the operative field dry, with no visible blood? How far along is the team? How much blood is in the suction bottle? What is the total blood loss on the wall board? What does the anesthetist's record show: Blood pressure? Stable pulse? Color of blood? Color of patient? Things like that."

"One last question," Austin Raymond said, laying down his notebook. "When can I go home?"

"I wondered when you'd ask. Let's see, tomorrow's the ninth day post-op. We'll give you a final examination tomorrow and, if all's well, discharge you on Sunday. How's that?"

"Great!"

Saturday, June 21

At a meeting on Friday with physicians from the Department of Medicine, we reviewed Austin Raymond's case. We felt that since the lymph nodes from his thoracic cavity were negative, no postoperative radiation was indicated.

The Saturday morning examination was unremarkable (doctor jargon for normal) and Raymond was scheduled for discharge on Sunday morning. Ordinarily, I do not make rounds on Saturday but this day I was in town for a meeting and I stopped by his room about 4 P.M. He was in a chair by the window reading our mimeographed newspaper, the *Playroom Times*, which is written and illustrated by our pediatric patients on the fifth floor and printed by volunteer workers in the Recreation Department.

"This is a remarkable little paper that the youngsters put out, Ted," Austin Raymond said, looking up from his copy. "Absolutely remarkable."

"Yes it is. It's an interesting combination of creative writing, humor, and perceptive observation."

"How old are the children who write and draw this material?"

"Oh, they range in age from 4 or 5 to 19 or 20. Some of them aren't children."

"And they all have cancer?"

"Yes. About half have leukemia. We treat most of these youngsters on an outpatient basis after they've been diagnosed and received initial treatment here at Memorial.

"The therapy is complex and childhood cancers should be treated only at a major cancer center which has specialized personnel and facilities. Once the treatment protocol is set, therapy can often be given locally. The youngsters write the *Playroom Times* while they're in Memorial."

"The spirit and humor of these youngsters is astonishing," Austin Raymond said, picking up the issues in his lap. "Listen to this, Ted.

"The best thing about the hospital is teasing the nurses and shooting waterguns. Chemo makes you naseasus.

J.Y., age 10

"I am almost as bald as my grandfather. I never thought that would happen!

H.W., age 7

"Thought for the Week: Courage is not the absence of fear but the conquest of it.

"Not all the night nurses are INCONSIDERATE. But the ones that are know who they are.

From a patient WHO WANTS RESPECT!

"Bulletin board sign. GOODBYE EVERYBODY. I'm going home!

Saul

"Worst TV commercials: Charman's toilet paper. Rice-a-Roni. Crest. Parkay. Meow-Mix.

"I like sticking the doctor dolls in the Playroom with needles. They all have leukemia.

C.O., age 8

"Here are more I like," Austin Raymond said.

"While you were being operated on the surgeon fainted and Josephine the plumber took over. Maybe that's why your pipes are leaking!

G.V., age 15

"Q. Do you think a physician should be allowed to practice after he reaches 65?"
"A. Absolutely not. By that time he should have the hang of it."

"Q. Who is the most popular doctor on the 5th floor?"
"A. Whoever signs the MOST DISCHARGE SLIPS!"

"*Doctor of the Week:* Dr. Zea because he is sweet. He always checks up on us. He has great interest in his patients.

"*Nurse of the Week:* Frances Hall—when we are in pain or upset, Frances takes our mind off it with her jokes and her Southern accent."

"I remember one memorable issue that announced: '*Doctor of the Week:* Nobody. *Nurse of the Week:* All of them,' " I said. "The fifth-floor nurses were gracious but the staff knew they'd read it."

Austin Raymond laughed. "Good for them. . . . Ted, I've got to read you just a few more.

"When you die your eyes are closed. You dont hear. You dont talk, You dont have to brush your teeth.

T.Y., age 6

"I've felt close to many doctors but I love Dr. Wollner. She's not only my doctor, she's my friend. She's concerned and patient. Patience is an important thing, especially with young children.

A.D., age 14

"X-ray escorts have a long walk. They talk when you don't want to.

"If you have to stay in bed you can watch TV. Or read. Well thats all. Have fun.

J.I., age 13."

"They're a great bunch of kids," I said, looking at my wristwatch. "Austin, I want to tell you about your discharge tomorrow . . ."

"One last quote, Ted," Raymond said.

"*Q:* What do you like most about this hospital?
"*A:* Loving people.

S.W., age 4."

"Bless her heart. Everyone here tries—I hope we succeed. . . . I thought you'd found the issue where the children wrote what kinds of animals the doctors reminded them of. I seem to remind them of a panda bear."

"Not bad," Raymond chuckled.

"I remember another amusing incident," I said. "On the day one young patient was admitted to our pediatric floor there happened to be several clowns from the Ringling Brothers and Barnum & Bailey circus entertaining our children in their beds. The new patient said he thought Memorial was a terrific hospital because it had clowns on its staff."

"Great!" Raymond laughed.

I outlined the discharge routine and explained our recommendation for chemotherapy which should have relatively few side effects; I told Raymond that we wanted to examine him again in 10 days.

"Tomorrow the house physician will see that you have pain pills and sleeping medicine with you when you leave. The pain will disappear gradually within 10 days and you should be able to resume normal activity at half speed within 2 to 3 weeks. Do as much walking as you can. It's okay to climb stairs and take a shower or a tub bath. Take your temperature at 4 P.M. and 8 P.M. If you have a fever, call us immediately. Let us know of anything unusual."

"How long does the follow-up period last?"

"After your first checkup, I'll want to see you every month for the first three months and then every two months for a year. After that, every three months for the next three years. If there's any recurrence, we want to catch it fast—we don't want to miss anything. After three years, we'll see you every six months for the rest of your life."

He nodded. There was a long silence.

"You know, I've led a life more interesting than most," Austin Raymond said slowly, "but this brush with death has had obscure and bizarre advantages. To say that I have a heightened awareness of life, an appreciation that I never held before, is a profound understatement. Minutes become precious when they may be numbered.

"I've learned about courage and kindness and optimism that I never knew existed and my memories of this hospital will defy time. I could never forget that lovely young woman singing softly to those sick children, the pale teenage girl walking slowly in the corridor pushing her I.V. stand, the spirit and resilience of the patients, and the love and fortitude and tears of their loved ones, who are also the victims of cancer.

"I saw the devotion of wives and husbands to their sick mates and was moved beyond words, and I thought of the Cassandra chorus of the fringe feminists. Human nature has not changed. Men and women still need love and devotion which endures through triumph and misfortune.

"I have never forgotten what Adlai Stevenson said about the knowledge of an older person, 'a knowledge not gained by words but by touch, sight, sound, victories, failures, sleeplessness, devotion, love—the human experiences and emotions of this earth; and perhaps, too, a little faith and a little reverence for the things you cannot see.'

"The older I grow, the more poignant life becomes. The past crumbles with change and the death of dear friends, but the future comes with the dawn. Life is not fading, it's becoming brighter and more intense. A glorious sunrise, stars in a velvet sky, a flaming sunset—these to me now are almost mystical. I don't feel older, but I am. Perhaps this is what the ancient Greek philosopher knew when he wrote, 'Better the old age of the eagle than the youth of the sparrow.' "

We stood up and shook hands. There were tears in his eyes.

"I know," I said. "I'll see you in 10 days, Austin. Good luck."

7

The Tobacco Industry
and the Government's Dilemma

AFTER ONE LIVES YEAR AFTER YEAR through draining ordeals like Austin Raymond's lobectomy, it is difficult to think clearly about the illness and death caused by smoking. Here was a man in his early fifties, who should have 25 years of life ahead of him, brought to the edge of existence by 30 years of cigarette smoking, a habit he enjoyed, never believing that it might cut short his life.

Yet this addiction brought him to the point of death and engulfed him and his loved ones in anguish, pain, and suffering, not to mention expenses of over $10,000. Your emotions are so raw at this point that you believe drastic action is the only solution: why not outlaw tobacco as a crop?

The situation, of course, is not that simple, nor is that a feasible solution in a free society.

Fifty-five to 60 million men and women in the United States, exercising their freedom of choice, continue to smoke, which is their right. But their freedom of choice collides head-on with the huge cost of providing medical care to smokers made sick by their addiction. After private payments by individuals, the remaining cost is paid by taxpayers who smoke—and by taxpayers who do not smoke.

One hardly needs to be reminded of the staggering cost of health care in this country, which is rising 10 percent a year. It is estimated that the nation's total health care bill in 1980 will add up to $225 billion in direct and indirect costs. Of this total, the illness and death caused by smoking accounts for about $20 billion ($20,000,000,000), which goes for doctor bills, hospital bills, disability payments, lost production, lost wages, and on and on. (Cigarette-related disease includes coronary heart disease, lung cancer, and chronic obstructive lung disease.)

Direct costs cover the prevention and treatment of disease, rehabilitation, research, and the construction and maintenance of health care facilities.

Indirect costs are the economic losses caused by disease and premature death, such as insurance payments, lost production, and lost wages.

By the year 2000—only 20 years from now—Georgetown University's Public Services Laboratory estimates that direct health care costs will reach an astounding $850 billion to more than $1 *trillion* a year, and that indirect costs will add another $1 trillion. Thus, the total cost of health care may reach $2 *trillion* annually by the turn of the century unless firm action is taken to control these skyrocketing costs. Such a plan would obviously include effective preventive medicine, tight control of inpatient hospital costs (one hospital staples the patient's bill to his medical chart so physicians can see the costs they are prescribing), and tight control of costs allowed by insurance companies and the government.

If tobacco-related disease remains at about 10 percent of total costs, then by the year 2000 these misfortunes will carry a price tag of $200 billion a year—most of which is an unnecessary expense.

Despite what some politicians and fuzzy-headed liberals apparently believe, this country cannot go on forever underwriting spiraling costs of this magnitude. There is an end point to what fiscal responsibility can countenance, and to what taxpayers will pay, as Proposition 13 in California proved.

Britain and Sweden, both nations with comprehensive national health care programs, have been forced by untenable costs to deny some types of health care to certain people. The National Health Service in Great Britain no longer pays for kidney dialysis, which cost it about $10,000 a year per person. In Sweden, expensive organ transplants are not available to people over age 70. Other wrenching restrictions are sure to follow, and it will not be long before the United States faces similar onerous decisions.

As an example of escalating costs in compassionate health programs, the kidney hemodialysis program subsidized by the federal government cost $200 million a year when it was enacted in 1972. By 1978, this program to keep alive 44,000 Americans afflicted with renal failure was costing U.S. taxpayers over $1 billion a year.

I am troubled by the philosophical implications of these formidable problems and have no ready-made solutions, nor do I wish to single out any one group. I mention the dialysis program only as an example of the perplexing implications of an ever-expanding health care program.

"Your Fault" Insurance

Dr. Keith Reemtsma of Columbia University's College of Physicians & Surgeons has suggested "your fault" insurance under which people who practice good health habits would pay lower taxes while those with dangerous health habits would be taxed to pay the medical costs of their own behavior. He proposes that taxes for medical care be added to tobacco and alcohol products, and that industries that produce products and pollutants that cause illness be taxed to help care for the people they make sick.

Dr. Reemtsma believes that medical costs such as immunization and treatment of diseases of unknown causes should be borne by society as a whole, but that when health hazards—such as cigarette smoking—have been clearly identified, the people who ignore the warnings should pay for the medical consequences of their own actions.

These proposals are enough to give tobacco and liquor industry executives cardiac arrest, but it may one day come down to whose will should prevail: that of the people or that of small groups with special interests.

George Will wrote in his *Newsweek* column, "It is irrational for Americans to spend so much to cope with illness when so much illness is the predictable consequence of habits. They are paying increasing sums of private and public money for *post facto* medicine which treats the consequences of dumb behavior."

One straw in the wind is that some far-sighted life insurance companies now give premium discounts of up to 20 percent to nonsmokers.

Tobacco Is Big Business

Those of us who witness day after day the sickness and death caused by tobacco, and who sometimes wonder whether tobacco should be banned as a crop, should nonetheless be aware of the leaf's place in the country's economy.

Federal, state, and local governments in 1978 collected $6.3 billion in taxes on tobacco products, 98.8 percent from cigarette taxes. By any standard, the tobacco industry is a major donor to the tax coffers.

Tobacco is grown on about 275,000 farms in 22 states and Puerto Rico, and more than half a million farm families are involved in growing the crop; farmers were paid $2.55 billion in 1978 for tobacco. The states with the largest incomes from tobacco crops are North Carolina, Kentucky, South Carolina, Tennessee, Virginia, and Georgia. Tobacco is the country's sixth largest crop after corn, soybeans, hay, wheat, and cotton.

The U.S. Department of Agriculture supports the price of tobacco through the Commodity Credit Corporation to the tune of $50 to $60 million a year. Horace Kornegay, president of the Tobacco Institute—which is supported by the cigarette companies—said, "The government is the biggest partner in the tobacco business in this country," and there is no reason to doubt his words.

While the per capita consumption of cigarettes was down slightly in 1978 for the fifth year in a row, Americans still smoked 620 billion cigarettes for which they paid $16 billion. Sale of other tobacco products added $1.1 billion in 1977.

About one-third of the U.S. tobacco crop is exported; exports of leaf tobacco and manufactured products in 1978 totaled $2.1 billion. The cigarettes sent overseas tend to have the highest tar and nicotine content and are the most dangerous to health. "We not only export a great many useful products," one researcher remarked, "we also export heart disease and lung cancer." Warning labels are not printed on export packages unless requested by the importing country.

"Conclusions Are Based Largely on Statistical Associations"

The tobacco industry likes to emphasize that the evidence against cigarettes is largely statistical in nature, and that "no one knows the root cause or causes of cancer." Let me answer this contention:

1. While there were a few earlier studies (Brosch in 1900, Abbe in 1915, Miller in 1939), the first major epidemiologic studies linking cigarette smoking and lung cancer were published in 1950 (Levin et al.; Wynder and Graham; Doll and Hill). Since then, thousands of studies have concluded that the link between cigarette smoking and heart disease and bronchogenic carcinoma is indisputable. The evidence is so overwhelming that no responsible scientist, in any country in the world, doubts for an instant that cigarette smoking is a health hazard of the first magnitude.

2. It is true that we do not know the cause or causes of cancer, or how carcinogens (cancer-causing agents) transform a normal cell into a malignant cell. But while seeking to unravel this complex secret of life itself, isn't the next wisest course to identify those acts or agents which cause many cancers so that the disease can be prevented?

The tobacco companies recently financed a $10 million study by the American Medical Association on the effects of cigarette smoking on health, for which they deserve credit. Understandably, their hope was that this unimpeachable research would conclude that cigarettes did not cause disease.

Unfortunately, this comprehensive study, released by the American Medical Association in 1979, concluded that cigarette smoking helped to cause irreversible heart damage, lung diseases including cancer, and a number of other ills. These conclusions were not quite what the tobacco companies were hoping for.

Health Risks Reduced

While still proclaiming their belief that cigarettes are not injurious to health, the tobacco companies nevertheless are switching to low-tar, low-nicotine, filter cigarettes—presumably to reduce health risks. (Interestingly, these cigarettes also cost less to manufacture.)

In the past 30 years the tar content of the average American cigarette has been reduced 50 percent and filter-tip cigarettes now account for 90 percent of sales, both steps in the right direction. (In 1955, the national average was 43 mg. tar per cigarette while today it is 17 to 18 mg.)

The death rates from heart attacks and lung cancer are somewhat lower among those who smoke filter cigarettes with the lowest tar and nicotine ratings. These cigarettes also cause fewer precancerous cell changes. But it must be underscored that while these cigarettes are an improvement, they are by no means safe. As Dr. Julius Richmond, the Surgeon General, said, "The only safe cigarette is an unlit cigarette."

Cigarette Companies Diversify Their Businesses

Although only about one-third of adult Americans now smoke, compared to 41 percent in 1966, the per capita consumption is down only from 209 packs a year to 200 packs in the past 10 years because of population growth. The percentage of adult males who smoke has dropped from 52.8 percent to 39.3 percent and that of females from 31.5 percent to 28.9 percent.

It is significant that every major tobacco company has diversified its product lines and the businesses in which it participates. This is the result of concern over the long-range future of the tobacco industry and the natural inclination of modern management to strengthen its base with products in markets that are growing.

Cigarettes, however, remain the most profitable product line that the tobacco companies market; 35 percent of the cost of a pack of cigarettes goes for federal, state, and local taxes. The profit margin on cigarettes is 20 percent or more, higher than on most other products.

American Brands (Lucky Strike, Pall Mall, Carlton, Tareyton) has broadened its business to include Jim Beam whiskey, Acme Visible Records, Franklin Life Insurance Company, Acushnet golf balls, Swingline staplers, Andrew Jurgens, and Duffy Mott foods.

Reynolds Industries (Camel, Winston, Salem, Real, Doral, Vantage) owns Sea-Land Service, the world's largest containerized shipping company, an oil company, and Del Monte foods.

Philip Morris (Marlboro, Benson & Hedges, Parliament, Merit) owns Seven-Up soft drinks, Miller and Löwenbräu beer, and is a real estate developer.

The *Liggett Group* (Chesterfield, L&M, Lark, Eve, Decade) markets Wild Turkey bourbon, J&B Scotch whiskey, Campari aperitif, Alpo pet foods, Super Pop popcorn, and owns a Pepsi Cola bottling company. At this writing, Liggett is trying to sell its tobacco business.

The Government's Dilemma

The U.S. Government presents an advanced case of schizophrenia where the health problems caused by tobacco are concerned.

On the one hand, it supports the price of tobacco, which costs taxpayers (smokers and nonsmokers) $50 to $60 million a year, and collects $2.3 billion in taxes on tobacco products.

On the other hand, the National Heart, Lung and Blood Institute, the National Cancer Institute, the Public Health Service, and the Office on Smoking and Health are working to find cures for smoking-caused illness and to educate the public on the hazards of smoking.

The Office on Smoking and Health, the government's principal antismoking agency, has a puny annual budget of about $2.5 million.

All told, the federal government spends only about $10 million a year for research and public education on the hazards of smoking while it spends $50 to $60 million a year to help grow tobacco.

"The Most Effective Lobby on Capitol Hill"

Since 1958, the tobacco companies have poured millions of dollars into well-planned, effective lobbying to hamstring antismoking efforts by the government and prevent any regulation of tobacco products.

"Hour for hour, and dollar for dollar, they're probably the most effective lobby on Capitol Hill," said Senator Edward M. Kennedy, a member of the antismoking forces.

The Tobacco Institute (1875 I Street NW, Washington, DC 20006), which was formed by the six largest cigarette companies, employs an estimated 65 lawyers, lobbyists, and public relations experts and has an annual budget of about $5 million. Additional special funds fight antismoking proposals such as Proposition 5 in California (1978), which would have severely limited smoking in that state.

Tobacco money is channeled into influential Washington law firms and the tobacco forces are aggressive politically, making contributions to numerous candidates for office. The Tobacco Tax Council notes attempts by states to increase tobacco taxes and opposes them; full-time industry spokesmen present arguments in favor of smoking.

On top of all this, the cigarette companies spend some $890 million a year on a barrage of advertising in magazines, newspapers, and billboards.

Two of the greatest victories for the tobacco forces are: (1) the fact that the federal tax of 8¢ per pack of cigarettes has not changed since 1951 in spite of numerous bills to increase it; and (2) every effort to regulate tobacco products and cigarette advertising has met with failure in the Food and Drug Administration, Federal Trade Commission, Environmental Protection Agency, Occupational

Safety and Health Administration, and the Consumer Product Safety Commission.

The influence of tobacco interests over Congress began in 1906 when it voted to declassify nicotine as an addictive drug to make certain that tobacco would not fall under the Food and Drug Administration. The tobacco lobby has successfully blocked every attempt at regulation and seen to it that more than 150 regulatory bills were buried in committee.

But the tug-of-war between the opposing forces has not been all one way. The banning of cigarette advertising from television, the warning label (weak as it is) in advertising and on cigarette packs, and the growing restrictions on smoking in public places and aboard aircraft are skirmishes won by the health advocates. (The removal of cigarette advertising from TV was probably a mistake since, under the FCC's Fairness Doctrine, it also removed most of the highly effective antismoking commercials.)

In fairness, it should be said that most tobacco company executives do not believe that cigarettes are hazardous to health, which is why, as the *New York Times* stated, they "spend considerable time and money trying to discredit the antismoking forces by challenging their research, motives, accuracy, and objectivity."

"Cigarette Smoking *OR* the Health of Americans?"

In October 1978, the American Cancer Society created the National Commission on Smoking and Public Policy to take testimony from knowledgeable people regarding cigarette smoking, assess antismoking activities, and recommend new approaches to this public health problem. The focus was on public policy and, in particular, the roles of the federal, state, and local governments.

The commission, which consisted of 23 members including three Nobel laureates, took testimony from 300 individuals around the country and examined published and unpublished data about the health effects of smoking.

The Tobacco Institute declined to appear at any of the public forums.

This study, which is in part critical of the role played by the American Cancer Society, recommends a far-reaching program to reduce cigarette smoking and make the tobacco industry accountable for the health consequences of its products.

In his letter of transmittal, Philip R. Lee, M.D., Acting Chairman, wrote, "The Commission believes that cigarette smoking is a clear and present danger to all who smoke . . . and it hopes that the responsible forces in the nation concerned with the well-being of its citizens will help to implement the recommendations . . . which can help people, particularly youngsters, from starting to smoke and assist those who now smoke to stop."

A "Doorstopper Report"?

The growing stream of reports over the past 20 years has spawned a new phrase in our language—the "doorstopper report." These are voluminous studies which, once completed, few people pay much attention to or bother to read regardless of how valuable the report may be.

While many studies deserve their fate as doorstops, others do not, and "A National Dilemma: Cigarette Smoking *OR* The Health of Americans," by the National Commission on Smoking and Public Policy, is one that deserves to be read and implemented. This slim report consists of 76 interesting, easy-to-read pages while the appendixes take 78 pages.

The Principal Effects of Smoking

The commission's report reaffirms the U.S. Public Health Service's finding that "cigarette smoking remains the largest single unnecessary and *preventable* cause of illness and early death."

Cigarette smoking is estimated to be related to:

- 80 percent of lung cancer.

- 80 percent of emphysema.

- 75 percent of chronic bronchitis.

- 30 percent of coronary heart disease (in men under 55).

The study concludes that smoking is:

- "A major factor in most cases of oral cancer and cancers of the larynx, pharynx, and bladder . . . and estimated to be related to 20 percent of *all* cancer deaths."

- A significant danger to unborn infants.

- "A major health hazard for women who use oral contraceptives."

Cigarette smoking in 1977 was related to:

- More than 320,000 deaths.

- More than 81 million lost workdays.

- Nearly 150 million days of excess bed disability.

"At a minimum, the current cost of cigarette smoking to society for medical and hospital bills and lost income from lost workdays is $18 billion [in 1977]," the study states.

The Principal Recommendations

The commission urged Congress to "place the interests of 218 million Americans above the interests of six major cigarette-producing companies" by passing legislation to:

1. Replace the federal excise tax of 8¢ a pack with an increased graduated uniform tax based on tar and nicotine content—a financial incentive to smoke low tar/nicotine cigarettes which would also curb cigarette bootlegging and increase tax revenues to the states.

2. Phase out tobacco price supports over 10 years; full payment to farmers for not growing tobacco; research into nonharmful tobacco uses and alternative crops, such as grains from which to distill alcohol for "gasohol" to help solve the energy problem.

3. Enact into law the Federal Trade Commission's recommended health warning label: "Warning: cigarette smoking is dangerous to health, and may cause death from cancer, coronary heart disease, chronic bronchitis, pulmonary emphysema, and other diseases."

4. Direct the Food and Drug Administration to regulate tobacco products including the additives in cigarettes.

The study recommended a comprehensive program by the Department of Health, Education and Welfare and its numerous agencies which includes a priority of funds for public education, antismoking advertising, a study of nicotine's addictive qualities, and regulation of the tar/nicotine and carbon monoxide content of tobacco products by the Food and Drug Administration.

Cigarette Advertising

"A purposeful and practical tack in regulating cigarette advertising," the report continues, should be pursued by the Federal Trade Commission which should seek voluntary agreement not to use models in advertising, and not to advertise cigarettes which exceed 10 mg. tar and 0.7 mg. nicotine. The levels of tar, nicotine, and carbon monoxide should be printed prominently on every package.

(Indeed, the persuasive cigarette advertising that associates beautiful women and rugged men who smoke with romance, health, and a zest for living bears scant resemblance to the real world. The truth is that the vigorous cowboy of this fantasy is more apt to be a pale, blue-lipped cowboy coughing his lungs out at the K.O. corral, scarcely able to stay on his horse.)

A Smoke-Free Workplace

The report urges that the Department of Labor support the policy that "the workplace should be a smoke-free environment," and that special areas be provided for smokers.

The Tobacco Institute agrees that "there are places (crowded elevators, to take the simplest example) where smoking is not appropriate. In closed and private places, the ancient courtesy of, 'Do you mind if I smoke?' is still the best rule."

The Department of Defense should stop encouraging cigarette smoking through the sale of tax-free cigarettes to the armed forces. "The military establishment is in effect underwriting future disability and death for . . . the armed forces and their dependents," the report states.

State and local governments should make "no smoking" the rule in all public places and enforce the laws banning cigarette sales to minors—laws that are seldom enforced.

Health Education Programs in Public and Private Schools

Perhaps the commission's most vital recommendations are those that concern youngsters and cigarette smoking. It urges that smoking not be permitted in elementary or secondary schools, and that the highest priority be assigned to developing an education program stressing health maintenance to be taught from kindergarten through twelfth grade as part of the required curriculum. "Use should be made of nonsmoking peers in stressing the social unacceptability of smoking" and communicating the "immediate and long-range disease consequences. . . . Smoke cessation clinics should be part of school health services," the report says.

Health Professionals Should Set an Example

"Health professionals, particularly dentists, obstetricians, pediatricians, and general practitioners" should inform their patients about the risks of smoking, the study says, and set an example by not smoking themselves. Health professionals ought to play a more active role with legislatures on policies related to smoking.

Hospitals should stop selling cigarettes and prohibit smoking in hospital rooms and public areas.

Reduced Insurance Rates

Insurance companies were urged by the commission to make available to nonsmokers, at substantially reduced rates, policies for life, health, accident, automobile, homeowners, and fire insurance. Certain insurance companies already do this on some policies and it is hoped the movement will spread.

Recommended Action by the American Cancer Society

In an encouraging show of independence, the commission urged the American Cancer Society to "accept responsibility for public policy activities, including legislative initiatives" and to establish a full-time legislative (lobbying) capability. "Within five years [the ACS] should be spending the maximum amount permitted by law for this activity." (Until 1976, tax legislation hindered nonprofit organizations where legislative activity was concerned. A new law now permits expenditures up to 10 percent of income or a maximum of $1 million a year for legislative programs.)

The commission also recommended expanded ACS capabilities to help smokers quit, special programs for school health education, and closer cooperation with health professionals.

Acting on this report, the American Cancer Society in November 1979 called upon the federal government to move aggressively through the Federal Trade Commission, the Food and Drug

Administration, and the Congress with a strong program against cigarette smoking.

What Smokers Should Do

Lastly, the commission said that smokers who cannot yet quit should be aware of the risks, sensitive to the needs of nonsmokers, and support education programs for children. Smokers should continue pressure on cigarette companies to produce less hazardous cigarettes.

I should add that high-risk groups ought to have a physical checkup once or twice a year, including a low-dose chest X ray and sputum examination, with bronchoscopic examination if carcinoma is suspected. High-risk groups are those who have smoked one pack a day for 20 years, and smokers in the asbestos, coal, rubber, textile, uranium, and chemical industries. Research is seeking to determine the optimum monitoring procedure for these groups.

What Are Foreign Countries Doing About the Smoking Problem?

Sweden has a program to make children born after 1974 the first generation of nonsmokers and to achieve a cigarette-free society by the year 2000. Within the next few years, the price will increase to over $2 a pack, which must list the levels of carbon monoxide, tar, and nicotine. Cigarette advertising was banned in 1976 and the sale of cigarettes in vending machines and food stores is being phased out. Schoolchildren at every level are taught the dangers of smoking.

Norway banned tobacco advertising in 1975 and regulates the content, weight, and filters of cigarettes. Finland prohibited advertising in 1976. Bulgaria is trying to reduce smoking among its youth. West Germany does not allow cigarette advertising on television.

Almost every European country (except Spain) prohibits smoking on public transportation and in hospitals and theaters.

China discourages young people from smoking and has linked cigarettes to cancer, the leading cause of death in that country according to the World Health Organization.

Egypt bans cigarette advertising on TV and forbids smoking in theaters and on airplanes.

The Soviet Union discourages smoking and in some industries, workers receive antismoking lectures and incentives to quit.

In 1978, Great Britain and its cigarette industry reached voluntary agreement banning the advertising of cigarettes with more than 17 mg. of tar.

Magazines That Refuse Cigarette Advertising

Among the U.S. magazines that do not accept cigarette advertising are: *Reader's Digest, Good Housekeeping, Better Homes and Gardens, National Geographic, The New Yorker, Scientific American, Parents' Magazine, Seventeen, Sunset, Natural History,* and *Yankee.* A number of newspapers also refuse cigarette advertising.

The Smoking Problem Is Complex and Worldwide

Clearly, the health hazards of cigarette smoking are acknowledged throughout the world, and forward-looking countries are doing something about the problem for both humanitarian and cost reasons.

As the National Commission on Smoking and Health stated, "Tobacco and nicotine are capable of inducing psychological or physiological dependence or habituation; cigarette smoking is characterized . . . by many as a form of compulsive drug use or drug addiction."

As noted in Chapter 1, smokers do not deserve abuse or scorn, or the stigma of second-class citizens; they need and deserve our understanding, sympathy, and assistance.

Smokers are hooked on a powerful and pernicious drug—*but nicotine addiction can be broken if motivation is strong enough.*

Regardless of how smoking may have affected their lives, or how strongly they feel, nonsmokers should always remember that informed adults have the right to smoke if they choose. "To suggest otherwise," the commission said, "would be to imply a prohibition that is neither enforceable nor desirable in a democratic society."

What is needed, in my judgment, is for Congress and the executive branch to reform our present irrational government policies, which are dictated by the tobacco industry. With the industry's virtual control of Congress and its expenditures of over $1 million a day, the scales are now tipped unfairly against the public interest.

It defies logic, for example, to understand why the government is so exercised over 50,000 highway deaths a year, yet pays inadequate attention to the nearly 350,000 deaths a year related to cigarette smoking—almost seven times the highway toll.

Our long-range national goal should be a nonsmoking society achieved over a period of years with minimum hardship to the tobacco industry and the people employed in it. To suggest less is to ignore the humanitarian needs of our people and the financial limitations of our society.

8

The Evidence That 33 to 50 Percent
of All Cancers Can Be Prevented

IN 1980, ABOUT 785,000* NEW CASES OF CANCER will be diagnosed in the United States. The prevention of about 50 percent of these new cases is, at this point in history, not within our power—*but responsible scientists believe that the other half of these new cases could have been prevented.*

Surprised? You have a lot of company.

Yet I suppose one should not be too startled. As former Senator J. William Fulbright observed, "It is one of the perversities of human nature that people have a far greater capacity for enduring disasters than for preventing them, even when the danger is plain and imminent."

While the proof that certain types of cancer are preventable is based upon solid medical evidence, the belief that other malignant neoplasms can be prevented comes from clues uncovered by epidemiologists—the medical "detectives" who study the patterns of disease occurrence by population groups and life-styles.

The evidence, for example, that polluted air and water, food contaminants, and the amount of fat in the diet may either cause cancer, or pave the way for it, is based largely upon epidemiologic studies, not laboratory research. Nevertheless, I believe that much of this evidence is sufficiently convincing to take action now even though all the answers are not in and future studies may disprove some of our present ideas.

One of our most troublesome problems in convincing people to take steps now to prevent cancer later is the long "latent period" between the igniting cause and the onset of disease. This latent period can vary from 5 to 40 years. If cancer followed the causative

---

*Figure does not include an estimated 400,000 cases of ordinary skin cancer, or carcinoma *in situ* of the cervix, both of which are almost 100 percent curable.

act by 6 months or a year, the cause-and-effect relationship would be clear and more people would be interested in prevention.

Another stumbling block is the statement that the "environment" causes 80 to 90 percent of all cancer. The clear implication is that we are at the mercy of our environment, and when we get rid of air and water pollution and chemical carcinogens that this will prevent almost all cancers—which is simply not true.

Understandably, people are confused as to what is meant by "environment." Dr. John Higginson of the World Health Organization points out that the concept of environment "includes the total background of a population such as its diet, social and cultural mores, etc. [life-style], as well as exposures to discrete chemical carcinogens." Under this broad definition, smoking habits are an integral part of the environment.

The final roadblock to interesting people in disease prevention is the innate belief that "it will happen to someone else, not to me." This mental opiate is vital to the soldier under fire but can be fatal where disease is concerned. The fact is that it can happen to any of us, particularly if we improve our chances of falling ill by ignoring preventive measures. Every last one of the thousands of men and women patients I have cared for thought that it couldn't happen to them—but it did.

Misleading Studies

It was Mr. Justice Brandeis who cited the danger of "drawing strong conclusions with dangerously few facts." Dr. William R. Barclay, editor of the *Journal of the American Medical Association,* said, "Many of the reports on carcinogenesis [the production of cancer] that have been made public have been flawed in both design and interpretation, but have been accepted by agencies that funded them, by the news media and the public." He pointed out that while ignorance of a hazard can be dangerous, "false information can be even more dangerous."

Part of the problem is caused by scientists some of whom, intentionally or unintentionally, publish premature, inconclusive data and exaggerate or misinterpret their findings. Simplistic answers to complex questions benefit no one and cause harm. One result in overemphasis on minor cancer risks and underemphasis on major risks (such as smoking).

Well-intentioned but poorly informed environmentalists often contribute their share of misleading information about carcinogenesis by mistakenly concentrating on chemical pollution in air and water.

The climate of cancerphobia is not calmed by the self-appointed "nutritionists," lay cancer "experts," and a few odd physicians who muddy the waters by parroting the nonsense that cancer is epidemic, that pollution causes most cancer, and that "alternative" cancer treatments produce miraculous cures. It all reminds me of the cartoon in the 1960s which showed a bushy-haired concert violinist standing at the footlights and saying to his audience, "Before the recital, I would like to make a statement on foreign policy."

It is no wonder that the public is confused and alarmed. As one housewife said, "Since it seems that just about everything causes cancer, I've given up paying much attention to news of the latest thing that causes cancer."

I doubt that ever in history has so much misleading information about one disease been unleashed on the public. Dr. James E. Enstrom of the UCLA Comprehensive Cancer Center, Los Angeles, wrote, "Some carcinogens that have been given a great deal of attention by the media . . . are not likely to have an important impact on reducing cancer mortality. These . . . include hair dyes, food coloring, saccharin, menopausal estrogens, and very low-level ionizing radiation."

What Causes Loss of Cell Control?

The cells in our bodies are constantly renewing themselves. In the course of life, cells die and new cells take their places. Cells that are injured are replaced. During its lifetime, a cell is either resting, or dividing and growing, controlled by its precise internal molecular mechanism.

A cell that gets stuck in the dividing state and reproduces itself uncontrollably is malignant (life-threatening)—a cancer cell. Cancer cells produce only more cancer cells, never normal cells.

While we do not yet know what triggers loss of cell control and thus causes cancer, we do know that loss of control can occur in two ways:

1. A biochemical breakdown within the body, either within the cell itself or possibly in some organ which produces a substance that

affects cell control. We can only speculate on what goes awry inside the minute cell (a million cells makes a clump the size of the head of a pin): damage to DNA (the master cell control material) may go unrepaired or be repaired inaccurately; the cell may miss a control signal; its surface sensors may malfunction; a defective gene may garble a message; one of its parts may wear out; it may receive too little, or too much, of an essential chemical; a slow-acting virus may sabotage the cell control system.

The basic disease mechanism, which seems related to aging, remains hidden in spite of millions of man-hours of research by scientists throughout the world. Since these cancers seem to arise spontaneously, we call them "blind accidents," but they obviously have a cause. You may read that the causes are "poorly understood," which simply means we do not have any idea what goes wrong.

2. The breakdown within a cell can be triggered by external influences—tobacco smoke (chemicals), diet, ionizing radiation, chemicals, drugs, alcohol, and so on. (A substance known to cause cancer is a carcinogen; a substance that causes cancer when combined with a second agent is a cocarcinogen; a tumor promoter is a substance that accelerates the action of a carcinogen.)

We believe that about 50 percent of all cancers fall into this second category, and that most of them can be prevented at a huge saving in human life and health care costs.

Simple Answers Are Often Wrong

Every so often you read in the popular press of the wonderfully low cancer death rates in Africa, India, Latin America, or the Soviet Caucasus. The implication is that these people live in a healthier environment and know something that we don't know. Secretly, perhaps, some of us wish we were members of these fortunate societies.

But there's an explanation for all this which they do not tell us.

In these countries, cancer is poorly diagnosed and underreported so actually it only appears to be low. Furthermore, the death rates from malnutrition, infectious diseases, and vague, unidentified causes are much higher than in the United States.

The right conclusion, which seldom reaches us, is that for the most part these populations avoid cancer by inaccurate records and by dying young. There is, of course, some variation in the occurrence of the different types of cancer in various parts of the world.

Then we are fed tantalizing news on how to avoid cancer of the gastrointestinal tract by simple changes in our diet.

The United States, England, and Denmark consume a high-protein, high-fat diet and have a high rate of cancer of the bowel and a low rate of cancer of the stomach. The implication is that if we reduced our fat and protein input, we would reduce the occurrence of bowel cancer.

But it is not quite that simple.

The Japanese and the Africans, who eat a low-protein, low-fat diet, experience a low rate of bowel cancer but a high rate of cancer of the stomach—far higher than the United States, England, and Denmark.

Thus, the control of risk for one type of cancer may increase the risk of another type of cancer. I am afraid that simplistic interpretations of complex questions are misleading and, in some cases, harmful.

Two Low-Risk Populations Prove Many Cancers Can Be Prevented

While we are bombarded by a barrage of nonsense about cancer these days, reliable epidemiologic studies of two population groups prove beyond doubt a great many cancers can be prevented.

Members of the Mormon Church (The Church of Jesus Christ of Latter-Day Saints) follow a doctrine which opposes the use of tobacco, alcohol, coffee, tea, and addictive drugs and encourages a nutritious diet, good health practices, and a closely knit family life. There are 3.7 million Mormons, many of whom live in Utah, which has a cancer rate 25 percent lower than the U.S. average (the lowest of any state). Accurate church records show the following:

• Church leaders and missionaries, who are more apt to follow faithfully "The Word of Wisdom" doctrine and who constitute 20 percent of Mormon males, have a cancer death rate about 50 percent less than the average for U.S. white males.

• Devout Mormon males living in California have 75 percent less of the cancers related to smoking and 35 percent less cancer of other body sites.

• Among Mormons, every type of cancer occurs less frequently except the leukemias, lymphomas, and cancer of the prostate.

Seventh-day Adventists

The Seventh-day Adventists, with 3 million members worldwide, are a deeply religious group who experience even less cancer than the Mormons. Adventists abstain from tobacco, alcoholic beverages, and pork products, and avoid coffee, tea, cola drinks, spices, and hot condiments (not every Adventist follows this regimen strictly).

About half the members of this faith are lacto-ovo vegetarians who eat eggs and milk products but do not eat meat, fish, or poultry. The typical lacto-ovo diet has about 25 percent less fat and 50 percent more fiber bulk than the average American diet. Relatively few Adventists are true vegetarians. This group also stresses general and health education and a strong family unit.

Studies show that Adventists have extremely low mortality rates from cancers related to alcohol and cigarette smoking and sharply lower rates for cancers not thought to be related to smoking or alcohol, such as neoplasms of the gastrointestinal tract, reproductive organs, and leukemia.

Adventist men and women have 30 to 40 percent less risk of death from cancer of the stomach, colon, and pancreas than the general U.S. population. Postmenopausal women have less cancer of the breast, ovaries, and uterus than the national average; diet is thought to play a role in these malignant neoplasms.

The Adventists living in California who were studied from 1958 to 1965 had an overall mortality rate from cancer 42 percent less than the average rate for U.S. whites, while the California Mormons experienced 38 percent less cancer than the general population.

Although the exact role of diet in cancer remains to be clarified, the investigators in these studies believe that diet plays a significant role in the lower mortality rates, in addition to the fact that devout Mormons and Seventh-day Adventists do not smoke. Some scientists have suggested that animal fats and lack of sufficient fiber bulk in the diet may be a factor in cancer of the breast, bowel, and other body sites; dietary fats do not cause cancer but may bring about metabolic changes that make cells in the breast and colon more likely to become malignant. Other studies have not supported the relationship of meat, fat, and caloric intake to these cancers.

What Percentage of Cancers Might Be Prevented?

No one knows precisely what percentage of all cancer cases can be prevented. The data from reliable studies vary from a low of 24 percent for U.S. white nonsmoking males (which did not include Mormons or Seventh-day Adventists) to a high of 52 percent in a study of 668 men and women in Alameda County, California, over a 9½-year period; in addition to not smoking, these individuals followed other good health habits.

Probably the most forthright estimate is that *at least* 33 percent of all cancer cases can be prevented if recommendations such as those in this book are followed, and it is quite likely that the figure could be as high as 50 percent.

The Great Cancer Mysteries

The tantalizing clues scattered about by cancer are tracked down by epidemiologists in the hope of learning what causes the different forms of the disease so that they can be prevented.

The first cancer epidemiologist was Percivall Pott, a surgeon at St. Bartholomew's Hospital in London. In 1775, he published an 800-word paper which attributed cancer of the scrotum in chimney sweeps to heavy exposure to coal soot (a hydrocarbon). Daily baths and changes of clothing helped to prevent this cancer.

Among the present enigmas are these:

• Why is the age-adjusted death rate from breast cancer among women in the Netherlands, England, and Denmark six times that of Japanese women?

• Why do nuns have such a high rate of breast cancer that it is considered their occupational disease?

• Why is cancer of the cervix rare among nuns and common in women with multiple sex partners?

• Why do Jewish women have a very low incidence of cervical cancer?

• Why does Scotland have the highest incidence of lung cancer in the world?

• Why is cancer of the nasal passages and esophagus high in China and low in Europe?

• Why has stomach cancer declined 80 percent in the United States in the last 50 years?

• Why is cancer of the esophagus four times as high in France as in Norway?

• Why do people who emigrate to a new country develop the cancers common to their adopted country?

• Why, in a few cases, do cancers stop growing of their own accord and disappear completely?

We know the answers to a few of these questions and suspect the answers to others, but have no clues to the remainder of these mysteries. The known and suspected answers are in the pages that follow.

9

The Causes and Prevention of Cancer

*It is a common axiom that the least costly illness in terms of
human suffering or of demands on the health care system is the
illness which does not occur.*

—David Schottenfeld, M.D., in
Cancer Epidemiology and Prevention

WHILE THE EXACT NUMBER of cancers produced by the various
carcinogens is not known, nevertheless I believe it is useful to
estimate the percentages of U.S. cancer cases which result from the
various causes as the first step in prevention; the percentages for
other countries will vary somewhat from these figures. Bear in mind
that these are only *approximations;* no one knows the precise
percentages.

The best combined judgment of physicians who have devoted
their lives to this field is that cancer in U.S. males and females
results from the following causes, and in an unknown number of
cases from interaction between two or more causes. An estimated
400,000 annual cases of ordinary skin cancer, largely the result of

Causes	Males (Percent)	Females (Percent)
1. Tobacco	30–35	10–15
2. Tobacco/alcohol	5	2–3
3. Diet (indirect or modifying influence)	25–30	40–60
4. Chemicals (workplace; air pollution)	10–20	2
5. Drugs	1	2
6. Radiation (X ray, etc.)	1	1
7. Iatrogenic (chemotherapy, radiation)	1	1
8. Life-style	—	15
9. Congenital	1	1
10. Unknown	15–25	15–25

ultraviolet radiation from the sun, are not included. In the table above and the discussion that follows, no percentage is estimated for males under "life-style," since these factors are included under other causes; the estimated percentage for females relates to procreation; see discussion of "life-style." "Chemicals" includes those in the workplace and in air pollution; sufficient data do not exist for separate estimates.

At this point, we need to keep matters firmly in perspective: there is no cancer epidemic (except for lung cancer); many of the things in the scare headlines are not significant causes of cancer; the cure rate is higher than most people realize; and three out of four people never get cancer.

On the other hand, it makes sense to know the principal causes of cancer, or any disease, and take reasonable steps to avoid illness and expense. It is wise for each of us to weigh our risk in light of our work, way of life, and family history, and then make our decision.

The sensible thing, it seems to me, is to live a satisfying and productive life founded on a sustaining philosophy. I do not believe that people should avoid every known and suspected cause of cancer or any other disease. That would mean a spartan, unenjoyable life—and might even put us at risk for a new illness. Anyway, a person who lived such a rigorous existence would probably have the misfortune to be knocked flat by a cornice falling off a building.

Just being alive puts us at risk.

So, as you read what follows, weigh the facts and then make up your mind. (I personally enjoy a martini and a charcoal-broiled steak on occasion.)

While Reference Information I in the back of the book sums up what is known about the major forms of cancer, and suggests preventive measures where they are possible, it would be helpful to comment on the causes listed in the preceding table.

1. Tobacco

Since lung cancer kills twice as many people a year as the next cause of cancer deaths, there is no single step that will prevent so much illness, death, and expense as stopping the use of tobacco. While cigarette smoking is the principal culprit, the other uses of tobacco also carry risk. In addition to bronchogenic carcinomas, the chemicals in tobacco smoke are linked to malignant neoplasms of the mouth, throat, vocal cords, bladder, kidney, and pancreas. "No one who smokes can be seriously interested in cancer prevention," wrote Dr. Daniel Miller of the PMI-Strang Clinic.

2. Tobacco/Alcohol

Most people are surprised to learn that smoking cigarettes and drinking alcoholic beverages at the same time is a dangerous combination. Heavy smoking and heavy drinking over a period of years is often lethal, especially when accompanied by a deficient diet. This combination leads to malignant lesions of the mouth, nasopharynx, larynx (voice box), and esophagus; the liver also may be affected.

We suspect that alcohol makes the cells more receptive to the carcinogens in cigarette smoke, or promotes their activity. Alcohol alone is not carcinogenic and animal tests with the residues of whiskey, sherry, sake, and ethyl alcohol were negative. Excessive amounts of alcohol, however, suppress the body's immunological defense system and that leads to disease. One physician defines heavy alcohol consumption for a medium-sized male as more than 6 oz. of whiskey, or five 4 oz. glasses of wine, a day.

I know of no research on which drinks cause the least harm, but I suspect that a long, well-diluted drink like a Scotch-and-water may be better than a strong, undiluted drink like a martini or a shot of whiskey. But that's a guess, there's no proof.

Moderate social drinking is not harmful to most well-nourished people and does not lead to cancer in nonsmokers. In fact, there is some evidence that very moderate drinking promotes well-being and longevity.

Homemade applejack is consumed heavily in Brittany and Normandy and apparently contributes to the high level of esophageal cancer in France. Italy follows in second place. The U.S. rate of esophageal cancer is 80 percent lower than France's.

3. Diet

What we eat, and do not eat, has a profound effect on the body's immune system, the aging process, general health, and whether we will contract cancer—yet surprisingly little is known about what constitutes a proper diet and the subject is incredibly complex.

Dr. Ernst L. Wynder, the distinguished epidemiologist, believes that nutrition in its broadest sense may relate to (but not cause) about 60 percent of the cancers in women and about 40 percent of the cancers in men. The cancers to which diet is related are malignant lesions of the breast, uterus, liver, esophagus, stomach, colon, and rectum.

Nutrition exerts mostly an *indirect* effect on cancer, either by setting the stage for cancer-causing substances, by promoting their activity, or by protecting us from them. Dr. Elizabeth Miller, a leading biochemist at the University of Wisconsin, pointed out that many of the agents considered carcinogens are actually precarcinogens and may be detoxified by the liver into harmless substances, or activated into genuine carcinogens.

Nutrition relates to cancer in three ways:

• *Nutritional deficiencies* that lead to biochemical malfunctions which start the neoplastic process.

• *Nutritional excesses* that induce metabolic abnormalities which initiate, or promote, cancer.

• *Nutrients, additives, and contaminants* which promote or speed up carcinogenesis or which, in relatively few cases, are actual carcinogens such as the aflatoxins, nitrosamines, and polycyclic hydrocarbons.

Chemicals That Block Cancer

A number of natural and man-made dietary substances block the formation of carcinogens in the digestive tract—contrary to what we are told by the alarmists. The food additives BHA and BHT, used as preservatives (antioxidants) in cereals and baked goods, block the formation of nitrosamines and polycyclic hydrocarbons and may well have contributed to the 80 percent drop in stomach cancer in the United States. Vitamin C (ascorbic acid) and vitamin E (alpha tocopherol) inhibit the formation of nitrosamines in animals, and probably in man. Vitamin A possesses anticancer activity.

The trace metal zinc is essential for the proper functioning of some 70 enzymes in the human body (enzymes regulate body processes). Zinc also has a profound influence on the effectiveness of the immune system. One oncologist found a zinc deficiency in 20 to 30 percent of his patients.

Chemicals called coumarins and indoleacetic acid, which occur naturally in the cabbage family, broccoli, turnips, Brussels sprouts, cauliflower, and many fresh fruits, inhibit the formation of certain carcinogens in the digestive tract.

The hue and cry raised about the nitrates and nitrites added to meat products to prevent deadly botulism poisoning was, to put it gently, ill-advised. (Nitrate can be reduced to nitrite which, if it combines with amines, can form nitrosamines.) What the alarmists fail to tell us is that most leafy vegetables contain high levels of nitrate, that nitrates can be formed in our intestines, and that 80 percent of the nitrite in our stomachs comes from our own saliva, not from food additives. Nitrate is absorbed quite rapidly by the body. It is possible, of course, that an excess of nitrite may increase our susceptibility to cancer—no one knows.

"Natural" and Processed Foods

"Natural" foods became a byword in the 1970s and most consumers believe that natural foods are safer and healthier than processed foods. There is no evidence to support this belief even though natural foods cost more. Some "natural" foods are composed largely of artificial ingredients. Other natural foods contain minute amounts of poisons which harm no one—arsenic in shellfish, solanine in potatoes, carotoxin in carrots. What counts is the *dose* of a chemical, not whether it is natural or synthetic. Foods are nothing but chemicals anyway, a fact that apparently escapes many people.

In the United States and Europe, where consumption of processed foods has increased the most, there is no evidence that food additives play any role in causing cancer—contrary to what we are told by excitable people without the facts. Stomach cancer is highest in the countries where processed foods are not consumed. Despite this, some of the coloring additives need further testing to make sure of their safety. Food additives, many of which are natural substances, are generally beneficial, almost all are harmless, and some protect us against dangerous contaminants. Additives keep the product safe and edible and sometimes improve its taste. Vitamin A is natural in butter but an additive in margarine. The most common additives are natural substances.

Ten years ago, Dr. Henry A. Schroeder pointed out that the hazard in some foods results not from contamination but from refinement which removes most of the trace elements essential for health. Milling wheat into refined white flour removes 78 percent of the zinc, 76 percent of the iron, 89 percent of the cobalt, 40 percent of the chromium, 86 percent of the manganese, 48 percent of the molybdenum, and 68 percent of the copper. The residue, Dr. Schroeder said, which is rich in these essential elements, is fed to animals.

Prevention Through Nutrition

Our increasing knowledge of nutrition is already helping to reduce or prevent some forms of cancer and decrease deaths from heart disease.

• In Japan, the program to reduce deaths from stomach cancer includes early diagnostic screening and increased consumption of ascorbic acid (vitamin C) and dairy products equal to two glasses of milk a day.

• In China, which has high rates of cancer of the nasal passages and the esophagus, vitamin C is used to block the formation of nitrosamines which results from eating pickled vegetables that are moldy; Chinese doctors are also discouraging consumption of scalding hot food and drink.

• In the United States, it is too early to know the effects of dietary changes on certain cancers, but the death rate from cardiovascular disease has dropped 24.1 percent since 1968. This encouraging progress is attributed to giving up smoking, eating less fat, control of weight, management of hypertension, and increased physical activity. The effective treatment of rheumatic fever and strep throat by antibiotics also has contributed to reduced heart disease.

Suggestions on dietary changes that may help to prevent some forms of cancer and reduce the risk of cardiovascular disease are given in Chapter 10—see "The Prudent Diet."

The undercurrent of interest in a diet stressing fresh fruits and vegetables is unmistakable and it is significant that our Stone Age ancestors who drew on cave walls were herbivores, not carnivores. They ate mostly plants, fruits, and berries, not primarily meat. The human digestive tract as it has evolved is not as long as a herbivore's but longer than the typical carnivore's. This is why the vast quantities of meat that Americans consume may overload the body's metabolic capacity and lead to diet-related health problems.

There is reluctance on the part of some physicians to accept the evidence that nutrition may lead to cancer. This may be because they know little about nutrition and are more concerned with active carcinogens and patient care than with factors that exert an indirect or modifying effect on the disease, as nutrition does.

"It should come as no surprise that a factor [nutrition] which can influence hormone production and retention, constituents and bulk of stool, the makeup of cell membranes and other cellular components, as well as affecting immunological factors, can be related to carcinogenesis," Dr. Ernst Wynder wrote in a professional paper, "Environmental Carcinogenesis."

4. Chemicals

The role of natural and synthetic chemicals in causing cancer, like the role of diet, is complex. Some chemicals cause cancer while others prevent it. Chemicals can cause disease but they are also a boon to mankind.

One needs to weigh the stream of government pronouncements that this or that substance causes cancer against the fact that the age-adjusted incidence of cancer in the United States in the past 50 years has remained about the same in spite of the huge increases in lung cancer—which means that most other cancers are decreasing. It also helps to remember the government warning of 21 years ago— just before Thanksgiving—that cranberry sauce might cause cancer because of contamination by a herbicide that caused thyroid cancer in rats. This prediction later proved false and healthful cranberry products are today more popular than ever.

The recent government report that some hair dyes are carcinogenic is not substantiated by a massive 20-year study by the American Cancer Society which showed that 5,000 beauticians had no greater risk of cancer than other women despite higher exposure to hair dyes.

The federal verdicts are based on tests with mice and rats in which the animals are given the highest doses of the test substance that they can tolerate without dropping dead. These massive doses—"the equivalent of drinking 500 cans of diet soft drink a day!"—are necessary, the experts say, so as not to miss a weak carcinogen that could remain undetected if lower doses were used, since all animals (and humans) are not equally sensitive to carcinogens. Perhaps so, no one really knows. Many people believe that huge doses of anything might cause cancer, but this is not true either.

Then there is the knotty question as to whether a safe "threshold" level exists below which a carcinogen in animals poses no threat to human health. Despite the abundance of statistical acrobatics brought to bear on this question, the fact is that no one knows the answer.

Authorities disagree on whether chemicals that cause cancer in rodents also cause cancer in man; most scientists believe they do since the majority of carcinogens in man also cause cancer in animals. But some agents that are carcinogenic in man do not cause cancer in animals, and the reverse is probably true.

For example, 2-napthylamine is a powerful carcinogen in man but not in animals. A study among diabetics, who use more saccharin than other people, showed no higher incidence of bladder cancer, yet at high levels saccharin caused bladder cancer in rodents.

The situation is further complicated by the long latent periods involved; exposure may not result in cancer for between 5 and 40 years, so a cancer time bomb might be ticking away, although this is unlikely.

People can be exposed to chemicals in the workplace, through air and water pollution, food and drink, and a few consumer products. In addition to cancer, chemicals can cause nervous system disorders, liver damage, miscarriages, and mental retardation.

The two dozen regulatory statutes that Congress has enacted to protect the public against toxic chemicals are administered by six government agencies since prevention is the best method of control. (The agencies are: Environmental Protection Agency; Occupational Safety and Health Administration; Consumer Product Safety Commission; Food and Drug Administration; Food Safety and Quality Service, Department of Agriculture; and Department of Transportation.)

The tragedy of Love Canal at Niagara Falls, New York, where buried toxic chemical wastes caused severe health problems, highlights the problem of dangerous chemical dumps. The EPA estimates that 1,200 chemical dumps are health threats and that the cost of cleaning up the worst of these might run into billions of dollars, some recoverable from the chemical companies responsible.

While we must rely on the federal government to a major extent, there are precautions that all of us can take to minimize the chance of harm from physical agents and toxic chemicals:

• Wood dust is carcinogenic; when using power saws, sanders, and other tools, wear a mask to avoid breathing in this dust.

• Do not refinish furniture using varnish or paint removers, sanders, or spray guns in a confined area; wear a mask and work in a well-ventilated area, preferably outdoors.

• When using sprays and other products, follow the recommendations on the labels with respect to ventilation, distance, and the like.

• Refrigerate food properly; never preserve food by home smoking; charcoal broiling may produce the carcinogen benzopyrene, so enjoy it sparingly.

• If you have doubts about the purity of your drinking water, have it tested by a commercial laboratory.

• Metallic particles from old pipes may leach into drinking water; if your plumbing is old, consider replacing it. In the morning, run the water hard for a few minutes to flush out residue that may have settled overnight.

Chemicals in the Workplace

Toxic substances in the workplace, which account for an estimated 10 to 20 percent of all cancers in men, enter the body by inhalation, ingestion, and contact with the skin. These agents include wood dust (furniture factories), asbestos particles floating in the air (not asbestos in solid form), arsenic, aniline dyes, solvents, plastic components, iron, nickel, and lead compounds and the like. The common sites of the malignant lesions caused by industrial chemicals are the lungs, bladder, liver, and GI (gastrointestinal) tract.

Preventive measures include containment of toxic liquids, dust, and fumes; protective gloves, masks, and clothing; "wash-down" facilities; laboratory medical tests; periodic physical examinations; and cooperation with epidemiologists.

Of the approximately 50,000 industrial chemicals in use, 40 are known animal carcinogens with 17 under federal regulation; several hundred more are suspect and need evaluation. Unfortunately, each animal test costs about $200,000 and requires three to five years. The Ames test, which measures whether a substance damages the genetic material in a bacterium cell (i.e., is a mutagen), may be a quicker, less costly way of flagging a potential carcinogen. All carcinogens are mutagens but not all mutagens are carcinogens.

Risk rises sharply when two or more carcinogens interact. Asbestos workers who smoke develop lung cancer at nine times the rate of asbestos workers who do not smoke. This synergistic effect may explain why the highest cancer death rates are in the heavily industrialized areas. For example, fine particulate air pollution containing sulfates, nitrogen oxide, and hydrocarbons may combine with the chemicals in tobacco smoke to increase respiratory disease and bronchogenic carcinoma.

Management obviously bears the principal responsibility for protecting its workers and the public, and most companies now have such programs, although in the past some have not. The Dow Chemical Co. in the 1950s found a health hazard in chloromethyl ether used in plastics manufacturing and took steps to limit worker exposure. Dozens of workers in other companies, which did not limit exposure, contracted lung cancer, according to government authorities.

Actually, the most dangerous chemicals occur naturally, such as the aflatoxin molds and nitrosamines which sometimes contaminate food, and the chemicals formed in our intestines by the interaction of bacteria with fecal matter. These natural compounds are responsible for many more cancers throughout the world than industrial chemicals which, to date, have not produced a significant cancer increase in the general population.

"I don't subscribe to the theory that we are on the verge of a cancer epidemic resulting from wholesale pollution of the environment," said Dr. Arthur C. Upton, former director of the National Cancer Institute, and most responsible scientists agree.

5. Drugs

The vast majority of drugs are not carcinogenic and those which are, or which may contribute indirectly to cancer, are evaluated and controlled by the Food and Drug Administration. Drugs are estimated to account for only 1 to 2 percent of cancers.

The synthetic female sex hormone estrogen has received the lion's share of attention because in birth control pills it increases a woman's chances of hypertension, blood clotting, heart attack, and stroke—and the danger increases if the woman smokes. Estrogen is also linked to cancers of the endometrium (lining of the uterus), cervix, and breast; one study connected estrogen to melanoma, a serious form of skin cancer.

Several years ago, at the request of the Food and Drug Administration, three pharmaceutical companies stopped marketing sequential birth control pills because of evidence that they increased endometrial cancer.

I am sometimes asked what, in my judgment, is the safest method of contraception, and my answer is the diaphragm, used correctly and conscientiously, and the condom, which also prevents venereal disease.

If estrogen is prescribed for postmenopausal symptoms, the risks should be explained to the patient and the dose kept to the lowest possible level and discontinued every so often to see whether it is still needed. The patient should be examined every six months, and if there is vaginal bleeding, a biopsy or D&C (dilation and curettage) should be performed. Endometrial cancer is detected by the Pap test only 40 percent of the time. A woman who has had breast or cervical cancer should not take replacement estrogen.

Another drug that has received public attention is DES— diethylstilbestrol—prescribed in the late 1940s and 1950s to prevent miscarriages. Twenty years later it was found that DES caused a serious, often fatal cancer of the vagina and cervix in some of the daughters of the women who took DES. It was a tragedy, but there was no way of knowing of the long-delayed effect. Late in 1979 the Food and Drug Administration banned DES from poultry and cattle feed, a long overdue step.

The immunosuppressive drugs given to kidney transplant patients to prevent rejection of the new kidney cause an increase in lymphoma and other cancers because the body's immune defense system is weakened.

The antibiotic chloramphenicol can depress bone marrow, which may lead to leukemia, and certain other drugs such as carbon tetrachloride and bleomycin, can produce liver and lung cancer respectively. Phenacetin, used in pain-relieving drugs, and amphetamines, used in weight reduction, increase the risk of cancer of the kidney pelvis, and Hodgkin's disease, respectively.

A few other drugs produce cancer in animals and may pose a risk for man, but this is uncertain, as discussed earlier. These include chloroform (used in some cough syrups), and methpyrilene (used in over-the-counter sleeping pills).

The overriding point to bear in mind is that if a drug's benefit is substantial and the risk slight, the physician and his patient may conclude that the drug should be used because of the relief it brings, or the life it saves.

6. Radiation

Although ionizing radiation is not a major cause of cancer, it is wise to restrict exposure to a minimum since little is known about the cumulative effects of low-dose radiation over a lifetime. Radiation beyond levels considered safe can cause cancer and genetic mutations which lead to birth defects and illness including leukemia.

Everyone on earth is exposed to radiation from three sources:

• Natural background radiation. This constant low-level radiation comes from the sun, cosmic rays from outer space, constituents of the body, and radioactivity in the earth's soil, sand, and rocks. People who live in Denver, Colorado, 5,000 feet above sea level, and those who fly at 40,000 feet in jet aircraft, receive considerably more natural radiation than someone at sea level.

Overexposure to the sun's ultraviolet rays often causes skin cancer, which can be prevented by wearing protective clothing and using an effective sunscreen with a high SPF (sun protection factor) number; many contain PABA—para-aminobenzoic acid. Outdoor people with fair complexions in sunny southern climates are at high risk—farmers, seamen, fishermen, construction workers. Skin cancer (except for melanoma) is almost 100 percent curable if treated promptly and properly, but untreated it can be a serious, disfiguring disease and can even cause death.

• Man-made radiation (nonmedical) from nuclear weapons fallout, nuclear plants, luminous watch faces, smoke detectors, X-ray inspection systems, TV receivers, and so on. Although this radiation should be reduced to the lowest level, it is not now a significant source—unless there should be a nuclear disaster.

It is obvious that nuclear power plants need tighter safety procedures and a safe method of disposing of nuclear wastes to avoid potentially hazardous radiation to the public. The two atomic bombs dropped on Japan in 1945 caused major increases in many types of cancer in that country.

Microwave ovens cook by RF (radio frequency) energy, not ionizing radiation, and properly designed, manufactured, and maintained, these ovens are not a health hazard. The oven door seals should fit tightly and as a precaution one should not unnecessarily place his face close to the door, even though the chance of RF leakage is slight. *Prolonged* exposure to *high power* microwave radiation, such as used in large radars, may cause eye cataracts and other tissue damage.

• Medical and dental X rays are man's principal source of ionizing radiation, and here effective precautions can be taken by physicians, dentists, and the public—although these precautions are sometimes ignored and X rays treated too casually. Every X ray carries an unknown degree of risk even though it may be slight; people vary in their susceptibility to radiation.

The following guidelines may be helpful in keeping radiation to a minimum:

• No diagnostic X ray for which there is an *important medical or dental reason* should be a source of concern.

• There should be a valid reason for every X ray; ask whether the X ray is essential to your well-being, and if another diagnostic test can be substituted. Good professionals welcome intelligent questions.

• There should be no "routine" X-ray examinations such as a dental X ray every six months. One young mother questioned her dentist about the wisdom of X-raying her young son at his six-month checkups. The dentist became angry and said if she did not trust his judgment, to find another dentist. She did. Her new dentist does not believe in routine X rays for children or adults.

In 1972, the American College of Radiology, the American College of Chest Physicians, and the U.S. Public Health Service recommended against chest X rays as a routine test for tuberculosis, and this practice has been stopped.

• Keep a record of your X rays by date and type, and know the location of the films; this may eliminate the need for new X rays.

• If you see a second physician or dentist, do not duplicate recent X rays (conscientious physicians and dentists ask about this).

• Radiation can be very harmful to a fetus. A pregnant woman should avoid all nonessential X rays, particularly in the pelvic region.

• Women of childbearing age should not be X-rayed or fluoroscoped, especially in the pelvic region, except during the first 10 days after the start of the menstrual period, to avoid possible damage to a fertilized egg.

• The genital area of a young adult should not be X-rayed without a sound medical reason.

• The potential for X-ray damage is greater among children and only essential films should be taken; because growing children are smaller, it is difficult to keep reproductive organs out of the main X-ray beam.

• Avoid examination by a fluoroscope if your doctor believes that an ordinary X ray will be adequate. X-ray studies using a fluoroscope expose patients to from 2 to 50 times more radiation than a standard X ray and their use demands a valid diagnostic reason; fluoroscopy should not be used for screening.

There is a wide variation in radiation dosage to the patient for the same study taken by a modern X-ray machine and by an old machine. In a mammogram (breast X ray) done with modern equipment, each breast absorbs about one rad while the dosage from an old X-ray unit can be up to 10 rads. The newest X-ray equipment films a mammogram with only a fraction of a rad—as low as 0.02 rad. The lower the dosage, the better. (A rad is a measurement of the amount of radiation absorbed by body tissue.) Chapter 10 gives mammogram recommendations.

Dose reductions of up to 90 percent with clearer films are common with modern equipment. This is achieved with new types of X-ray tubes, higher voltages, narrower, more intense beams, electronic timers, faster film, and shorter exposure times. These improvements are particularly important in fluoroscopy. The X-ray machine should be inspected yearly to be certain it is delivering the calibrated amount of radiation, and periodic radiation protection surveys should be made. In December 1979, the Bureau of Radiological Health of the FDA issued a report stating that about one-third of the dental X-ray machines and 46 percent of the X-ray units used for mammograms emitted unacceptable levels of radiation.

According to the Bureau of Radiological Health, between 130,000 and 170,000 technicians operate medical X-ray equipment but only 80,000 are licensed; in the dental field, more than 150,000 persons perform X-ray examinations. Only 10 states (Arizona, California, Florida, Hawaii, Kentucky, Montana, New Jersey, New York, Oregon, and West Virginia) and Puerto Rico license X-ray machine operators.

It is difficult for a layman to tell whether the X-ray equipment in a hospital or radiologist's office is modern. The best thing is to ask the radiologist. In a dentist's office, however, it is a different story.

• Ask your dentist.

• If a short, pointed plastic cone is placed against your cheek for bite-wing films, the X-ray machine is not modern. Modern equipment uses a collimator—a long, shielded, open-ended tube that restricts beam width and reduces scatter radiation.

• A lead apron should be placed over your chest, abdomen, and genitals; this is particularly important for children and patients in their reproductive years.

In 1978, the American people were subjected to an estimated 540 million medical and dental X rays in 278 million examinations. Experts differ on how many of these X rays were unnecessary, but estimates run from 30 to 50 percent—shocking figures. Physicians and dentists can render a significant service to the health of their patients, and reduce health care costs substantially, by limiting X rays to those that are *essential*. Reducing X-ray studies by 30 percent would save the public about $2 billion a year.

In answer to the question, "Would you recommend that physicians be more cautious in their use of X rays?" Dr. Arthur C. Upton, former director of the National Cancer Institute, replied, "Yes, I would recommend that." Clearly, the indiscriminate use of X rays is bad medicine and bad dentistry.

7. Iatrogenic

This refers to new cancers that may result from the medical treatment of patients by chemotherapy (drugs) and radiation therapy (X ray, cobalt-60, etc.). The critics, who are not physicians and have no clinical experience, state that chemotherapy and radiation destroy healthy cells and suppress the body's immunological defense system, which leads to new malignant lesions.

Well, as H. L. Mencken said, there is something to this but not much. These allegations are, for the most part, outrageous exaggeration, but since I am sometimes asked about them by anxious patients and their families, it is worthwhile to set the record straight.

I think the first thing to remember is that we are treating men, women, and children who are seriously ill, that every effort must be made to save their lives, and that few things in medicine—or life—are without some degree of risk. Chemotherapy and radiation have impressive cures to their credit, something the critics conveniently ignore, but like other forms of therapy, they pose some dangers.

The powerful drugs used in chemotherapy are toxic and improper administration can cause death. The side effects are often severe but disappear after treatment. These drugs, and radiation, do damage healthy cells while destroying cancer cells, but the damaged cells are replaced and no permanent damage is done if treatment is properly controlled. Chemotherapy is usually "pulsed," that is, the patient is given the drug combinations for, say, one week and then no treatment for three weeks, which lets healthy cells regrow and the immune system regain strength.

Chemotherapy tends to suppress the body's immune system, but again this can be controlled by frequent tests of immunologic competence. Chemotherapy also can restore the immune response by destroying a bulky tumor that has depressed it.

Chemotherapy is the primary method of killing malignant cells that have metastasized (spread), and in some cases oncologists can either cure the cancer or control it. Because of advances in chemotherapy, for example, 90 percent of the young boys and girls with acute leukemia are in complete remission in three years at major pediatric cancer centers, and we hope to cure at least 50 percent of these youngsters; only one or two decades ago, most of these children died within six months.

Ionizing Radiation

High doses of uncontrolled radiation can cause cancer. Early experimenters, unaware of the danger, developed cancers because they frequently X-rayed their hands and other parts of their bodies.

New machines and techniques, such as rotating the source of radiation around the patient, reduce the exposure of normal cells and concentrate the beam on the tumor to destroy it.

Ignorant critics speak of "burning" the patient with radiation, which is gross misrepresentation. If a patient is ever burned, it is because the radiologist is incompetent. Radiation may produce a red blush on the skin, as with a sunburn, but it does not burn the patient.

If you could attend surgical grand rounds at Memorial Hospital, which is held weekly for our staff, listen to the case histories, and see the color slides of patients "before" and "after" radiation treatment, you would be astonished—and encouraged. The case of one 52-year-old woman is typical. Her disfiguring facial tumor completely disappeared and the "after" photograph, taken six months after treatment began, showed an attractive woman whose face looked almost normal. In her case, this result could have been achieved only with radiation therapy.

Administered properly, chemotherapy and radiation therapy cure a number of cancers, and if cure is not possible, these therapies often enable patients to live years of productive life.

Ten or twenty years after treatment of a life-threatening tumor it is possible that a relatively small number of people will develop another cancer from the effects of the therapy. But isn't this an acceptable risk when they would have died years sooner if treatment had been withheld? Our patients think so.

8. Life-Style

Life-style is a vague but important concept that is difficult to study except in homogeneous populations such as Mormons and Seventh-day Adventists. It includes factors already discussed such as diet, tobacco, alcohol, personal habits, occupation, and so on. The carcinogenic effects of many of these stimuli are not well defined, and fall into three categories:

• *Proven risk*—e.g., the chemical 2-naphthylamine in the workplace.

• *Potential risk*—e.g., the possibility that cyclamates, which in high doses are carcinogenic in rodents, may cause cancer in man.

• *"Additive" risk*—two or more substances which, when combined, greatly increase risk (e.g., smoking and alcohol act together to increase risk beyond that of smoking alone).

Two things compound the difficulty of evaluating the effects of life-style:

• Social and cultural habits vary widely around the world (chewing betel nut quid is carcinogenic and a problem in India and Pakistan but not in most other countries).

• Each individual's susceptibility to cancer varies by age, sex, genetic predisposition, general health, status of immune system, and so on. Two cocarcinogens that cause cancer in Mrs. A might not cause cancer in Mrs. B.

Life-style has an important influence on two types of female cancer:

Cancer of the Cervix

Cancer of the cervix (the opening to the uterus at the end of the vagina) is rare among nuns and other women who do not engage in sexual intercourse. There is no relationship to the frequency of intercourse but there is a relationship to the number of different partners a woman has. Prostitutes have a high incidence of cervical cancer; women with only one partner also get this disease but at a low rate.

Sexual intercourse at an early age increases risk and a woman should start annual Pap tests as soon as she commences sexual activity. Cervical cancer is close to 100 percent curable when detected early by the Pap test and properly treated; yet 40 percent of U.S. women in the years of peak risk never have a Pap test.

Jewish women have a very low incidence of cervical cancer, which is attributed to the fact that their sexual partners are usually circumcised. The wives of uncircumcised males are three times more apt to contract cervical cancer, according to one study.

Epidemiologists believe that cervical cancer is related to poor penile hygiene and probably results from some agent passed into the cervix during intercourse. Circumcision and good habits of male cleanliness probably would eliminate cancer of the cervix.

(A modern woman who knew these facts asked her gynecologist what preventive steps could be taken. "Well," he replied, "it might raise a few eyebrows, but before going to bed you could suggest that your partner urinate, take a shower, and wash his genitals thoroughly with hot water and soap." This is good medical advice but hardly likely to encourage romance—unless they shower together.)

Breast Cancer

Epidemiologists discovered that breast cancer occurs more frequently among these groups:

• Women who either have no children, or who bear children after age 30.

• Women who consume a diet rich in fats; Dutch women with their consumption of cheese, butter, eggs, and whole milk have the highest incidence of breast cancer.

• Women overweight by about 40 percent have a higher rate of cancer of the uterus (endometrium) and ovaries, and somewhat higher rates of cancer of the breast, gall bladder, and kidney. (Men 40 percent or more overweight have a higher risk of prostate and colon-rectum cancer.)

• Women who start menstruation early and continue to a late age.

These and other factors are believed to set the level of the female sex hormone estrogen and its fractions in a woman's body throughout her life. Estrogen is produced by the endocrine glands, present in birth control pills, and may be prescribed for postmenopausal women.

Pregnancy at an early age, and artificial menopause before age 40 by removing both ovaries (for other reasons), affect estrogen level and provide protection against breast cancer. Japanese women who eat a low-fat diet and menstruate a fewer number of total years have the world's lowest incidence of breast cancer, but it is rising as their diet changes.

About 60 percent of breast tumors contain "estrogen receptors," which means that the cancer needs estrogen to grow. If this hormone were not present at a high level, it is possible that these tumors would be less likely to develop, or might not develop at all. The presence of estrogen receptors is detected by a tissue study called an estrogen receptor assay, which should be made for every patient. But the basic cause of breast cancer remains a mystery.

The only preventive measures against breast cancer, at present, are these:

• Consume less fat in the diet. Stay at normal weight.

• The estrogen in birth control pills is linked to female cancer including cancer of the endometrium and in one study to melanoma, a serious form of skin cancer. While the risk may be slight, it is probably prudent to use another form of contraception.

• Estrogen should be taken by a postmenopausal woman only after her physician has explained the risks clearly and where the benefits outweigh the risks. A woman who has had breast or cervical cancer should not take estrogen.

The two methods of detecting breast cancer at an early and highly curable stage—self-examination and mammography—are described in Chapter 10.

9. Congenital

Cancer is not inherited and many descendants of families with a history of cancer never get the disease. However, certain cancers do tend to run in famillies and if many of your close relatives had cancer, your chances of one day contracting cancer are somewhat greater than those of someone whose family tree shows little trace of the disease. This occurs both for genetic reasons and because families may live in the same places and follow the same life-styles.

The cancers associated with increased familial risk are those of the breast and colon.

Susceptibility to cancer varies from one person to the next. This is due, in part, to the biological inheritance from our ancestors. It may be due to an inherited exchange of genetic material between chromosomes, enzyme deficiencies, variations in hormonal output, or defects in the immune system. (Genes are the building blocks of heredity and make up each chromosome; each female egg houses 23 chromosomes and each male sperm carries 23 chromosomes.)

A chromosomal abnormality thought to be acquired, not inherited, the Philadelphia chromosome, is linked to chronic leukemia. In 1979, an inherited genetic defect was found to cause kidney cancer in 10 members of the same family. Before there were any signs or symptoms, three members had small malignant tumors removed with good expectation of cure because of early diagnosis and treatment.

A rare inherited condition, familial polyposis, in which members of a family develop multiple intestinal polyps, leads to cancer of the colon (ordinary single polyps may be precancerous and should be removed as a precaution).

The tendency for certain cancers to run in families is nothing to worry about, simply something to be aware of so that those at somewhat increased risk can take intelligent precautions, including conscientious checkups every year using the newest screening techniques (see Chapter 10).

10. Unknown

This refers to cancers that appear to be "blind accidents," where we have no idea of the cause but which probably result from a biochemical breakdown within the body or from an intricate synergistic action between external and internal events.

Viruses are known to cause cancer in animals but it has never been proved that viruses cause cancer in man. There is strong evidence, however, that viruses are a factor in causing at least two human cancers: Burkitt's lymphoma, which primarily affects African children, and nasopharyngeal cancer, which strikes adults in southern China and parts of Southeast Asia. Antibodies to a Herpes virus have been found in some cancer patients, and viruses are suspected in Hodgkin's disease, cancer of the cervix, and neuroblastoma (a childhood cancer).

One intriguing idea is that there is no mystery virus but that the guilty parties are the common viruses which infect most of us at some point in our lives, and which only infrequently result in cancer. Virologists who believe this point out that the polio virus infected many people but caused paralysis in comparatively few. This would explain why no one has been able to isolate a cancer virus despite the vast amounts of time and money expended in this quest.

The intriguing mystery remains: Do viruses cause cancer in man, and if so, what is the mechanism?

The increased emphasis on preventing cancer is a progressive step forward but it should not be at the expense of fundamental scientific research to uncover the basic disease mechanism of cancer and conquer it once and for all.

10

The Promise of Preventive Medicine—
You and Your Physician

CENTURIES AGO IN CHINA PREVENTIVE medicine was practiced in a novel manner. You paid your doctor to keep you well and if you became ill, you stopped paying him. If too many of his patients fell ill or died, the doctor's scroll authorizing him to practice medicine was confiscated and his head was chopped off.

There would be thousands of doctors' heads rolling in the squares today if this quaint custom prevailed here because few physicians practice much in the way of preventive medicine. They are more interested in disease—but then so are their patients. Most people go to a physician to be cured of illness, not to stay healthy. And there is a real question as to whether people can be motivated to take better care of themselves even if it means being healthier, happier, richer, living longer, and paying so little to doctors, druggists, and hospitals that it does not qualify for an income tax deduction.

But there is always hope. Conditions are changing because of the mountainous increases in health care costs, more effective communications, and a growing interest in health on the part of a segment of the public. The dramatic decline in cardiovascular disease from 1968 through 1977 shows that preventive measures can work.

In those years, total cardiovascular disease decreased 24.1 percent; stroke decreased 32.4 percent; and rheumatic fever and rheumatic heart disease, 38.9 percent.

What the medical profession needs is more intelligent patients who care about themselves. And patients need physicians interested in health and prevention as well as disease and cure, who do not display "weary indifference to the patient's sensitivities."

Six months ago a 68-year-old woman whose larynx (voice box) had been removed to save her life came to see me. She suspected a recurrence of her cancer. I referred her to a specialist in head and neck lesions.

"Dr. Beattie," she told me later, "what a wonderful man he is. He pulled his chair up close and sat right in front of me. He was gentle and friendly and sympathetic, and I felt confident and at ease. He said, 'Now, Mrs. _____, tell me all about yourself. Don't worry, I have plenty of time.' "

This inspiring woman, who has mastered esophageal speech and now instructs others, was given a clean bill of health. But what impressed her most was the warmth and interest of this renowned physician after the cold, impersonal treatment she had received from a less sensitive doctor.

Man Is a Tough Species

Intimidated as we are these days by the prophets of doom who tell us that we live "in a sea of carcinogens"—which is not true—we are apt to lose sight of a reassuring truth: man is not a fragile entity who falls apart at the slightest breath of disease, and he recovers faster than any other species. I would rather operate on a man than a sheep any day—you are always worrying whether the sheep will make it. (Surgeons operate on anesthetized animals in research studies and to develop new techniques to save human lives.)

Dr. Lewis Thomas, in his award-winning book *The Lives of a Cell*, voices this truth in a memorable paragraph:

"It is a distortion to picture the human being as a teetering, fallible contraption, always needing watching and patching, always on the verge of flapping to pieces; this is the doctrine that people hear most often, and most eloquently, on all our information media. . . . [We should celebrate] the absolute marvel of good health that is the real lot of most of us, most of the time."

The body's built-in biomechanism to resist disease borders on the miraculous, provided we treat our bodies with reasonable care and judgment. Many medical scientists believe the day will come when the body's immunological defense system can be marshaled to conquer cancer.

There is an interesting, if mildly disturbing, theory that each one of us regularly produces cancer cells that are routinely destroyed by our immune system before they can gain a foothold—which is why three out of four people never get cancer.

On autopsy, pathologists sometimes find small malignant tumors in people who died from unrelated causes; these tiny lesions never caused trouble. The medical literature documents several hundred cases of advanced cancers that stopped growing and disappeared, leaving the individual to live out a normal span of years. The body's natural defenses apparently destroyed these malignant lesions.

Man has powerful systems that fight disease if we seize opportunity and give ourselves a chance. "Four things come not back," the proverb says, "the spoken word, the sped arrow, the past life, and neglected opportunity."

The Four Paths to Prevention

There are four separate but interrelated pathways to disease prevention:

> 1. What you do for yourself.
>
> 2. What your physician does.
>
> 3. What health organizations do.
>
> 4. What the government does.

What each of us does for ourselves is 80 percent of the outcome; what the other groups do is much less important.

1. What You Do for Yourself

There is a long chain of events over many years from one atypical cell to a malignant tumor that you can feel or see. And there are steps that each of us can take to intervene in the neoplastic process, if our motivation is strong enough.

The Prudent Diet Since it is believed that diet is related indirectly to 40 percent of the cancers in women and 25 percent of the cancers in men, and since diet is easily modified, it is obviously the place to start. The earlier in life these suggestions are implemented, the better, but starting them later is still beneficial.

• Consume alcoholic beverages moderately, if at all.

• There are 55 known nutrients in the four basic food groups—dairy products, fruits and vegetables, grains and cereals, and protein (eggs, fowl, fish, meat, and legumes high in protein such as peas and members of the bean family). Balance your intake of these groups; a deficient diet suppresses the body's immune defense system and may lead to disease.

• Most people eat too much. Eat less at each meal; serve smaller portions; go to each meal hungry. Animal studies show that reducing caloric and protein intake inhibits the development of cancer; this also probably applies to man.

• Increase consumption of fresh fruits and vegetables.

• Eat less fat (the body needs *both* saturated fat and unsaturated fat); avoid meat heavily marbled with fat; trim off visible fat; eat lean cuts—veal, eye of round, lean London broil; select fish and poultry more often than beef; spread butter lightly.
A certain amount of meat is beneficial because of its high-quality protein, vitamins, and minerals. Oven broiling or baking is preferable to pan frying, deep-fat frying, and charcoal broiling.

• Drink skim milk; go easy on cookies, pies, cakes, and rich desserts; enjoy sherbet instead of ice cream.

• Consume 10 to 15 grams of fiber bulk daily. Fiber is provided by fruits and vegetables, whole grains, and nuts. Beets, carrots, broccoli, sweet potatoes, cabbage, and cauliflower give good bulk and other benefits. Apples, whole-wheat bread, whole-grain cereals, oatmeal, and brown rice are excellent. Bran is concentrated fiber; two tablespoonfuls a day provide needed bulk.
(A high-fiber diet should not be followed by individuals with colitis, ulcerative colitis, disease of the small bowel, and diverticulitis; these people should consult their physicians.)

• Reduce intake of salt and sugar. Although not related to cancer, salt is linked to high blood pressure and sugar to cavities in teeth. Most people use salt and sugar to excess, and there are usually excessive amounts in processed food.

• Avoid overweight; obese people are more prone to disease. Eating and drinking less, and exercising sensibly with your doctor's okay will take off excess pounds.

• Maintain adequate intake of vitamins and minerals, which should come from your daily diet. After age 50, a vitamin-mineral supplement is probably a good idea; do not cancel out its effects by excessive alcohol or by taking mineral oil or any other laxative. There is some evidence that vitamins A, C, and E and the minerals zinc, selenium, and iron may have anticancer properties. Where vitamins and minerals are concerned, it is not true that "more is better." In fact, more may be worse—too high an intake may be as hazardous as too little. Vitamins A and D in excessive amounts are toxic. The whole complex subject of nutrition, including vitamins and minerals, requires further competent, unbiased study.

The optimum diet probably lies halfway between the American high-fat, high-protein diet and the historic low-fat, low-protein diet of the Japanese.

What About Cholesterol?

The cholesterol story is complex, misunderstood, and usually oversimplified. Cholesterol, a waxy alcohol in the bloodstream, is needed for more than 100 vital chemical processes and is essential for life and health. About 80 percent of the cholesterol is made by your liver; only 20 percent comes from food. Reducing your intake of cholesterol has a relatively minor effect on its blood level, although reduction is advisable for certain people on the advice of a physician.

Cholesterol has long been suspected of being a factor in heart attacks because deposits are often found in the coronary arteries but it's not quite that simple.

Two types of cholesterol circulate in the blood, and each joins with a protein molecule to create a lipoprotein—a fat molecule. Low-density lipoproteins *increase* your chances of a heart attack while high-density lipoproteins *decrease* your chances. What is important is the ratio of total cholesterol to high-density lipoproteins, not whether your cholesterol level is high or low.

The level of desirable high-density lipoproteins increases when you stop smoking, eat less, reduce fat intake, and exercise regularly. The moderate use of alcohol also increases the level, according to some studies, I am happy to say.

It is wise to restrict, to some extent, the intake of foods high in cholesterol but not at the expense of sound nutrition. The much maligned egg, for example, with its cholesterol-rich yolk and abundant nutrients, is one of nature's finest gifts of food and should be part of every diet. Some physicians believe that if cholesterol in the diet decreases, the liver increases its output. Shedding excess weight and engaging in regular physical exercise is the best way to reduce the cholesterol level.

People who engage in strenuous physical activity—such as farmers, athletes, construction workers, and African tribesmen,—

need higher levels of blood fats to sustain them; they burn up the fats in physical exertion. But people who roost at desks need nowhere nearly as much fat to fuel their muscles, and it is these men and women in whom high blood fat levels cause trouble.

Your State of Health

While I know of no scientific studies that relate an individual's general health to his incidence of illness, it is obvious that people in vigorous health are less prone to illness than those in precarious health. Your state of health affects how well your various organs carry out their life-sustaining tasks, their output of enzymes, hormones, and other vital substances and—most important—the vigor with which your immunological defense system protects you against the inroads of disease.

When we test the strength of a cancer patient's immune response, we almost always find it weaker than normal except in the early stages of disease. In people with advanced cancer, it is usually seriously deficient. In kidney transplant patients, whose immune system must be suppressed to prevent rejection of the new kidney, the risk of developing certain cancers is far higher than normal. In one case, a transplant patient who received a kidney with an undiagnosed cancer deep inside it developed thyroid cancer which disappeared after the diseased kidney was removed, the immunosuppressive drugs stopped, and his own immune system reverted to normal.

Millions of words have been written about how to achieve health, but they boil down to these essentials:

• Do not smoke.

• Consume a nutritious diet; stay at normal weight.

• Use alcohol in moderation, if at all.

• A close, happy family life promotes well-being.

• Engage in work you enjoy.

• There are two kinds of stress: healthy and unhealthy. Avoid unhealthy stress.

• Sleep seven to eight hours a night.

- Go away on regular vacations.

- After a stress test and your doctor's okay, exercise at least three or four times a week. Work up gradually to "continuous action" exercise such as brisk walking, bicycling, swimming, and sensible jogging (walk-jogging for older folks). Exercise strengthens your heart muscle, reduces cholesterol, sheds excess weight, and makes you feel great.

- Pursue a relaxing, change-of-pace outside interest, whether tropical fish, growing orchids, or amateur radio. Famed neurosurgeon Wilder Penfield summed up: "Real rest from the day's job is doing something that brings you delightful preoccupation such as comes to a child at play. . . . Superlative achievement comes most often for the man who broadens the basis of his own culture all through life without lessening the intensity of work in his chosen field."

- Have physical checkups by your physician according to a graduated schedule:

Young children	Frequently, as recommended by pediatrician.
Young adults, early 20s	A comprehensive base-line examination with personal history.
Young women	Annual Pap test with start of sexual activity.
Age 27–28	A comprehensive base-line examination.
Age 35–36	A comprehensive base-line examination.
Ages 40–60	*Women*—Pap test and breast examination yearly. *Women and men*—tests of vision, hearing, tests for hypertension, colon-rectal cancer, etc. every 2–3 years. Comprehensive examination every 5 years.
Ages 60–75	Comprehensive examination every 2 years.
Over age 75	As recommended by physician.

See Reference Information I for recent American Cancer Society recommendations on cancer detection examinations for people with no symptoms and not at high risk. However, since each individual is different, the advice of your personal physician should take priority over the ACS guidelines.

Thorough, low-cost health checkups with emphasis on cancer screening are available through the CANSCREEN program listed in Reference Information II. Checkups are worthwhile because a condition detected early usually can be cured, or if not cured, controlled by patient and physician. One spry 77-year-old farmer on leaving the hospital for the third time said, "If I'd known I was going to live this long, I'd have taken better care of myself."

Cancer's 10 Warning Signals

It is wise to know cancer's warning signals and see your doctor without delay should you notice one of them. It's probably not cancer, but check it out so you don't worry. Remember that most of the discouraging statistics are created by people who put off seeing a physician. Most cancers detected early and treated properly have a good cure rate.

1. Involuntary weight loss.

2. A sore that does not heal; sore or white patches in mouth.

3. Persistent indigestion or difficulty in swallowing.

4. Persistent swollen glands in neck or armpit.

5. Thickening or lump in breast or elsewhere.

6. Change in cough; nagging cough; hoarseness; spitting up blood.

7. Change in bowel or bladder habits that lasts more than two weeks.

8. Unusual bleeding or discharge; blood in urine, stool, or sputum.

9. Change in wart or mole (color, size, bleeding).

10. Headache that wakes you from sleep regularly; changes in vision, balance.

Some of these warning signs are not early, which is why periodic physical examinations are important. The best time to pick up cancer, of course, is when it is asymptomatic (not causing symptoms).

2. What Your Physician Does

Several years ago a successful 54-year-old businesswoman with cancer of the colon told me the day before her operation, "I had a physical examination by my internist every year—and now this happens. I thought checkups detected cancer early."

Questioning revealed that her physician did not feel that periodic examination with a proctoscope was indicated, and the simple Guaiac test for occult (hidden) blood in the stool was not done. (A "procto" exam is where a small lighted tube is inserted gently up the rectum for 8 to 10 inches and the lower bowel walls examined.)

When the physician recommends a proctoscopic examination, which takes only two or three minutes, some people refuse because they fear pain and embarrassment. Undignified—yes. Painful—no. This vital precaution, together with examination by the physician's gloved finger, and the simple test for occult blood, *could eliminate 75 percent of the 53,000 annual deaths from colon-rectum cancer in the United States.*

Confronted with an unexplained lump or lesion, some doctors are prone to say, "Let's watch it for six months." This delay can be fatal if it turns out to be malignant. Lumps and lesions should be diagnosed immediately, and biopsy (study of a sample of the tissue) is the only sure way.

COLON-RECTUM CANCER strikes men and women equally and is the number two cancer killer in the United States (114,000 new cases in 1980, 53,000 deaths). The tragedy is that this cancer is 75 percent curable if it is caught early and treated properly. Increasing the amount of fiber bulk in the diet, and decreasing the amount of fat, may help guard against this disease. A bulky, medium-fat diet keeps the intestinal bacteria in healthier balance, reduces the concentration of bile acids, dilutes substances that may be carcinogenic, and promotes more rapid passage through the tract.

The physical checkup for men and women should include:

• Examination every year of lower rectum with physician's gloved finger.

• Proctoscopic examination every two to five years after age 40.

• Guaiac test for occult blood in stool. In this simple home test, small stool samples are put on special paper with an applicator; a reagent is applied by the doctor or nurse; a color change indicates occult blood. Ninety percent of blood in the stool is from benign disease, not cancer; red meat and vitamin C are avoided for three days prior to test as they may lead to false results.

• If indicated, examination of the entire large intestine with fiberoptic colonoscope, and X-ray studies.

Symptoms: blood in stool; change in bowel habits for more than two weeks; abdominal distress (gas, cramping, pain).

LUNG CANCER is the number one cancer killer (117,000 new cases in 1980, 101,300 deaths) and the number one cancer we give ourselves. It is the number two cancer killer of women but in the 1980s will probably replace breast cancer, now in first place.

A change in cough is about the only symptom of lung cancer; by the time the lesion causes significant symptoms it is usually too late to save the patient. A National Cancer Institute plan to detect lung cancer earlier in heavy smokers is underway at the Mayo Clinic in Rochester, Minnesota, at Johns Hopkins Hospital in Baltimore, Maryland, and at Memorial Hospital in New York. The program uses sputum tests and low-dose chest X rays. To date, the yield rate is three to four early lung cancers per 1,000 men and there is a question whether such a program can be cost-effective even though the probable cure rate of early lesions will be more than 60 percent contrasted with the present low national rate of less than 10 percent.

Not many physicians include a lung function test using a spirometer in a health checkup, but they should because it provides important information on how efficiently the lungs are working (vital capacity). Impaired lung function makes the heart work harder and may indicate respiratory disease. (A spirometer is a small tank that measures your lung capacity when you breathe in and out.) A quick test of lung function: if you can hold your breath for one minute, your lungs are in good shape (people with heart trouble should not attempt this test).

A natural question is, "Why doesn't every cigarette smoker get lung cancer?" There are two answers: (1) Perhaps if they lived long enough, all smokers eventually would develop bronchogenic carcinoma. (2) Another theory is that the level of an enzyme, aryl hydrocarbon hydroxylase (AHH), which is released when cigarette smoke enters the lungs, may determine a person's susceptibility to lung cancer. Individuals with a low level of AHH may be less likely to develop a lung lesion while a high level may promote lung cancer—but this is not certain. And even if it were true, this would not affect the other damage caused by smoking.

BREAST CANCER is the number one cancer killer of women (109,000 cases in 1980, 36,000 deaths); a few men get breast cancer but account for only one-half of 1 percent.

Symptoms: lump or thickening in breast (80 percent of breast lumps are benign cysts and occur monthly at the time of menstruation); change in shape of breast; nipple discharge or change in nipple; pain.

Breast cancer is 80 percent curable when discovered early and localized (no spread to the lymph glands). More than 90 percent of breast lumps are found by self-examination (BSE) and every woman should examine her breasts monthly after her menstrual period although only 20 to 30 percent do.

If lumps are found during self-examination, a physician may be able to rule out breast cancer by palpation, or by aspirating fluid from a benign cyst; or a biopsy may be needed for diagnosis. Physicians should instruct their women patients in breast self-examination (perhaps with the exception of women who are obese, have chronic cystic mastitis, or who suffer from extreme anxiety). Self-examination is done as follows:

HOW TO EXAMINE YOUR BREASTS

 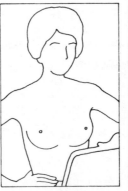 

1 —IN THE SHOWER:

Examine your breasts during bath or shower; hands glide easier over wet skin. Fingers flat, move gently over every part of each breast. Use right hand to examine left breast, left hand for right breast. Check for any lump, hard knot or thickening.

2 —BEFORE A MIRROR:

Inspect your breasts with arms at your sides. Next, raise your arms high overhead. Look for any changes in contour of each breast, a swelling, dimpling of skin or changes in the nipple.

Then, rest palms on hips and press down firmly to flex your chest muscles. Left and right breast will not exactly match—few women's breasts do.

Regular inspection shows what is normal for you and will give you confidence in your examination.

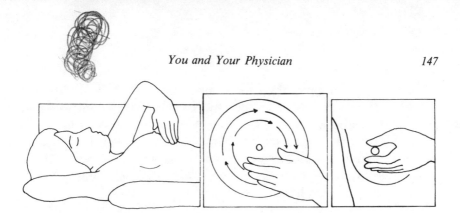

3 —LYING DOWN:

To examine your right breast, put a pillow or folded towel under your right shoulder. Place right hand behind your head—this distributes breast tissue more evenly on the chest. With left hand, fingers flat, press gently in small circular motions around an imaginary clock face. Begin at outermost top of your right breast for 12 o'clock, then move to 1 o'clock, and so on around the circle back to 12. A ridge of firm tissue in the lower curve of each breast is normal. Then move in an inch, toward the nipple, keep circling to examine *every part of your breast,* including nipple. This requires at least three more circles. Now slowly repeat procedure on your left breast with a pillow under your left shoulder and left hand behind head. Notice how your breast structure feels.

Finally, squeeze the nipple of each breast gently between thumb and index finger. Any discharge, clear or bloody, should be reported to your doctor immediately.

The information on breast self-examination is from the American Cancer Society and is reprinted by permission.

How to Examine Your Breasts

This simple three-step procedure could save your life by enabling you to find breast cancer early when it is most curable.

Follow the same procedure once a month about a week after your period, when breasts are usually not tender or swollen. After menopause, check breasts on the first day of each month. After hysterectomy, check your doctor or clinic for an appropriate time of the month. Doing BSE will give you monthly peace of mind and seeing your doctor once a year will reassure you there is nothing wrong.

What to Do If You Find a Lump or Thickening

If a lump or dimple or discharge is discovered during BSE, it is important to see your doctor as soon as possible. Don't be frightened. Most breast lumps or changes are not cancer, but only your doctor can make the diagnosis.

Low-dose mammography (X-ray picture of breast) is an efficient method of detecting early lesions, but its principal use is screening women with above-average risk (a previous breast cancer; family history of breast cancer; persistent benign breast disease; no children; childbearing after age 30; early onset of menstruation).

• *Women 35–39:* one base-line mammogram; annual mammogram only if you have a personal history of breast cancer.

• *Women 40–49:* annual mammogram if you or your sisters or mother had breast cancer; consult personal physician.

• *Women over 50:* mammogram every year (two-thirds of breast cancers occur in women over age 50).

Thermography to locate breast lesions by heat detection is no longer widely used. A new technique that does not involve X ray, graphic stress telethermometry (GST), may prove useful.

PROSTATE CANCER will strike 66,000 men in 1980 and claim 21,500 lives. Many cases are never diagnosed because the tumor grows so slowly that there are no symptoms. (The prostate, a gland the size of a chestnut, is part of the male genitourinary system and surrounds the urethra where it joins the bladder, the urethra carries urine from the bladder to the penis.)

Symptoms: difficulty in urinating—trouble starting urination, need to urinate frequently, weak or interrupted flow, painful or burning sensation. Pain in the pelvis, lower back, or upper legs may occur.

Benign enlargement of the prostate gland, which occurs in well over half of all men over age 50, frequently causes these symptoms and is not precancerous.

Most of these tumors occur in the rear lobe of the prostate gland which is readily felt by the physician's examining finger at the time he examines the rectum for lesions. This examination is quick, painless, and of great value. Other tests may include X ray, urine, and blood studies. A biopsy is needed to determine whether a tumor is malignant.

CANCER OF THE UTERUS is of two types, cancer of the cervix (the opening to the uterus) and cancer of the endometrium (the body of the uterus). Some 61,000 cases of cervical lesions will be diagnosed in 1980 and of these 45,000 will be either carcinoma *in situ* or precancerous conditions, both of which are almost 100 percent curable. The balance of 16,000 cases are serious invasive cancer and will cause 7,400 deaths—*which could have been prevented by a Pap test* (40 percent of U.S. women at peak risk never have a Pap test). The Pap test, which examines cells shed from the uterus, is quick, simple, painless, and inexpensive. Symptoms of pain and bleeding usually mark a late stage of disease.

Cervical cancer is more common in low socioeconomic groups and among black women (over twice the rate of whites).

Cancer of the endometrium (38,000 cases, 3,200 deaths in 1980) occurs most often in women ages 50 to 64. The Pap test detects these lesions only about 40 percent of the time, which is why women at menopause should have a pelvic examination and palpation of uterus and both ovaries by the examining physician in addition to the Pap smear; endometrial tissue may also be examined. Menopausal women at higher risk include those with a history of obesity, uterine bleeding, and estrogen replacement therapy.

The death rate from cancer of the uterus has decreased more than 70 percent in the last 40 years because of the Pap test and improved treatment.

Cancers of just these five sites account for nearly 60 percent of the new cases diagnosed in 1980 and 55 percent of the cancer deaths. The preventive steps that you take to avoid most of these illnesses can have an impact on your chances of contracting these neoplasms. And should you detect a suspicious symptom, your forthright action in visiting your physician promptly will increase your chances of a cure. Reference Information I gives further details.

Other Preventive Steps

Among the other checks your physician will make are these:

Skin Examination of moles, warts, lumps, and areas of increased pigmentation or chronic bleeding. Skin cancer often appears as a pearl-like nodule that may ulcerate and develop a crust, or as a red scaly patch. The most common skin condition that may be precancerous is keratosis, a scaly thickening which is easily treated. Common skin cancer is almost 100 percent curable. More serious, with a much lower cure rate because it metastasizes more rapidly, is melanoma. A black mole that changes size or color, or bleeds easily, suggests melanoma and needs immediate attention.

Oral cavity Cancers of the oral cavity and pharynx are among the most curable lesions when detected early by the individual or by his dentist or physician. The death rate is too high considering how accessible these sites are to frequent visual inspection. Symptoms are sores that do not heal, white patches, thickening of tissue, sore throat, and difficulty chewing or swallowing. Tobacco, heavy drinking, dentures that do not fit properly, poor dental hygiene, and jagged teeth that irritate gums or cheeks are linked to oral cancer.

Electrocardiogram   A "resting" EKG with you lying flat on the examining table detects heart chamber enlargement and abnormal rhythm but not coronary artery disease. A "stress" EKG shows how your heart performs under physical exertion and provides valuable information. It is a "must" before starting an exercise program since 10 to 15 percent of the population has a silent heart defect and does not know it.

Your First Line of Defense

You are the first line of defense against disease—not your physician—which is why it is wise to have an idea of important symptoms that need conscientious investigation.

As part of your checkup your doctor will take a "history" by talking with you, asking questions about your way of life, and counseling you on prevention. Most physicians point out the important difference between a known carcinogen and a carcinogenic risk factor such as excessive fat in the diet, lack of fiber bulk, obesity, multiple sexual partners, and so on.

A patient's history furnishes valuable clues, but physicians have learned there is often a big difference between what a person does and what he says he does.

When asked about his drinking habits, one man told his doctor that he had "about 10 drinks a day."

Knowing that his patient was a very heavy drinker, the doctor asked if he was sure that 10 drinks was the correct number.

"Of course," his patient added, "that's in the morning."

While cancer is largely a disease of the last half of life—75 percent of cancer cases are people over 50—malignant lesions do occur in the middle years and in the very young on a reduced scale.

As a major aid to prevention, epidemiologists constantly analyze factors that increase cancer risk and publish impressive professional papers packed with statistics, graphs, and challenging conclusions. At a cancer symposium, after listening to papers on cancer of the pancreas, a difficult disease to diagnose and treat, a surgeon was asked to sum up from the data given his profile of a typical candidate for pancreatic cancer.

"I would seek a male, black, diabetic, Jewish, smoking, alcoholic chemist with gallstones," the surgeon replied to the amusement of his distinguished audience.

Each of us is at the mercy of our genes, our body chemistry, our immune system, and the stray viruses and bacteria we encounter by sheer chance. We cannot select our ancestors but we can minimize our chances of paying thousands of dollars into the health care system.

Quite simply, this means not taunting our body's defenses by smoking, overeating, overdrinking, underexercising, undersleeping, being constantly overtired, enduring unhealthy stress, and ignoring measures to maintain health.

11

The Promise of Preventive Medicine
—Health Groups and the Government

AT A RECENT DINNER PARTY, the soaring cost of health care came up and debate waxed hot on whether preventive medicine could ever keep these costs down by creating a healthier population.

"You can't sell preventive medicine," one industrialist said in the positive tone he used in his office. "The public isn't interested. They'll pay to get well, but they won't pay to stay well."

One of the physicians agreed. "There's a negative attitude toward preventive medicine," he said. "A prominent physician—I forget who—said that to most doctors preventive medicine was intellectually dull, emotionally unrewarding, and financially unremunerative. I think that's how many physicians look at it.

"And many of us believe, with justification, that advice on how to stay healthy isn't wanted, or followed, by most of our patients."

"Hell, Larry's right," said an internist, sipping his Irish coffee. "Look at the millions of parents who've neglected to have their children immunized against childhood diseases. I read where one-third of all preschool children are unprotected.

"The problem is complacency on the part of parents and physicians," he continued. "They forget that epidemics of old diseases that have been conquered can flare up, and that these diseases can have serious side effects—mumps can cause brain damage and deafness, measles can lead to mental retardation. . . ."

There was more than a little truth in this conversation, but the picture is not as black as it was painted. True, for preventive medicine to be highly effective there needs to be a change in attitude by the public and the medical profession. But conditions constantly shift, and attitudes do change even after they appear cast in concrete. The substantial decrease in heart disease in the past 10 years is a good example.

President Dwight D. Eisenhower once opposed family planning. Years later, he made effective TV commercials in behalf of planned parenthood. Once, Americans would not buy small automobiles. Now you put your name on a waiting list to get delivery on a small, gas-efficient car. And so it goes.

3. What Health Organizations Do

On the encouraging side are four examples of successful health maintenance programs now at work in this country.

• In the "well baby" program, obstetrician and pediatrician look after the health of mother and child over a long period of years with scheduled checkups and preventive medical measures. Their goal is a healthy mother during pregnancy, a safe delivery, and a healthy mother and child afterward. The pediatrician immunizes the child against measles, mumps, rubella, scarlet fever, diphtheria, poliomyelitis, whooping cough, and tetanus. As recently as 50 years ago, infectious diseases swept away thousands of precious young lives.

• The pioneering Kaiser-Permanente Medical Care Plan in California is a prepaid health maintenance program with the objective of keeping people healthy. Under it, members undergo periodic health screening to detect any abnormalities at an early stage. Experience proves that this plan works and is cost-effective. (A cost-effective program is one in which the money spent in preventing disease is less than the cost of treating those diseases and the economic losses that those illnesses create.)

• The Preventive Medicine Institute-Strang Clinic, 55 East 34th St., New York, NY 10016, is a nonprofit diagnostic, research, and educational organization which develops innovative programs to extend the benefits of preventive medicine to as many people as possible. Among its projects: the CANSCREEN program for early cancer detection in people at risk; the do-it-yourself Health Action Questionnaire, a preventive step taken at home; education of health specialists in cancer prevention; and distribution of health information for the layman.

• The Know Your Body program of the American Health Foundation, 320 East 43rd St., New York, NY 10017, is another example of prevention in action. It involves schoolchildren in the awareness and maintenance of their health with emphasis on the results of cigarette smoking. Risk factors such as smoking, drinking, blood pressure level, relative weight, and serum cholesterol are recorded in a Health Passport for each child. There is annual reexamination and results are compared with those of previous years. Programs such as this are of tremendous value and should be integrated into school and college curricula throughout the country as part of a total health care system.

The American Cancer Society, 777 Third Ave., New York, NY 10017, makes available a variety of excellent teaching materials including booklets, posters, displays, slides, filmstrips, audio tapes, radio and television spot announcements; effective professional material for nurses and physicians is also available. The American Heart Association provides educational materials.

So something *is* being done about preventing disease by private groups—but there is no concerted, nationwide health education program in schools and colleges and for the public. Sweden, for example, is far ahead of the United States in preventive medicine programs.

The Problem of "Health" Insurance

A serious related problem is that most "health" insurance is actually "disease" insurance since it pays only for the diagnosis and treatment of illness in a hospital, and offers no incentive for disease prevention. The result is little incentive to reduce medical costs. Nor, for the most part, does this disease insurance pay for less expensive, but in many cases equally effective, outpatient care which is suitable for many patients. To collect on your disease insurance you must be admitted to a hospital at anywhere from $150 to $300 a day plus.

This, obviously, is an absurd way to keep health care costs under control.

Research and Prevention Neglected

In 1978, the United States spent nearly $200 billion on health care. Of this staggering amount, only 3 percent went for prevention, 2 percent for research, and less than 1 percent for education.

The government now spends $1 billion a year to treat miners with black lung disease (preventable), $7 billion a year on the diseases caused by cigarette smoking (preventable), and $14 billion a year on cardiovascular disease (50 percent preventable).

When a national health insurance law is enacted, as seems probable within this decade, health care costs can only increase. At this writing, *none of the proposed national health insurance programs includes any significant provision for disease prevention—* a ridiculous misordering of priorities in a supposedly advanced country.

4. What the Government Does

There appear to be three logical tasks for the government, areas where private organizations are not in a position to perform as effectively.

• *Basic research* The planning, financing, and general direction of scientific research by private groups to discover basic disease mechanisms which lead to effective prevention. This is what Dr. Lewis Thomas in his book *The Lives of a Cell* calls "the genuinely decisive technology of modern medicine." When medical science understands the basic mechanism of a disease, it becomes possible to manage that disease effectively at a fraction of the former cost. As Dr. Thomas points out, "The price is never as high as the cost of managing the same disease during the earlier stages of no technology or halfway technology." (Cancer is today managed by halfway technology.)

Proof: after John Enders and his colleagues at Harvard isolated the poliomyelitis viruses, it was possible to develop vaccines to prevent polio which closed the polio hospitals, ended the fund drives, and conquered this disease.

Other decisive technology: immunization against the infectious childhood diseases; antibiotics to cure bacterial infections; INH and streptomycin to cure tuberculosis.

As mentioned earlier, the stronger emphasis on cancer prevention is encouraging but should not be pursued at the expense of basic research to discover what triggers loss of cell control and causes cancer. Only when this is known will we be able to treat cancer with truly effective technology.

The United States spends less than $2.5 billion a year on all medical research, or only about 1.5 percent of the health dollar instead of 5 percent. Put another way, we should be spending 5¢ of each health dollar on research instead of 1.5¢.

• *Pollution control* Regulations to control environmental hazards to health, prepared with the cooperation of the industries affected, are clearly the government's domain. These hazards include nuclear wastes and the discharge of toxic substances into the air, water, and ground. Tobacco smoke contains toxic chemicals and ought to be regulated exactly like other hazardous substances.

Progress is being made in control of air and water pollution but not in control of the carcinogens in tobacco smoke.

• *Public policy* In the area of public policy, certain healthful changes could be made. Dr. Ross Hall, a Canadian professor of biochemistry, said, "If the governments of the United States and Canada wanted to promote better nutrition, they could promote the raising of leaner meat animals, stop basing milk price supports on butterfat content, and encourage farmers to produce a wider variety of grains and fiber crops."

• *Public education* Preventive medicine and health education are closely linked and, if one looks very far into the future, both are clearly indispensable. Dramatic, continuing educational programs for schools, colleges, and the public should be part of a national health insurance plan. Yet in the past, education has been a stepchild.

Without doubt, the quickest, most efficient way to get an effective program off the ground is to use the private groups that are already involved in health education with the newest techniques. As someone said, "You'd better learn from the mistakes of others, because you'll never live long enough to make them all yourself."

Perhaps the screening of people at high risk for cancer or heart disease to help contain health care costs can be cost-effective; certainly many thousands of these cases are preventable.

A well-designed and implemented health education program would save literally billions of dollars a year for the American people—both as individuals burdened with bills from doctors, druggists, and hospitals and as taxpayers who foot the bill for the care provided by the government. But even more important are the illnesses, suffering, and premature deaths that such a program would prevent.

One would think that health professionals, medical associations, labor, industry, and government officials could agree that an approach of this sort is plain common sense. But then I recall the story told by Dr. Karl Compton, a former president of M.I.T. His sister, living in a foreign country, engaged a local electrician to install new wiring and fixtures in her home. He appeared particularly stupid and kept returning for instructions. Finally, exasperated, she said to him, "Why do you ask questions all the time? Why don't you use your common sense?"

"Madam," he replied, "common sense is a rare gift of God. I have only a technical education."

12

What the Experts Do—
Unofficially—to Dodge Cancer

HAS A FRIEND ever said to you, "My doctor gave me good advice but you should see him—he's overweight, never exercises, and smokes like a chimney."

You've no doubt heard this, and so have thousands of others.

So you are on target if at this point you wonder, silently, what physicians in the cancer field do—if anything—to guard against cancer.

Medical Tribune, a publication for physicians, was curious, too, and surveyed selected cancer experts to see if they practiced preventive oncology (the study of tumors).

Many do, but those polled were quick to point out that their strategies "are based only on scanty scientific evidence and are not to be taken as gospel by the public." The one thing the scientists polled agreed upon: they did not smoke cigarettes.

Here, with the generous permission of *Medical Tribune,* are the replies to its poll with the "I won't swear this is good science" disclaimers by the respondents omitted.

Fred Rapp, Ph.D., Professor and Chairman, Department of Microbiology, and Director, Specialized Cancer Research Center, Pennsylvania State University College of Medicine, Hershey, Pennsylvania:

"I gave up smoking 10 or 11 years ago. I was a heavy cigarette smoker, I smoked cigars for a while, and gave them up last July. My wife also stopped smoking. In a department I chair with 75 people, we no longer have a single authentic smoker. We haven't particularly tried to change our diet, although I don't eat a lot of eggs and try to keep my weight down, not completely successfully."

Dr. Arthur C. Upton, former Director, National Cancer Institute, Bethesda, Maryland; Chairman, Department of Environmental Medicine, New York University Medical School, New York, New York:

"I take vitamin C and a multiple vitamin preparation; I do not drink heavily, although I'll have an occasional drink. I minimize my intake of animal fat. I also take a substantial amount of fiber, including a large amount of green leafy vegetables, and I eat bran for breakfast, and try to control my weight. I do not smoke. I guess you might say I try to hedge my bets."

Thomas J. Slaga, Ph.D., Head, Skin Carcinogenesis and Tumor Prevention Group, Oak Ridge National Laboratory, Oak Ridge, Tennessee:

"In terms of the food I eat, and on the basis of the studies that I've made, I would select [preservative] BHA over BHT right now in food products, just because there have been some negative effects with BHT. It's been shown to be a tumor promoter in the liver and the lung. I drink a lot of orange juice. I eat a lot of vegetables like cauliflower and things like that which have certain flavones that may have an inhibitory effect against cancer, and I try to select some diets that have a number of vitamins in them, like vitamin A and that type of thing. In terms of diets, in general I try to stay away from high-fat diets, and high caloric foods. If I drink my beer and eat my sausage, which might have the relationship of making nitrosamines in the stomach, I try to counteract that with a glass of orange juice, or mix my beer with tomato juice."

Dr. Ernst L. Wynder, President, American Health Foundation, New York, New York:

"Current evidence suggests that in cancer of the colon total fat, by affecting the formation of bile acids, is of etiological significance, and that a high fiber diet that contributes to increased stool bulk can have a protective influence. Most of us consume sufficient vitamins and minerals in our diets and do not require vitamin supplements as a possible protection against certain types of cancer. Like others who are proponents of disease prevention, I do not smoke and if I were to drink I would do so only in moderation. In fact, moderation as it involves all aspects of our life styles should be the key to our healthy behavior."

Dr. Benjamin F. Byrd, Jr., Professor of Clinical Surgery, Vanderbilt University School of Medicine; past president, American Cancer Society; Chairman of the American Cancer Society Task Force on Breast Cancer:

"I think the dietary habits in our household have changed completely over the past five years. Maybe I should tell you that my wife is doing something to prevent cancer, but she is taking a bit of the outline that Dr. Wynder gave us, and that is to avoid excessive dietary fats, and to avoid for the most part the food additives which have some evidence of being potential carcinogens, and this is the main thing."

Dr. Philip R. Lee, Director, Health Policy Program, University of San Francisco; former Assistant Secretary for Health and Scientific Affairs, Department of Health, Education and Welfare:
"I eat what I consider to be a prudent diet, along the lines of what Ernie Wynder's been advocating for a number of years. I eat considerably less meat than I used to eat. Part of that is what I read in the literature, part of that is being influenced by my own kids. I haven't changed it explicitly with colon cancer in mind, but that is certainly one of the things I thought about, and also with alcohol consumption. I am not a heavy drinker, but I don't abstain."

Elizabeth M. Whelan, Sc.D., Research Associate, Harvard School of Public Health and author of a book on preventing cancer:
"I certainly don't smoke, and would never dream of having anyone around me or in my family who would smoke. I stay out of the sun, except when I'm using a sunscreen, as that is a tremendous threat, especially for a person with my coloring. I also watch my diet now, because I think that while the evidence is not totally convincing, I am suspicious enough that something is going on. I can't explain the major world differences in breast cancer, for instance, without bringing in the high fat, overnutrition. As for mammography, I heartily recommend it for any woman over 50, and personally if I were in a high-risk category, I would consider having it after age 40."

Roger J. Williams, Ph.D., biochemist, University of Texas in Austin, who first isolated pantothenic acid and has done much work with the B vitamins:
"I try to eat wholesome foods and avoid sugary things and too much alcohol, and try also to avoid contaminated foods. I take vitamin supplementation in the form of an insurance formula I devised which is put out by Bronson Pharmaceuticals in LaCanada, California. In addition to this, I take extra vitamins C, E, B6, folic acid, calcium, and magnesium. I also exercise by walking about three miles daily."

Dr. Arthur Holleb, Director of Medical Affairs in the national headquarters of the American Cancer Society:

"I think the most important thing we're doing in my family is not smoking. In terms of my wife, she has an annual physical examination, and does a monthly breast examination, and she has an annual Pap smear and a mammogram once a year.

"I personally do not take anything but a diet which provides me with the minimum daily requirements of vitamin C and all the other vitamins. In terms of obesity, if my wife were obese, and she is not, I would certainly try to get her to lose weight because there's a strong relationship between obesity and breast cancer."

Dr. Warren Winkelman, Jr., Dean and Professor of Epidemiology, School of Public Health, University of California, Berkeley:

"The most important thing anyone can do is not smoke. Beyond that, I don't think there's anything I do in a conscious way, and that's partly related to the fact that I don't really know of any particular agents outside of radiation, but no one goes around exposing themselves to ionizing radiation unless it's necessary. I don't think the evidence is very good on diet. Also, I don't like to be around smokers. Until recently I was comfortable around them and tolerant of them, but lately this has changed. My daughter has made a little sign for our front door, which says, 'Please Smoke Outside.' Of course we live in California now. Maybe we couldn't have done that when we lived in Buffalo."

The editors of the *Center News,* Memorial Sloan-Kettering Cancer Center's employee newspaper, did a similar survey among the center's health professionals. Like the scientists interviewed by *Medical Tribune,* those who replied noted there was insufficient scientific evidence to support most of their actions but were willing to share their thoughts. The one area of unanimous agreement: don't smoke!

Dr. William G. Cahan, Attending Surgeon, Thoracic Service, Department of Surgery:

"When walking near a bus or automotive fumes, I now automatically hold my breath. Similarly, I avoid cigarette smoke and other irritating inhalants.

"To eliminate carcinogens from our diet as much as possible, we eat bacon without preservatives and avoid charcoal-broiled meat. Hamburgers are cooked resting on a piece of toast rather than in direct contact with the pan.

"Our meat intake has been reduced and fresh fowl, fruits and vegetables, and fiber cereals have been increased. We exercise frequently (tennis singles) and sunlight is screened."

Dr. David Schottenfeld, Attending Physician and Chief, Epidemiology and Preventive Medicine Service, Department of Medicine:

"The single most important thing one can do to guard against cancer is to stop smoking. Cigarette smoking accounts for 30 percent of cancer mortality in men and slightly more than 5 percent in women. In addition, excessive alcohol consumption in combination with tobacco now contributes to more than 10,000 cancer deaths each year in the United States, specifically within the upper digestive tract.

"I've always tried to stay slim by maintaining a low-fat diet. I keep caloric intake down and eat high-fiber foods like cereals, nuts, and beans, and I usually eat yogurt for lunch. In our relative state of ignorance, I also take vitamin C. A moderate degree of physical activity gives one a sense of well-being that is important for the quality of life."

Dr. Nael Martini, Attending Surgeon and Chief, Thoracic Service, Department of Surgery:

"I gave up smoking eight years ago. My mind is at ease and as a lung surgeon, I now find it much less difficult to tell patients not to smoke."

Dr. Paul Sherlock, Attending Physician and Chairman, Department of Medicine:

"I probably don't do enough to dodge cancer. However, I do not smoke and I have decreased my beef and fat intake because of the possible relationship to colon cancer. I have been eating a bit more fiber for the same reason. Although there is no major evidence for it, I am intrigued with the possibility that vitamin C exerts a protective effect against the development of certain types of cancer. I therefore eat more citrus fruits and, sporadically, take 500 mg. tablets of vitamin C."

Dr. Thomas J. Fahey, Attending Physician and Associate Chairman for Patient Care, Department of Medicine:

"I do think that there is something to eating a high-fiber breakfast, and I usually start my day with some raisin bran and orange juice. I also avoid saturated fats: hard cheeses, creams, and fatty meats. It would appear that a low-residue, high-fat diet contributes to bowel cancer."

Roger N. Parker, R.N., Director, Department of Nursing:

"I try to follow good health habits. I get regular exercise, practice yoga, and eat a modified vegetarian diet—more out of a conviction that it is good to do it than a fear of cancer."

Dr. Jane W. Magill, Director, Employee Health Service:

"Personally, I believe that being turned on to life and enjoying it to the fullest is the answer to many health problems. I stopped smoking when I worked at Memorial previously in chemotherapy at the insistence of my director, Dr. David Karnofsky. I ride my bicycle every day and go to the health club two or three times a week for calisthenics and dance exercises. I do my best to keep my weight down. I'm into a vegetarian diet, though not on a strict basis."

C. Chester Stock, Ph.D., Vice President and Associate Director, Sloan-Kettering Institute:

"The causes of cancer have been defined to a relatively small degree. We cannot do anything about causes which are unknown, but it is common sense to avoid known hazards. For me, this means no smoking, minimizing intake of foods containing added nitrates, and eating a diet low in fats, high in vitamins and roughage, and a larger reliance on fowl and fish for proteins. I believe this diet has considerable value beyond possible cancer prevention aspects."

13

How Cancer Is Treated

ON JUNE 14, 1979, Robert Fisher, age 51, pedaled up to the entrance of Memorial Hospital's outpatient building, completing a 3,600-mile cross-country trip on his 10-speed bicycle. He had started from Venice, California, in early March.

Why did Fisher's achievement attract widespread publicity in newspapers, magazines, and on television when others had made the trip before? Because there was one big difference:

In 1974, Robert Fisher was diagnosed at Memorial Hospital as having leukemia and has been on chemotherapy ever since; blood tests along the way proved he was in excellent health. Robert Fisher wanted to dispel the widespread idea that cancer patients are sick, tired, and run down, and that chemotherapy knocks you out.

Contrary to popular opinion, there are literally hundreds of different treatment combinations depending upon the type of cancer (over 100), its stage of progression, the patient's age, sex, and physical condition. The right treatment for one type of cancer may be ineffective for another; what works for one age group may not be the treatment of choice for another; a combination of therapies may be indicated for one patient but not for another. Some therapies are unpleasant, others cause moderate discomfort, while still others hardly bother the patient at all.

While we are forced to treat cancer by "halfway technology," still the cure rate of many neoplasms is high and 50 percent of all cancers can be cured with early diagnosis and prompt, competent treatment—in addition to the 33 to 50 percent of cancers that could be prevented.

Ten-Year Lag Time

It is not often pointed out that it takes 10 years for the increased effectiveness of new treatments to be reflected in the overall statistics from the National Cancer Institute. These years are needed for clinical testing, distribution of information, adoption in the field, and prolonged evaluation. So the statistics that you read today reflect only the effectiveness of the treatment methods of 10 years ago. Today's improved treatment methods will be reflected in the statistics you read in 1990.

One Patient Is Not a Statistic

Another point one is apt to lose sight of is that a single patient is never a "statistic." Statistical data cover thousands of cases nationwide and an individual patient may do better, or worse, than the national average. If you are cured, your cure rate is 100 percent and if you are not, it is zero. Even if one has cancer with a low cure rate, all is not lost. And statistics are sometimes misleading, or even wrong, as the lumberjack fond of numbers found when one of the two female cooks in camp married one of the 50 lumberjacks. He duly noted in his diary that "50 percent of the women married 2 percent of the men."

So many variables influence the outcome that it is almost impossible for a physician to predict the course of cancer. We all know stories like that of the cancer patient given six months to live who died 20 years later of a heart attack while cheering at a football game. A physician's most valuable diagnostic instrument is often the "retrospectoscope."

Can Cancer Be Detected Years Before It Shows Any Symptoms?

I am afraid that we are seeing and diagnosing many cancers in the middle or end of their life cycles when the chances of a cure are greatly reduced. Tests to detect the presence of atypical or malignant cells many years before a tumor causes signs or symptoms would be a tremendous step forward. Medical scientists are pursuing two approaches to such tests, with limited success because of the complexity of the problem.

• New instruments to examine internal body organs. Example: the fiberoptic bronchoscope and the colonoscope that use smooth, flexible glass fibers which conduct light and visual images along their lengths and around corners. Low-dose mammography, correctly interpreted, picks up early asymptomatic breast cancer about 80 percent of the time, tumors which are too small to palpate. Graphic stress telethermometry (GST), a new, non-X-ray screening test for breast cancer, may prove effective.

• Sophisticated analyses of body fluids and products (blood, lymph, discharges, sputum, urine, stool, lung and stomach washings) to pick up atypical cells, malignant cells, or unique "markers" that indicate the presence of cancer. The Pap test to detect early cervical atypia, which has saved the lives of a million women, is an example of this technique at its most productive. The simple, inexpensive Guaiac test to detect occult blood in the stool is another test of great significance which promises to save thousands of lives.

New techniques by which body fluids and products are examined include fluorescent cytology, isotopic labeling, new staining techniques, radioimmune assays, and automated equipment that screens thousands of samples rapidly and selects abnormal specimens for study by trained personnel.

But the breakthrough tests which scientists seek are those that detect unique markers indicating the presence of malignant cells somewhere within the body in the very earliest stage. These markers may be hormones, enzymes, antigens to specific tumors, proteins, or other blood constituents—and there is some progress here. Alpha fetal protein (AFP) is a compound usually found in the blood only when primary liver cancer (hepatoma) is present. If high and rising levels of AFP are detected, the surgeon promptly explores the liver; the cure rate of liver tumors found this way is over 50 percent. Human choriogonadotropic hormone (HCG) is secreted by germ cell tumors of the ovaries and testes.

What is urgently needed are markers like these for the major neoplasms, without false positives and false negatives.

Method of Treatment Depends on the Type of Cancer

Cancer is treated by surgery, radiation, chemicals (drugs), hormones, and immunotherapy, or more likely by some combination of these modalities. The type of cancer and other variables determine the treatment selected. The days when surgery and radiation were the only weapons against cancer are long gone.

Surgery

Surgery is the most common method of treating solid tumors within reach of the scalpel; a few tumors are so entwined with the heart or other organs that resection is impossible and they are treated with radiation and perhaps chemotherapy. Surgery can prevent cancer by removing polyps of the colon, rectum, and larynx that may be precancerous; deeply pigmented moles are usually removed as a precaution. Surgery may be used to alleviate pain or discomfort in patients with advanced cancer.

When a tumor is localized (*in situ*), or encapsulated in its own fibrous cocoon, with no metastasis, and can be removed with a safety margin of surrounding tissue, the cure rate is close to 100 percent. Nearby lymph nodes that may contain malignant cells are usually removed as a precaution. Even if the entire tumor cannot be resected, removing most of the growth may enable the body's natural defenses to destroy the remaining cells.

Major improvements make surgery safer and more effective than ever before when done by a competent surgeon. These include new surgical techniques, safer anesthetics, accurate monitoring, improved blood transfusions, replacement of plasma, platelets, and electrolytes, antibiotics, and vigilant postoperative care.

Breast Cancer Surgery

There are three types of surgery for breast cancer and a question exists as to which is the most effective with the least trauma to the patient. There is no easy answer because it depends on the woman's age, type of breast cancer, and whether malignant cells have spread to the axillary (armpit) lymph nodes. The alternatives are:

1. *Standard radical mastectomy*—removal of breast, lymph nodes, and the two large muscles attaching the breast to the chest wall.

2. *Modified radical mastectomy*—the same as standard radical except that there is no removal of the chest muscles and somewhat less disfigurement.

3. *Local excision (lumpectomy, tumorectomy, tylectomy, segmental mastectomy)*—removal of only the tumor, preserving the breast, usually followed by radiation of the breast and lymph node areas. Biopsy of axillary nodes is essential to determine whether there is metastasis beyond the breast.

Chemotherapy may be used in women whose cancer has spread to the lymph nodes.

The problem in evaluating the effectiveness of these three procedures is that 10 years is needed for a conclusive study. The present controversy concerns whether limited surgery plus radiation therapy will be equally curative compared to modified radical mastectomy. In early Stage I disease (localized, noninvasive) they seem equal, but the lymph nodes in the axilla have to be studied microscopically for accurate staging. More advanced Stage II disease has a better 10-year survival with modified radical mastectomy than with local excision plus radiation. The present question is how adding chemotherapy will alter the above statements. The modified radical is the procedure used most frequently today since U.S. women are coming to their physicians with earlier breast cancers than before.

With the results of the tumor and lymph node biopsies and hormone receptor assay in hand, the physicians on our Breast Service discuss the situation with the patient and try to answer her questions. A single treatment for all types of breast cancer is not good medicine and the biopsy should be separate from surgery to give the patient time to consider the alternatives (65 percent of the breast biopsies done at Memorial Hospital are negative—no breast cancer).

Patients sometimes ask me what happens when a biopsy is done during surgery and the pathologist's report 15 minutes later says the tissue is "borderline"—he cannot be certain whether the cells are malignant. The answer is that we stop the operation, close the incision, send the patient to the recovery room, and wait for the final pathology report in a day or two. The organ in question is never removed as a preventive measure.

There are questions about how effective surgery is in difficult cases, and there is no pat answer. I have seen very ill patients respond to treatment and live out their normal life spans, and I have seen others who I thought would do well, die. Imponderables such as state of mind, the will to live, the support of loved ones, and luck, affect the outcome.

I once took care of a little girl who had 4 chest operations and 11 metastatic bone cancers removed. It is now 12 years since her first surgery; she is doing fine and recently got married. She could have given up many times but she chose to fight.

A Chicago businessman asked for only one extra year of life so he could see his lovely daughter married—yet he was still around to see his grandchildren enter college.

In 1965, a patient was diagnosed at another hospital as having osteosarcoma (bone cancer) with metastasis to his lungs and a tumor in his leg. They suggested that he go home and prepare to die—but he was not quite ready for that so he came to ask what I thought.

"Well, you can't cure cancer without trying," I said, "and I don't know whether we can cure you or not but I think we should try."

"Can you guarantee I'll be around for Christmas with my children?" he asked.

"I can't guarantee anything," I told him, "but with aggressive treatment, and a generous amount of luck, there's a chance you'll see Christmas."

We treated his osteosarcoma and removed the lung tumors and the growth in his leg. He went home, did well, and enjoyed Christmas with his beloved family.

The following year he visited Memorial for regular checkups and in October asked whether he would see the approaching Christmas.

"I think so," I told him.

By December 1979, this man had celebrated Christmas 14 times with his family and his children were grown.

Radiation Therapy

The patient, draped in a white sheet with her head on a pillow, lies comfortably on a treatment table in the colorfully decorated room. A green leafy tree stands in one corner.

But this is no ordinary room. The concrete walls are 12 feet thick in places, and lead and steel shielding are embedded in the massive walls. A pair of three-ton steel and lead doors seal the room.

The white-coated radiation technologist positions the patient precisely beneath the overhanging eye of the 20-million-electron-volt linear accelerator and leaves the room.

In the control room, behind steel and concrete shielding, the radiotherapist watches the patient over closed-circuit TV, programs the computer, and presses a button.

The accelerator eye rotates slowly around the patient, who hears a low hum but feels no pain or discomfort.

Thirty seconds later, the treatment is over.

This powerful linear accelerator delivers either X rays to treat deep-seated cancers or an electron beam to destroy shallow tumors near the body's surface. It can treat a tumor in a woman's breast without harming the chest wall or lungs behind the breast because the precise electron beam penetrates only short distances. Treatments last from 30 to 120 seconds.

Surgery and radiation are both very effective in treating localized cancer; surgery excises the lesion and radiation destroys it. Surgery is preferred for younger patients and radiation for older individuals because, years after treatment, radiation may induce cancer in a small percentage of patients. Cancer of the cervix, for example, is usually treated by surgery in a younger woman and by radiation in an older woman.

Radiation therapy is particularly effective in destroying tumors near the surface such as lesions of the head and neck and cancer of the vocal cords. Early, localized cancer of the larynx (voice box) can be treated effectively by radiation and the voice preserved. Larynxes have been removed unnecessarily by surgeons who did not know that radiation is often just as effective in treating these early lesions.

In head and neck lesions, where surgery might be too disfiguring, radiation therapy is the treatment of choice. The only way to believe the remarkable results often achieved by radiation, which leaves only a small scar, is to see "before" and "after" photographs of patients.

A patient should be treated by the modality best suited to his type of lesion, not necessarily by the specialty of the physician whom the patient sees. That is why it is advantageous to be cared for at an institution where all the different skills are available.

Radiation may be used to shrink a tumor before surgery and to destroy malignant cells that may remain after surgery. It can also prevent metastases and relieve pain in advanced cases.

The powerful beams are generated by X rays, electrons, neutrons, gamma rays, and atomic particles from radioactive materials. High-energy sources such as pions (pi-mesons), protons, and fast neutrons promise still greater destructive power with less effect on normal tissue.

Certain types of cancer (those of the lymph glands and blood-forming tissues) are very sensitive to radiation while other forms—lesions of the stomach, liver, and intestines—are radiation resistant. Malignant cells are more susceptible to radiation than normal cells, and are particularly vulnerable when they are dividing rapidly. Slow-growing tumors are less sensitive to radiation.

The increased cure of Hodgkin's disease (cancer of the lymphatic system) by extended radiation therapy, pioneered by Dr. Henry Kaplan of Stanford University, Palo Alto, California, was a major achievement.

Internal Radiation

Tumors come in all sorts of shapes and sizes and may be mixed in with the body's tissues and organs, making surgery and external radiation impossible. In these cases, internal radiation can be used to destroy the lesion:

• Tiny radioactive seeds are implanted inside the tumor in the operating room.

• A "radium bomb"—radium in a shielded container—is placed in the body for a day or two.

• In "after loading," a tiny catheter is positioned in or next to the nonresectable tumor during surgery; later, radioactive seeds on a tiny wire are inserted into the catheter for a short time.

The side effects of radiotherapy are often unpleasant—temporary loss of hair, loss of appetite, nausea and vomiting. This is unfortunate, but one must weigh the benefits against the side effects, which stop when treatment stops.

Drawing on his knowledge of physics, mathematics, and medicine, the therapeutic radiologist plots a treatment protocol in consultation with other oncologists. At Memorial Hospital, our radiation oncologists work with many hospitals in devising the most effective treatment strategies for their patients. Radiation therapy, now the second most common method of treating cancer, is certain to become even more effective in the future.

Chemotherapy

The treatment of disease by chemotherapy (drugs) is not new. Ancient man used arsenicals to treat disease. At the turn of the century in Germany, Paul Ehrlich, the father of chemotherapy, made his successful attack on syphilis with Salvarsan. Meningitis, tuberculosis, and a host of infectious diseases have fallen before the onslaught of chemotherapy.

The worst characteristic of cancer is that microscopic malignant cells may break off from the primary tumor and travel by the bloodstream or lymphatic fluid to other parts of the body where they seed new lesions. Surgery and radiation rarely cure cancers that have metastasized, or cancers of the blood (leukemias). The primary way of attacking systemic disease is with toxic drugs which destroy the cancer cells.

More Than 50 Effective Drugs

There are more than 50 groups of drugs with proved anticancer activity in man and hundreds more are under investigation. Like radiation, chemotherapy is most effective against rapidly dividing cells. In the last five years, we have learned a great deal about how to administer chemotherapy, the value of combining different drugs, and the importance of using chemotherapy along with radiation and surgery.

These drugs work three ways: *alkylating agents* poison cancer cells; *antimetabolites* mimic normal nutrients, but once inside the cell they starve it and the cell dies. Some *antibiotics* possess anticancer activity; actinomycin D is an important drug in treating ovarian and testicular cancer. Chemotherapy protocols are designated by the initials of the drugs used, such as the CMF (cyclophosphamide-methotrexate-5-fluorouracil) protocol used in breast cancer.

Eleven fairly rare cancers, formerly incurable, now are controlled by chemotherapy and many patients are cured of them. Several drugs plus radiation result in 76 percent of Memorial Hospital's young Hodgkin's disease patients being free of disease for an average of 3½ years. At major cancer centers, 90 percent of the youngsters with acute leukemia are in remission in three years and we hope to cure more than 50 percent; a decade ago most of these children died within a year. Chemotherapy cures 90 percent of the young women with choriocarcinoma, a rare cancer of the placenta, and is becoming effective against advanced melanoma (a serious form of skin cancer).

Combining chemotherapy with surgery and radiation promises to improve survival rates of cancers of the breast, lung, and colon— major cancers where formerly drugs were ineffective. Nearly 50 percent of patients with metastatic colon cancer now respond to a new four-drug protocol devised at Memorial Hospital.

Treatment by these poisonous drugs is often lengthy and unpleasant; common side effects (which are temporary) are loss of hair, nausea, vomiting, diarrhea, and depression; the drugs also reduce production of blood cells which weakens the immune system. Chemotherapy should be given only by experienced oncologists who test frequently to see how the patient is responding. Close, supportive nursing care is essential. There are physicians who are simply not informed about the latest advances in chemotherapy and who should not use it.

Uninformed critics of chemotherapy—who do not have cancer and are not physicians—say that the treatment is worse than the disease and causes cancer by suppressing the body's immune system. This criticism ignores reality.

Most patients do not agree that chemotherapy is worse than cancer and if they do, they have the right to refuse treatment. Much, but not all, chemotherapy is rigorous and unpleasant but the distress disappears when treatment stops. The immune system is suppressed by the drugs which may lead to a new neoplasm years later in some patients; we try to avoid this by not giving the drugs continuously and by monitoring the patient closely.

If one of these irresponsible critics comes down with cancer, it would be interesting to know whether he accepts chemotherapy or ineffective treatment based on fruits, vegetables, and distilled water.

The Tragedy of Chad Green

The case of Chad Green, the two-year-old Massachusetts child with acute lymphocytic leukemia, received nationwide attention in 1979 when his parents refused chemotherapy and took him to Mexico to be treated with laetrile and "nutritional therapy." The courts tried to force his parents to reinstitute treatment, without success, and Chad died.

There are disturbing aspects to this sad case. Acute childhood leukemia is no longer a death sentence, and Chad had an excellent chance of disease-free survival had the physicians at Massachusetts General Hospital been allowed to continue treatment. The statement by the Mexican doctor that Chad's death "was not nearly as painful as it would have been had only chemotherapy been administered" is unfortunate and inaccurate. Most of the children on chemotherapy

lead fairly normal lives during treatment and are not in pain except
for the prick of a needle from time to time.

But not all children do well and in those cases the compassionate
physician, consulting with the family, stops the treatment, relieves
any pain, and provides continuing emotional support to the child
and his parents.

The Chad Green tragedy might well have been avoided had his
parents understood more about chemotherapy and permitted a full
course of treatment. Chad's doctors had no objection to a special
diet, provided it was nutritious, but pointed out that it was of no
value in treating his leukemia.

One physician estimates that only 25 percent of children with
acute lymphocytic leukemia are receiving the treatment with the
greatest potential for cure.

Immunotherapy

Of all the cancer enigmas, none is more puzzling and challenging
than those cancers which disappear spontaneously for no known
reason, leaving the patient healthy with no recurrence.

• Years ago in Chicago I knew a man who presented osteosarcoma
with lung metastases. Suddenly, the tumors started to decrease in size
and finally disappeared. X rays 15 years later showed no signs of
disease.

• A woman operated on for breast cancer was well for three years
and then developed bone metastases. She was treated with radiation,
hormones, and removal of her ovaries; a few years later she became
an alcoholic and stopped the hormone therapy, taking only
Antabuse for her alcoholism. Surprisingly, her bone cancer faded
away. The woman died 10 years later in an accident, and on autopsy
small pockets of malignant cells were found in the bone marrow,
their growth halted years before.

• An aircraft plant worker diagnosed with a malignant chest tumor
became ill with a serious infection and ran a high fever. Slowly, the
infection subsided. X rays showed the tumor was smaller and
ultimately it disappeared.

While these spontaneous regressions are exceedingly rare—since
1900 there have been only a few hundred documented cases in the
world—they are an important clue and there is renewed interest in
them today.

The body's natural defense mechanism against disease—the immune system—almost certainly destroyed these malignant lesions. Many of the regressions occurred after the patient became ill with an unrelated disease that stimulated the immune system to heightened response which also wiped out the cancer.

Most medical scientists believe that each of us produces cancer cells regularly which are destroyed by a healthy immunological system. This complex, finely orchestrated system surveys the body for foreign invaders and attacks them with lymphocytes, antibodies, and other weapons. When the system becomes weak, breaks down, or is outwitted, malignant cells gain a foothold, which leads eventually to a detectable cancer.

Tests show that in most cancer patients the immune system is not functioning properly. Immunotherapy is aimed at stimulating the immune system into more vigorous action in the hope that it will destroy the malignant cells. There are three approaches:

1. *Nonspecific immunotherapy* tries to shock the patient's system into stronger reaction by injecting "immunomodulators" such as BCG (attenuated tuberculosis vaccine), C. Parvum (killed bacteria), Poly A, Poly U and Levamisole.

2. *Specific immunotherapy* involves preparation of a compound from the patient's tumor and administering it in the hope of preventing recurrence; the cancer cells are inactivated by heat or radiation.

In an interesting animal experiment, mouse sarcoma cells were injected into a sheep which manufactured antibodies to the mouse tumor. These antibodies were then injected into the mouse and the cancer disappeared. But unfortunately the tumor returned and the mouse died. So, impressive as this is, it is not a cure for cancer but promising research.

This experiment was tried in man by Dr. Peter Alexander and his colleagues at the Royal Marsden Hospital in England. But using sheep lymphocytes in man is a heterologous transplant (between different species), with resulting problems such as graft-versus-host rejection.

3. *Passive immunotherapy* in which lymphocytes "sensitized" to cancer cells, extracts from these cancer cells such as transfer factor, and natural body substances such as interferon, are administered to the patient to strengthen his immune response.

Interferon was discovered in 1957 by Alick Isaacs and Jean Lindenmann, virologists at the National Institute for Medical Research in London; it is thought to be a major component in the body's defense against viral infections. At present a rare, expensive drug, interferon is being clinically tested at 10 medical institutions in this country against various cancers and the early results are encouraging. Interferon, a protein produced by body cells in tiny amounts, warns other cells of impending invasion, which enables them to produce protective proteins. Unlike other anticancer drugs, interferon works best against malignant cells in their resting stage. Should interferon prove to be a major cancer drug, it probably will be used as a supplement to surgery and radiation in treating most forms of the disease. Years of research and evaluation lie ahead of this promising natural substance.

While immunotherapy has produced some encouraging remissions, the overall results to date have been disappointing and the primary cancer treatments remain surgery, radiation, and chemotherapy. Immunotherapy is sometimes used in combination with these modes.

Unless there is a major breakthrough—which is always possible— it appears that immunotherapy will be an adjuvant mode which may destroy malignant cells missed by other methods of treatment. But if immunotherapy can ever correct the defect that allowed the cancer to get started in the first place, it will be the major method of treatment and possibly of prevention.

Other Methods of Treatment

1. *Hormones* The place of hormones in treating, and causing, cancer is complex and many questions remain unanswered. Removing the pituitary and adrenal glands, and the ovaries—all hormone sources—causes remission in one-third of all breast cancers; these neoplasms contain hormone receptors and are dependent on hormones for growth. The female sex hormone, estrogen, is used to treat cancer of the prostate. Most cancers do not respond to hormonal manipulation, but a few common neoplasms do and in these cases hormone therapy can be effective.

2. *Hyperthermia* Intense heat kills malignant cells. High-frequency radio waves are used to heat tumors which become much hotter than normal tissue because of their sluggish blood flow.

Marked reduction in tumor size has resulted but usually not complete destruction. Hyperthermia may become an additional modality in conjunction with surgery and radiation. Total body heat is also under investigation.

An ingenious application of heat is in chemotherapy. The toxic chemical is encased in a fatty outer coating which dissolves when it encounters a heated area. Thus, the drug can be released only in or near the lesion heated by high-frequency energy.

3. *Cryosurgery* Intense cold, as well as intense heat, kills malignant cells. The idea of cryosurgery is not new, but at Memorial Hospital a unique application is the use of liquid nitrogen at –196° C to treat benign and malignant bone tumors and avoid the need for limb amputation.

4. *Plasmapheresis* Dr. Lucien Israel, a French oncologist, is experimenting with blood plasma replacement in terminal cancer patients. The plasma is replaced with fresh plasma and the white blood cells are washed and returned to the bloodstream. Partial tumor regression occurs in about one-third of the cases. Dr. Israel speculated this was due to removal of "blocking factors" in the plasma which suppressed the immune defense system.

5. *Vitamins A and C* Retinoids, synthetic vitamin substances which are distant relatives of vitamin A, are being investigated as a possible cancer preventive and a method of treatment. But people should not take more than the recommended amount of vitamin A (5,000 I.U. daily) because in excessive amounts it is toxic to the liver.

Vitamin C has anticancer activity but many questions remain to be answered. We have long used vitamins A and C along with standard modalities in treating cancer (which does not support the statement by nutritionists that cancer centers have little interest in nutrition).

A recent Mayo Clinic study failed to find that massive doses of vitamin C had a therapeutic effect in patients with advanced cancer, contrary to the report of Dr. Linus Pauling and Dr. Ewan Cameron. Drs. Pauling and Cameron challenged the Mayo report because the patients had already been treated with chemotherapy or radiation which could have suppressed their immune systems. It would be difficult, I think, to find advanced cancer patients in the United States who had not received some form of more conventional treatment in an effort to cure or arrest their disease.

Better Nutrition During Cancer Therapy

Eating Hints—Recipes and Tips for Better Nutrition During Treatment is an excellent booklet to help cancer patients eat well and enjoy eating when cancer treatment or the disease itself causes problems. The appetizing, nutritious recipes are easy to prepare and were selected to solve specific problems. The booklet (NIH Publication No. 80-2079), written by the Yale-New Haven Medical Center, is available from the Office of Cancer Communications, National Cancer Institute, Bethesda, MD 20205.

A Look into the Future

Late in 1979, a team of scientists at Rockefeller University and the National Institutes of Health successfully injected a single gene into a defective cell, and cured a genetic flaw. This brilliant achievement, using mouse cells, may one day lead to the repair of defective human genes, the basic chemical units of inheritance.

The failure of human genes to function properly leads to several hundred diseases including hemophilia and sickle cell anemia. Genetic defects can lead to physical deformity, mental retardation, and create a predisposition to cancer.

Recombinant DNA (deoxyribonucleic acid) research allows scientists to splice genes from plants, animals, and humans into bacteria where they can be studied more easily. This work will lead to increased knowledge of genes and the production of body substances such as insulin, the absence of which results in disease.

"Genetic engineering" has exciting potential but is not close to practical application and probably will not be for many years. Dr. Robert A. Good, director of the Sloan-Kettering Institute, believes this research is "one of the most powerful tools ever introduced for analyzing the mechanisms of cellular disturbance and disease."

The Truth About Laetrile

It is impossible to discuss cancer treatment without mentioning laetrile, which has created much controversy in recent years.

The National Cancer Institute and the Food and Drug Administration policy is that before a drug is tested clinically in man, it must first possess anticancer activity in animals. Under NCI auspices, laetrile was tested in the Sloan-Kettering Institute laboratories for anticancer properties in mice. This pilot study was conducted by Dr. Kanematsu Sugiura, an experienced investigator who joined the Memorial Hospital staff in 1917. He used a strain of mice with breast cancer which develop lung metastases.

In the mice that received laetrile, all the mice eventually developed lung metastases and all the mice died. However, Dr. Sugiura thought there was some delay in the time frame before pulmonary spread developed in a small percentage of the mice, and that the animals looked better and ate better.

When the experiment was repeated in a "double blind" study in which Dr. Sugiura did not know which animals received laetrile and which did not, he found that lung metastases were not delayed and he could not tell one group from the other.

In 11 other experimental test systems, which collectively demonstrate the activity of drugs now being used against clinical cancer, laetrile had no effect.

The animal evidence on laetrile was so weak that it did not qualify as a test drug in the standard screening techniques used to find new therapeutic drugs. Since there are more than 50 drugs with known anticancer activity, there was no interest in taking laetrile to the bedside of man.

Unfortunately, the information in 1978 on these tests was mishandled, which resulted in inaccurate or misleading stories in some of the media. A few individuals, capitalizing on the confusion, alleged that Sloan-Kettering Institute was concealing the positive results of the laetrile test, which simply is not true.

In spite of these observations the laetrile controversy continues. The National Cancer Institute has discussed with four institutions, including Memorial Sloan-Kettering Cancer Center, the possibility of carrying out human clinical trials using laetrile to settle this dispute. Our institution has indicated a willingness to cooperate with the National Cancer Institute.

The Dangers of Quack Treatment

Quacks promising a miraculous cure for cancer exist in almost every country and each year a number of ignorant, frightened people put themselves in the hands of these fakers. No one knows how many needless deaths quacks cause by their irresponsible treatment, or by delaying effective medical care, but the figure is probably in the thousands. Some states now have made medical quackery a criminal offense punishable by imprisonment.

The quack is easily recognized:

1. He calls himself "doctor," but most quacks are not M.D.s.

2. He treats patients without obtaining a medical history, and diagnoses without a thorough physical examination including, where necessary, biopsies.

3. His single remedy for every type of cancer is a dark secret often involving worthless medicines and fake machines.

4. He claims that the medical profession is persecuting him for his unorthodox methods which challenge accepted theories.

5. He has published no scientific papers in professional journals describing his treatment for peer review, yet he claims the "medical establishment" will not listen to him because it does not want a cure for cancer.

6. His "cures" are testified to by excitable people some of whom did not have cancer, simply an undiagnosed lump or a vague shadow in an X ray. Those who did have cancer are usually dead.

"Alternative" Cancer Treatment?

There is a second group not quite as pernicious as the outright quacks but who nonetheless pose a threat to the cancer patient. These are the lay people, and a few physicians and nutritionists, whose battle cry is "alternative" treatment with "freedom of choice"—something everyone has anyway. They urge those ill with cancer not to submit to orthodox treatment but instead to rely on "metabolic therapy," a special diet, a positive frame of mind, massive doses of vitamins, or laetrile, hormones, or enzymes.

There are fragments of validity in some of these ideas but by no means enough to warrant abandoning the medical treatment that gives the best chance of recovery. A nutritious diet is essential to health, but there is no evidence that diet can cure cancer. A person's mental outlook is important and affects health; it can upset hormonal balance, overstimulate the autonomic nervous system, and alter the output of corticosteroids which weakens the immune system. A positive outlook aids recovery.

Certain vitamins appear useful in treating cancer. Hormones are effective in treating some types of cancer but should be administered only by an experienced oncologist. Laetrile has not been shown to be an effective anticancer drug.

It is stark tragedy for sick people to gamble with their lives by accepting quack treatment, or "alternative" treatment, instead of consulting an oncologist who has spent his life learning the best ways to fight cancer—and winning about half the time with early diagnosis.

A Challenge to Anyone Who Claims to Have a Better Cancer Treatment

Throughout the world there are people who claim to have discovered a superior method of treating cancer and who say that no one in established medicine will listen to them. To these individuals I offer the following challenge:

1. Submit to me, in writing, a study that you have carried out, using accepted scientific procedure, which details your method of treating cancer, and I will guarantee to get it published in a professional journal with you as the author.
2. Like every such study, your study must include:
   a. A significant number of patients.
   b. Documentation of diagnosis of each patient: diagnostic method; type of cancer; stage of disease.
   c. Methodology used to assure that the results were unbiased (blind; double blind).
   d. Details of treatment: components; length; side effects, and so on.
   e. Results in treated group and in control group over a stated and sufficient period of time.
   f. Names of professional journals, if any, to which your study was submitted and which declined to publish it.

Physicians reporting the results, good or bad, of new treatment modalities routinely provide the above data for publication. Others then follow the procedure and endeavor to duplicate the results, then in turn publish their findings. There are no secrets in the accepted scientific method. New drugs can, of course, be patented.

Cancer quacks and advocates of "alternative" treatment are not able to publish documented scientific studies. Their claims are based on anecdotes and vague statements which cannot be verified by others and which, in all probability, have no foundation in fact.

An Outrageous Lie

Few things anger physicians more than the allegation that they do not want a cure for cancer because it would throw many of them out of work. This outrageous lie, which crops up in the irresponsible minority of the information media, is an affront to every physician and scientist working to prevent cancer, cure patients, and discover the basic cause of the disease.

Physicians and their loved ones become ill with cancer and every year we admit doctors to Memorial Hospital as patients.

Physicians have sacrificed their lives trying to conquer cancer. Unaware of the hazards, many of the early experimenters with radium and X rays died of malignant neoplasms induced by intense, uncontrolled radiation. Until safety precautions were understood, radiologists suffered a higher incidence of leukemia. Dr. David Karnofsky of Memorial Hospital, a pioneer in chemotherapy, died at age 55 of cancer caused by his investigations of nitrogen mustard, now used in cancer therapy. Before his death, Dr. Karnofsky wrote, "The triumphs . . . in the fight against cancer will come from doctors who do too much—who continue to treat the patient when the odds appear overwhelming—and not from those who do too little."

Unfair Job Discrimination Against Ex-Cancer Patients

It is estimated that 90 percent of cancer patients experience discrimination problems with their employers in returning to their jobs after treatment, even though most of them resume full-time work. At a cancer conference, Dr. J. Herbert Dietz observed that cancer patients are better able to resume their job responsibilities than workers who suffered a heart attack or stroke.

A 14-year study by the Metropolitan Life Insurance Company concluded, "The employment record of the cancer treated group is good relative to non-cancer employees of the same age and position. . . . We conclude that the selective hiring of persons who have been treated for cancer, in positions for which they are physically qualified, is sound industrial practice."

The American Telephone & Telegraph Co. found that 81 percent of its employees treated for cancer returned to work after treatment lasting an average of 80 days.

Dr. Guy Robbins of Memorial Hospital, who for years has fought discrimination, says, "There is still great resistance by business to employees with cancer and there is much to be done to remove the remaining stigma. This can only be done through education and legislation, which requires greater activism by health professionals."

As ignorance and fear of cancer are replaced by knowledge and optimism, the unjust barriers of job discrimination will pass into history.

Social Discrimination

Cancer patients and ex-cancer patients sometimes experience another form of discrimination which is poignantly expressed in this letter to Ann Landers; it was published in her widely read newspaper column and is reprinted with permission:

Dear Ann Landers:

I am dying. But don't become alarmed, and please don't feel sorry for me. After all, we are ALL dying.

Three years ago I learned I have chronic leukemia. (I was 31, then.) The news came at a crisis time in my life. (I had just gone through a divorce and had young children to raise.)

Would you believe I had to move to a larger city because people would not accept me as a normal person? I was devastated, not by the disease, which has been controlled by drugs, but by the way I was treated. Although I could play tennis, ski, dance, hike, and take part in community activities, the people at work made my life miserable. (One woman refused to use the same washroom!) Men wouldn't date me. I was treated like some sort of social outcast—a pathetic, hopeless case.

After I moved here my life changed dramatically. No one here knows of my illness. I work part-time, attend college, have many friends, am involved with community activities and participate in sports.

Although I feel well and look fine, I know it can't last forever. I dread the day my friends must be told of my illness. I don't want to be pitied or deserted as I was before.

The purpose of this letter is to help educate people, should they encounter someone in the same spot I'm in right now. Yes, folks—you can help. How? Here are the ways:

1. Treat me the same as a well person. Don't ask me, "How are you doing?"

2. Include me in your activities. I need friends just as you do.

3. Stay off the subject of funeral arrangements and insurance. (Relatives are especially guilty of this.)

4. Forget I have a disease. I'll do better if I don't know it's on your mind.

5. Ask me out. Develop a relationship with me. You can even marry me. I might live another 20 years. (Today that's longer than most couples stay together!)

6. Hire me. If I'm productive I will live longer. If I'm forced to go on welfare or disability, it will raise your taxes.

7. Give to the American Cancer Society. They support research and alert the public to cancer signs.

8. Get a checkup this week. Many forms of cancer can be cured if caught early.

9. Treat me as you would like to be treated under the same circumstances.

10. Love me! Enjoy me! I have a lot to give—I Could Be Anybody.

Dear Anybody:
What a beautiful and courageous letter! Thank you for educating millions of people today. You've made an enormous contribution.

Ann Landers

As knowledge about cancer becomes widespread, the kind of distressing social injustice illustrated so movingly in this letter will fade into the past.

Half of All Patients Can Be Cured

Cancer is an expensive, demanding disease to treat but one day will come under control as a result of basic medical discoveries. It will then cost relatively little to manage with "effective technology"—or perhaps it will be prevented entirely.

Meanwhile, with our present knowledge one-half of all cancer patients can be cured *if they are diagnosed early and receive prompt, effective medical treatment.* So, if you are the one person in four who eventually will contract cancer, don't let it throw you. Your chances of being cured and back on the golf course are one in two or even higher—not bad odds.

14

The Truth About Pain

Dr. Raymond W. Houde and his associates at Memorial Sloan-Kettering Cancer Center have been pioneers in studying pain control in cancer patients. Over the years, they have evaluated nonnarcotic and narcotic drugs and determined their efficacy, dosages, and side effects when given orally and by injection. The published works of Dr. Houde and Dr. Kathleen M. Foley, noted in this chapter, are basic references in this field and I am indebted to them for permission to use their data.

In no area are the misconceptions by patients and physicians greater than about the mechanism of pain, the pain caused by cancer, and the effective control of pain.

• In spite of what you read, not all cancers are painful; some never cause pain; others cause pain only in the last stages.

• Should a cancer patient develop pain, it can be controlled and the patient made comfortable.

• Pain is controlled poorly by many physicians in the United States and thousands of patients suffer needless pain, which is a medical disgrace.

Surveys of inpatients at Memorial Hospital revealed that only about 33 percent had severe enough pain due to cancer to require analgesic (pain-killing) drugs. Of those patients in the last stages of disease, only 60 percent had significant pain and that was controlled by adequate medication or other means. Almost no cancers cause pain in the early stages.

Certain types of cancer are more likely to cause pain than others.

For example, in the Memorial Hospital survey 85 percent of patients with primary bone tumors and 52 percent of those with advanced breast cancer had pain. Pain in a cancer patient usually does not remain constant, or continue to worsen, nor does it necessarily mean a recurrence of disease.

It is important to understand the mechanism—the cause—of the patient's pain. If the pain caused by a tumor can be relieved or eliminated by surgery, radiation therapy, or chemotherapy, these are the treatments of choice. If, on the other hand, these modalities cannot give relief, then pain-killing drugs are necessary. The knowledgeable use of narcotic analgesics can relieve 90 to 95 percent of the patients who suffer pain. In the few patients not relieved by drugs, surgical procedures such as nerve blocks, or severing selected nerve pathways, provide relief.

Dangers of Narcotics Overrated in Treating Cancer Pain

Nonnarcotic analgesics (pain-killers) are administered first in an effort to control mild to moderate pain. If these do not provide comfort, then narcotics are used without delay. In some cases, narcotics should be used immediately without first resorting to weaker analgesics.

In our drug-conscious society, with the social abuse of drugs and the stigma of drug addiction, there is an understandable but unfortunate apprehension among both patients and physicians regarding the legitimate use of narcotics to relieve pain.

Narcotics, like all other drugs, can produce undesired side effects which must be handled with knowledge and skill. Some of those caused by narcotics are excessive sedation, constipation, and tolerance to or physical dependence on the drug.

Morphine and morphinelike drugs, such as methadone, are important and effective in managing severe pain and, contrary to popular opinion, when intelligently prescribed do not have many of the dangers that most people—including too many physicians—associate with them. Research at one widely respected hospital disclosed that 90 percent of its medical staff failed to prescribe the proper drugs and/or dosages for adequate pain relief, and did not know the differences between doses administered orally or by intramuscular injection (doses must be higher by mouth to give the same relief).

By far the most serious problems are caused by the widespread misconceptions of drug tolerance, physical dependence, and addiction. It is these misconceptions which lead to the poor management of patients with pain in this country.

Tolerance Patients who take a narcotic every two hours over a period of weeks require increasing doses to provide the same degree of relief. This is termed tolerance and is not a serious problem since the dosage can be increased as necessary without ill effect.

Physical Dependence When a narcotic is taken over a considerable period of time (weeks or months), physical dependence on the drug develops. Physical dependence is present if the patient experiences signs of withdrawal when the drug is stopped abruptly. These signs and symptoms include restlessness, muscle cramps, excessive sweating, nausea and vomiting, diarrhea, and some elevation of temperature, pulse, blood pressure, and respiration.

Tolerance and Physical Dependence Are Not Drug Addiction

Many patients and physicians are reluctant to use narcotics for pain relief because they fear drug addiction.

It is essential that patient and physician understand that tolerance and physical dependence do not imply drug abuse.

The distressing failure to understand this pharmacologic fact leads to the tragic mismanagement and needless suffering of patients with pain. Compounding the problem are the strict federal and state regulations for prescribing and dispensing narcotics.

Drug addiction is characterized by major behavioral changes, a craving for the drug, personality disorders, and concern with the source of supply. Dr. Kathleen Foley, coordinator of the Pain Clinic at Memorial Hospital, notes, "Addiction is not an issue in cancer patients. The patient receiving a drug for relief of pain is quite different from the person we know as a drug addict who is both psychologically as well as physically dependent on the drug. Although tolerance and physical dependence occur in the cancer patient, the psychological factors associated with addiction do not occur.

"Some of our patients are sent home on large doses of oral narcotics to keep them comfortable. Our experience is that these men and women do not abuse the narcotics, do not attempt suicide, and can be withdrawn from narcotics without any significant problems."

Factors That Influence the Choice of Drug and Dosage

Keeping a patient with severe pain responsive and comfortable is a complex task which involves more than simply writing a prescription or a medication order in a chart. Among the factors which must be weighed:

• The mechanism of the pain—whether caused by tumor, therapy, or unrelated to either.

• Patients are not equal in their responses to the same medication for a number of reasons including variations in size, weight, age, sex, and metabolism, for which adjustments can be made.

• Caution must be exercised in changing from one drug to another because narcotic analgesics include some with antagonistic properties which act differently on the brain receptors. If an agonist or morphinelike drug is replaced by an antagonist, such as Talwin, it can bring about an acute withdrawal state and fail to relieve the patient's pain.

• As stated, whether a drug is given by mouth or injection is an important consideration and equivalency tables are available. For the same relief, higher doses must be given orally and gross errors are frequently made by physicians who are not aware of this fact. For example, many are surprised to learn that 50 mg. of Demerol by mouth has the same efficacy as two aspirin tablets.

On the other hand, Levo-Dromoran and methadone are relatively effective by mouth: 4 mg. of Levo-Dromoran by mouth has the same effect as 2 mg. by injection; 20 mg. of methadone by mouth equals 10 mg. by injection. The equivalent doses by mouth and by injection have been determined in controlled studies by Dr. Raymond Houde and widely published.

The degree of ignorance that exists is illustrated by the following story. A patient of ours was told by a pharmacist when he presented a prescription for methadone for pain relief, "Get out of here, you hophead!" Although methadone is a valuable pain-relieving drug, in the public's mind it is primarily associated with drug addiction programs and the rehabilitation of heroin addicts. In this case, the pharmacist—unlike most of them, who are highly competent—did not know that methadone is an accepted, effective analgesic in a cancer patient.

An even more shocking case involved a 63-year-old woman who suffered excruciating pain because her physician, who should have known better, had prescribed two aspirin tablets and 50 mg. of Demerol orally every four hours. Her husband brought her to Memorial Hospital where an effective analgesic protocol was prescribed. When she showed her local doctor the new prescriptions, he told her to stop the methadone immediately because it was "a dangerous, habit-forming drug." Fortunately, she was smart enough to ignore his advice and was comfortable—for the first time—until her death two months later.

SPECIAL SECTION FOR PHYSICIANS:

Principles of Effective Pain Relief

The following is a brief summary of the principles that govern the practical application of narcotic pharmacology and is from the listed reference articles by Drs. Houde and Foley.

1. *Know the pharmacology of the drugs prescribed.* Start with the drug which is the most effective for the particular type of pain.

    a. *Mild pain.* Nonnarcotic analgesics such as aspirin and acetaminophen, or narcotics such as Darvon, are the drugs of choice.

    b. *Moderate pain.* Codeine, meperidine (Demerol), and oxycodone (in the form of Percodan or Percocet) are commonly prescribed.

    c. *Severe pain.* Morphine (by injection), methadone, and levorphanol (Levo-Dromoran) are the drugs of choice.

2. *Prescribe medication by the clock rather than on demand.* This reduces patient anxiety, keeps pain relief at a steady level, and allows reduction in total amount of drugs needed. The next dose should be given before the previous one has worn off. Medication should be given throughout the night even if the patient must be awakened; this prevents the patient waking in the morning with severe pain which may require increased dosage. Drugs should not be given rigidly "every four hours" out of stubborn habit but administered over whatever time span is correct to maintain steady relief.

3. *Use a combination of drugs.* Drugs like aspirin and acetaminophen combined with narcotics produce an additive analgesic effect. In some cases, muscle relaxants and antianxiety drugs are helpful but may limit the amount of narcotic analgesic that can be safely given; care must be taken not to overuse such medications. Sleep medication may be required in about half of advanced cancer patients.

The "Brompton cocktail" as employed at St. Christopher's Hospital, London, is a very effective mixture of varying amounts of heroin (5–10 mg., as indicated), cocaine (10 mg.), alcohol (1.25 ml.), chloroform water (to 10 ml.), syrup (2.5 ml.), and a phenothiazine. It achieves impressive pain and anxiety relief in 90 percent of the hospital's patients. Heroin (diamorphine) is illegal in the United States although it is being studied as an investigational drug. However, similar mixtures containing morphine and methadone are being administered to patients with terminal cancer in this country.

4. *Adapt drug administration to the needs of the patient.* Intramuscular, subcutaneous, or intravenous routes of narcotic administration should be used in patients who require rapid pain relief. Narcotic suppositories can be effective if other methods of administration are not tolerated, and can be adjusted to the patient's needs.

5. *Treat side effects early.* The inevitable constipation that accompanies use of narcotics can be managed through diet (increased fiber bulk, increased fluid intake, and so on) and cathartics, which should be started at the same time as medication. Excessive sedation can be countered by amphetamines and by reducing narcotic dose but increasing frequency of administration.

6. *Watch for development of tolerance.* The first sign of tolerance is the patient's complaint that the duration of relief has decreased; this occurs within a few days of starting narcotics. Tolerance is overcome by increasing the frequency of administration or increasing the dosage. Changing to an equivalent dose of an alternative narcotic may increase analgesic effect because cross-tolerance is seldom complete. Stopping narcotics abruptly produces withdrawal symptoms which can be avoided by reducing doses gradually.

Application of these proven principles can assure the physician of effective pain management, assuming adaptation to each patient's needs. These principles have enabled us to manage pain in inpatients and outpatients with excellent results and without major complications over many years. For detailed information, physicians are referred to these texts:

Houde, R. W. "Cancer Pain in the Head and Neck: Role of Analgesics and Related Drugs." In J. J. Bonica and V. Ventafridda, eds., *Advances in Pain Research and Therapy,* vol. 2. New York: Raven Press, 1979, pp. 533–35.

―――――. "Systemic Analgesics and Related Drugs; Narcotic Analgesics." Ibid., pp. 263–73.

―――――. "Visceral and Perineal Pain: Role of Analgesics and Related Drugs." Ibid., pp. 593–95.

Foley, K. M. "The Management of Pain of Malignant Origin." In H. R. Tyler and D. M. Dawson, eds., *Current Neurology,* vol. 2. Boston: Houghton Mifflin Co., 1979.

―――――. "Pain Syndromes in Patients with Cancer." In J. J. Bonica and V. Ventafridda, eds., *Advances in Pain Research and Therapy,* vol. 2. New York: Raven Press, 1979.

The Team Approach to Managing Pain

Hospitals are turning increasingly to the use of pain teams or pain clinics in managing severe or intractable pain. This has the advantage of bringing the special expertise of a number of medical scientists to bear on the patient's problem. At Memorial Hospital, the Pain Clinic under Dr. Raymond Houde is made up of oncologists, neurologists, neurosurgeons, anesthesiologists, pharmacologists, and nurses.

"A Sleepy, Sedated Patient Who Hurts"

It is important for the physician to understand the patient's complaint and distinguish between sleeplessness, anxiety, and pain.

Not infrequently people are given increased doses of sleeping medicines or tranquilizers in an effort to use less pain medication. Instead of having a patient free of pain, we have a sleepy, sedated patient who still hurts.

Other Methods of Relieving Pain

In addition to surgical techniques to relieve pain, another approach is transcutaneous electrical stimulation (TCS). Low-voltage stimulation of peripheral nerves can activate the large, non-pain nerve fibers which block the pain impulses carried by the smaller pain nerve fibers which act more slowly. This is the "gate" theory of pain described by R. Melzack and P. D. Wall. Small, portable nerve stimulators are available for those patients in whom it works well. It is interesting to note that shocks from electric eels were used to relieve pain in the first century A.D.

Acupuncture for pain relief is based upon the same theory of pain transmission. Unfortunately, our results with the use of acupuncture to relieve chronic pain have not been very successful.

Hypnosis, meditation, biofeedback, and psychological assistance are effective in relieving pain under some conditions and are well worth consideration in selected cases.

In a departure from normal practice, we have taught selected patients in Memorial Hospital's neurological unit to administer their own pain-killing drugs. Our experience shows this is a safe, effective method of treating those patients who have the required alertness, judgment, and physical ability plus a desire to be in the program. Patients are taught the principles of pain control, given a supply of drugs, and asked to keep accurate records of administration. In the past three years, about 75 patients have participated in this program and have reported decreased anxiety and pain and increased feelings of control and self-esteem.

The Body's Own "Morphine"

One of the most fascinating and important discoveries of recent years is that the human brain and spinal cord have special opiate receptors for natural substances secreted by the brain which act like morphine. These powerful natural chemicals, called endorphins, explain why terribly wounded soldiers and mangled victims of automobile accidents very often feel no pain until hours later. These amazing chemicals also seem to be nature's way of providing peace and comfort to the dying.

This major scientific discovery explains the puzzling "placebo" effect in which 30 to 40 percent of people with pain receive genuine relief from sugar pills or salt water which exert no direct pain-killing effect. In some people, the taking of these inert substances apparently triggers the release of the natural analgesic chemicals in the brain and perhaps in the spinal cord.

New, More Effective Drugs for Pain Control

Four new synthetic drugs that are expected to have little or no potential for addiction have given an exciting new dimension to the treatment of pain by drugs.

Two of these drugs, butorphanol (Stadol, Bristol Laboratories) and nalbuphine (Nubain, Endo Laboratories), are approved by the Food and Drug Administration and are currently available in injectable form.

As of January 1980, the other two, propiram (Dirame, Schering-Plough, Inc.) and buprenorphine (Temgesic, Eaton Laboratories), are being evaluated and are not yet approved or available in the United States. Buprenorphine, currently in use in England, is 30 times as potent as morphine. Propiram is almost as effective by mouth as morphine is by injection, and is equally effective by mouth and injection.

These four new synthetic drugs have the pain-killing effect of the most powerful narcotics, but their full value will be realized when they can be taken by mouth instead of by injection; oral forms are being developed by the drug companies.

Another advantage of these new drugs is that there is little decrease in their pain-killing potential over a long period of time; tolerance is slow to occur, or does not occur at all.

Unfortunately, every drug causes side effects of one sort or another and large doses of these new substances create psychological disturbances in some patients which may limit their usefulness. Years of clinical trials lie ahead of these promising new drugs.

New Natural Substance Discovered

Late in 1979, a remarkable new chemical in the human brain was discovered by scientists at Stanford University and the California

Institute of Technology. Called dynorphin, this substance proved 200 times as powerful as morphine in a standard laboratory test of drug activity, and 50 times more potent than beta endorphin.

While it is still too early to know, scientists believe that dynorphin may be of great importance in developing new drugs to control pain.

Contrary to popular belief, it is not true that cancer is always a painful disease. Many cancers never cause any pain at all. And if pain does occur, it can always be controlled and the patient made comfortable—if the attending physician is knowledgeable and compassionate. For the future, the new drugs now under clinical test hold the promise of even more effective pain relief with minimum side effects.

15

How to Get the Best
Medical Treatment

STUDIES BY MEDICAL AUTHORITIES REVEAL wide variations in the quality of medical care from one physician to another, and from one hospital to another.

Nearly one-third of the 7,000 hospitals in the United States do not meet the minimum standards of the medical profession's Joint Commission on Accreditation of Hospitals with respect to safety and adequacy of patient care.

In tests of proficiency by the Federal Center for Disease Control, a distressing number of the 14,350 clinical laboratories in the United States failed to evaluate a number of specimen slides correctly; about half these laboratories are in hospitals and half are independent organizations. Some are licensed and regulated while others are not.

An explosion of new medical knowledge has taken place since most doctors graduated from medical school 10, 20, or 30 years ago. If he is to practice the best medicine, a physician must keep his medical education up to date through medical conferences, contacts with colleagues, refresher courses, and continuing study of the voluminous medical literature. In several specialties, board-certified physicians must pass a requalifying examination periodically; recertification is an excellent idea because it requires doctors to keep abreast of current medical knowledge.

(A "board-certified" physician is one who has taken special study and training in a particular medical field such as pediatrics, internal medicine, or surgery and passed a rigorous examination; see Reference Information III for a list of the medical specialties. While board certification does not guarantee excellence, it is an important clue to a doctor's attitude and training. Twenty-three boards constitute the American Board of Medical Specialties. There are, of course, competent physicians who are not board-certified.)

Ten states now require that a doctor keep up his medical education in order to renew his license to practice medicine and this sound idea is spreading.

Your Own Judgment Is Important

My reason for stating these facts is simply to emphasize what many people already know, and what everyone should know: that medical care is not of equal quality, and that patients should ask more questions of their physicians and be willing to judge whether they are receiving the most effective care.

Far too many patients accept with blind faith whatever a doctor tells them and are reluctant to seek explanations of treatments or to ask that another physician be brought in for consultation. Doctors are human and fallible—no doctor is right 100 percent of the time. Every competent physician welcomes consultation; if your doctor resists consultation or resents your questions, perhaps you should find another doctor.

Which reminds me of the three factory workers in Europe who were accidentally exposed to a deadly gas. The doctor told them he could not save them, but that each would be granted one final wish. The Englishman wanted tea with the Queen, the Frenchman wanted a night in Paris with a beautiful actress, and the Israeli wanted to see another doctor.

Medical competence is, obviously, the first quality to seek in a physician, whether primary-care physician or specialist. But there is a second quality which, I think, is just as essential, and that is compassion—the intricate and elusive human qualities of sensitivity, understanding, and *caring* about every patient. It is these qualities which, by their very nature, are so difficult to teach in medical school yet which bear so crucially on the patient-doctor relationship and the outcome of an illness.

Many years ago I operated frequently beside one of the most brilliant, skillful surgeons I have ever known—yet this man had a 60-degree-below-zero personality. He was arrogant and paternalistic to his patients and saw them as little as possible. Was this man a good physician? I don't think so. He was a good technician.

I can think of no greater compliment to a physician than what one grateful patient told her surgeon: "You are as skilled with your heart as you are with your hands."

Selecting Your Physician

The choice of a physician can be a life-or-death decision. In selecting your family doctor while you are healthy, the following may be helpful.

• Choose a board-certified internist or a physician board certified in family practice, not a specialist.

• There should be good personal rapport between you and your doctor. If you believe he is unsympathetic or does not understand your problem, you would be better off with another physician.

• Many doctors will see a potential new patient for a 10-minute initial interview to get acquainted. You have a right to know about his fields of interest, medical training, board certification, hospital affiliation(s), and special qualifications, such as association with a medical school. Ask who covers for him when he is away, whether he works with a group of physicians (an advantage). Avoid a physician with no hospital affiliation or who is affiliated with a small, unaccredited hospital.

• Before any treatment, your doctor will have an "informed consent" talk with you and answer your questions. Discuss frankly what is on your mind; make up a list of questions ahead of time.

• You have the right to refuse treatment.

• You have the right to a consultation.

• You have the right to have your records transferred to a new physician (usually done by mail).

Names of primary-care physicians can be obtained from several sources: your county medical society; hospitals; medical schools; consumer guides in some areas; friends and associates; and the *Directory of Medical Specialists,* discussed later.

Dr. Arnold S. Relman, editor of the *New England Journal of Medicine,* suggested in 1978 that state and county medical societies publish directories of practicing physicians in each community to dissolve the information barrier between doctors and the public. The directories would include complete data about the physician— medical school, residency, special training, certification, hospital affiliation, and the like. This excellent idea probably will become a reality by the turn of the century.

Your Two Most Important Steps

Should you one day be told that you might have cancer—and one out of every four of us will—the first and most crucial step toward recovery is to get yourself under the care of a competent physician experienced in the disease. This might be a physician certified by the American Board of Internal Medicine in the subspecialty of medical oncology. A medical oncologist, with his special training in cancer diagnosis and treatment, is more qualified than a general-care physician to see that you benefit from the latest and most effective treatment.

Your second most important step is to shift yourself into a *positive and optimistic* frame of mind because this makes your life much easier and affects the outcome of the disease. Not easy, but you can do it. You have an excellent chance of being cured if you were diagnosed reasonably early or, failing that, of long-term remission with a good quality of life which reduces cancer to a livable chronic disease, like diabetes or heart disease.

Diagnosis Can Be Difficult

The first thing your oncologist will do is to confirm the diagnosis, perhaps using a consulting oncologist and additional diagnostic tests. Without accurate diagnosis there can be no effective treatment.

Diagnosing cancer can be tricky and mistakes can be made, particularly in borderline cases where even the most experienced pathologist examining body cells under a microscope cannot be certain whether the cells are benign or malignant. In these cases, experienced pathologists consult with other pathologists and cytologists; at Memorial Hospital our pathologists are frequently asked to consult on these "gray area" diagnoses.

I am sorry to say that we see a certain number of patients every year who have been diagnosed incorrectly. Some do not even have cancer—a diagnosis we are always pleased to reverse.

One 38-year-old woman was treated for 14 months for a "benign" tumor of the abdomen which, in fact, was highly malignant. A man in his forties was told that the swelling in his knee was only a cyst; he was operated on twice but his distress became acute. By the time we saw him the tumor had regrown and there was metastasis.

An athletic woman, age 53, noticed a bump the size of a grape on her neck below her ear. Her doctor told her it was an infection, prescribed an antibiotic, but the lump grew larger. Six months later the woman saw a second physician who sent her immediately to Memorial Hospital where the lesion was biopsied. It was a malignant tumor which our surgeons removed; later she was placed on chemotherapy to destroy any malignant cells that might have remained behind in her bloodstream or lymphatic system.

"Caretaker" Treatment vs. Modern Treatment

A number of physicians, confronted with cancer, resort only to surgery or radiation therapy as "standard" treatments based upon knowledge which is 15 or 20 years old. This is "caretaker" treatment and does not give the patient the best chance of cure. If all we ever did was give the standard, best-known care, we would be doing today what was being done in 1890.

In the past decade, as discussed, we have learned that "combination therapy" is frequently more effective than a single modality such as surgery. The oncologist sees that his patient receives the best possible treatment even if it is not his own specialty, and he avoids fragmentation of care through full communications among members of the coordinated team. *The patient should not necessarily be treated by the physician, surgeon, or radiation therapist who sees him first.*

Depending upon the type and stage of disease, the oncologist might plan a strategy of preoperative radiation to shrink the tumor, surgery to remove it, followed by chemotherapy using a combination of three or four drugs. Or, he might use immunotherapy, hormone therapy, perhaps supplemented by vitamins, or some combination of these modalities. With over 100 different types of cancer what works against one may be ineffective against another.

How to Find an Oncologist

If your family doctor is not a board-certified oncologist—and he probably is not—he can locate one for you and will no doubt suggest this. If he does not, then suggest it to him.

Patients sometimes confide, "I was afraid I would hurt my family doctor's feelings if I insisted on treatment by a cancer specialist."

This very human reaction is easy to understand but there are two answers to it. First, a conscientious family physician will insist that an oncologist be consulted and, second, when a life may be at issue is no time to worry about hurting a doctor's feelings.

Finding an oncologist is not difficult:

1. Your doctor may know one in whom he has confidence; there is probably at least one on his hospital staff.

2. Oncologists' names may be obtained from local medical societies, hospitals, and medical schools (see Reference Information III).

3. Your doctor may telephone a Comprehensive Cancer Center or Clinical Cancer Center (see Reference Information II) and obtain referral to an oncologist.

4. He may telephone the Cancer Information Service (see Reference Information II); if there is no number for his area he should call the Office of Cancer Communications, National Cancer Institute, (800)-638-6694 or (301)-496-5583; this office also can furnish the name of an NCI physician with whom your physician can consult.

Several state cancer offices offer physician-to-physician telephone consultation service:

University of Alabama Comprehensive Cancer Center, (205)-934-4011.

New York Cancer Information Service, 1-(800)-462-1877.

Florida Cancer Information Service telephone numbers for Spanish-speaking callers: 1-(800)-432-5955 (for persons in Florida) and (305)-547-6960 (for residents of Dade County and other states).

Texas Cancer Information Service, (713)-792-2300.

American Cancer Society divisions and units may be of assistance although furnishing the names of physicians is not one of their functions.

5. Your physician can consult the *Directory of Medical Specialists* published by Marquis Who's Who, 200 East Ohio St., Chicago, IL 60611, for names of oncologists in your area. This massive, three-volume directory contains the names, addresses, and brief biographies of about 200,000 board-certified doctors in the United States. It is available in some doctors' offices and in more than 7,000

public libraries; you may buy a copy direct from the publisher for $99.50 plus shipping.

Examples:

A *medical oncologist* should be certified by the American Board of Internal Medicine in the subspecialty of medical oncology.

A *therapeutic radiologist* should be a diplomate of the American Board of Radiology (therapeutic radiology).

A *surgeon* should be certified by one of several surgical boards, and, ideally, be a Fellow of the American College of Surgeons (FACS). The only surgical board, to date, which has established oncology as a subspecialty is the American Board of Obstetrics and Gynecology. However, most surgeons active in cancer therapy belong to one or more oncology societies; the *Directory of Medical Specialists* lists society memberships of its diplomates.

A *pediatrician* treating cancer should be certified by the American Board of Pediatrics in the subspecialty of pediatric hematology-oncology.

The biographical material in this directory includes name and board certification; recertification dates; date and place of birth; medical school; intern and residency training; hospital affiliation(s); teaching positions; military record; society memberships; office address and telephone number. The compressed biographies are difficult for the layman to decipher, but your family doctor can translate for you.

If, for some odd reason, your family physician will not locate an oncologist for you, you will have to do this yourself following the preceding suggestions. While the groups listed prefer contact by a physician (except for the Cancer Information Service), they will counsel a patient or a member of his family—but this is your doctor's responsibility and it is better that he makes these contacts.

I think it is unforgivable that a few doctors, after telling a patient that he has cancer, leave him high and dry. Three years ago a schoolteacher in a suburb of New York City was told by her internist that she had breast cancer and to "see a surgeon"—but he offered no guidance. A concerned friend who is not a physician arranged for her to see a physician on our Breast Service. After an examination in his office he was able to rule out breast cancer; she had a benign cyst, which is quite common among middle-aged women.

Where Should a Cancer Patient Be Treated?

In most cases, treatment can be given in an accredited community hospital under experienced direction. If the physician has questions he can consult with specialists at a Comprehensive Cancer Center, a Clinical Cooperative Group, or with the Clinical Center of the National Cancer Institute.

If the cancer is a difficult or uncommon type, the patient's condition should be evaluated and the cancer should be treated initially at a major cancer or medical center even though this means traveling hundreds of miles. Often, after initial treatment, the patient can return home and continue treatment at a local hospital or medical center, frequently as an outpatient.

Under "outreach" programs the Comprehensive Cancer Centers and Clinical Cooperative Groups share their knowledge and experience with the staffs of community hospitals. We look at the kinds of cancers they are treating, their facilities, how their cases are progressing, and then collectively agree on what they should do and how we can help them, and how they can help us.

A number of centers offer seminars and refresher courses lasting from a few days to several weeks to keep primary-care physicians informed of new developments. From 500 to 1,000 "observer physicians" attend Memorial Hospital's refresher programs every year.

The major centers are also available for consultation by telephone or visit and their pathology departments evaluate tissue biopsies. At Memorial Hospital we are assisting more than 50 hospitals from coast to coast in devising the most effective radiation therapy for their patients, a demanding task involving physics, mathematics, computers, and medicine.

The One Exception: Childhood Cancer

There is one strong exception to the preceding paragraphs. Childhood cancer, which fortunately is quite rare, should be treated *only* at a Comprehensive Cancer Center or other major medical center where the expertise and supportive nursing care are available.

Treating cancer in young children is a delicate—even dangerous—medical and nursing problem, and local treatment, no matter how devoted, should not be attempted. Further, it is vital that the correct treatment be given right from the start since the chances of a cure are greatly diminished by improper initial treatment.

In many cases, after treatment for a few weeks at a major center, the therapy can be continued on an outpatient basis and the child can live at home with his loved ones. Treatment with powerful anticancer drugs is rigorous and unpleasant but that phase ultimately passes and the youngster is out playing and riding his bike again. One seven-year-old girl showed her spirit by scrawling a sign which she taped to the door of her hospital room: BALD IS BEAUTIFUL! (The hair grows back when treatment stops.)

Yul Brynner and Telly Savalas (Kojak) have popularized bare heads and bolstered the spirits of youngsters who lose their hair from chemotherapy. One young patient's friends so envied his bald head that they shaved off their own hair.

The encouraging news is that major progress has been made in treating acute lymphocytic leukemia, the most common cancer that strikes young boys and girls. More than 90 percent of these youngsters are in remission in three years and we hope to cure the majority of these children. Other childhood cancers with good cure rates are Wilm's tumor (kidney), neuroblastoma (central nervous system), retinoblastoma (eye), lymphomas, and bone tumors.

Should a Physician Tell the Truth?

You no doubt know that some excellent physicians, motivated by the deepest compassion for their patients, do not tell the truth about serious illness. They believe that the very sick patient does not want to know the truth about his condition; they do not wish to destroy hope and they fear the consequences of candor. These physicians put on a cheerful front and radiate false optimism which is almost impossible to sustain as time passes.

All our experience at Memorial Hospital proves that this viewpoint is not valid and that patients can understand and put up with a lot more than many physicians think. In her book *Lying: Moral Choice in Public and Private Life,* Sissela Bok writes: "The damages associated with the disclosure of sad news or risks are rarer than physicians believe; and the *benefits* which result from being informed are more substantial. . . . Pain is tolerated more easily; recovery from surgery is quicker, and cooperation with therapy is greatly improved. . . . It is what patients do not know but vaguely suspect that causes corrosive worry."

The truth of this observation is borne out by our experience at Memorial Hospital where our policy is to tell our patients the truth in a gentle, compassionate manner without going into clinical detail or figures of survival time. Hope is never withdrawn prematurely or unwisely.

The only exception to telling the truth is if the patient or his family specifically ask not to be told, which is rare. One study found that more than 80 percent of patients want the truth.

We are also candid with the young boys and girls whom we treat. Dr. Denis Miller, chairman of Pediatrics, who has a high regard for his small patients, says, "There is no effort to withhold the diagnosis, the treatment, or the rationale for procedures such as surgery or radiation. We draw pictures, show them X rays—whatever might help."

Ruth Johnston, head nurse in Pediatrics, says, "We realized it was better to deal with this in the open where we could talk to the patient about his fears . . . rather than trying to hide it away where the patient had to deal with it scared and alone."

Telling the truth in a calm, compassionate manner builds a bridge of trust and confidence between patient and physician. It enables the patient to make informed decisions about treatment alternatives, his personal life, and, if death appears inevitable, his personal and business affairs.

Deceiving a patient leads to an almost intolerable situation for doctors, nurses, family, and friends—it is a game of charades played on quicksand. The emotional needs of the very sick patient need to be nourished with the same devotion and competence as his physical needs, a skill not easily acquired. Nothing is more reassuring to the gravely ill than truth, understanding, and love from his family and physician.

The truth helps to remove the mystery from cancer and the fear that is its companion. Truth can increase the cure rate by encouraging open discussion and earlier visits to a physician should one of the warning signals light up. It is encouraging to see that, according to one survey, there has been a major shift in the attitude of physicians in recent years, with the majority now in favor of telling patients the truth.

Answers to Questions About Surgery

After diagnosis, some patients are referred to a surgeon while others are treated by specialists in radiation therapy, chemotherapy, or combination modalities. Surgery is the most common method of treating cancer but there are lesions where surgery either cannot be used or is not the treatment of choice.

As a surgeon who has taken care of cancer patients for many years, I am often asked these questions about proposed surgery:

Is it a good idea to see a surgeon first if one is diagnosed as having cancer?

Not necessarily. I'm afraid that some surgeons might recommend surgery when another mode of treatment would be more suitable, and that the alternatives might not be explained.

How can I be sure that surgery is necessary?

If you have confidence in your doctor, and in your surgeon, their recommendation should be sufficient. If you would like a second opinion—which is often a good idea—then by all means request a consultation by another experienced physician, preferably someone who is not a close friend of your doctor to assure his independence. *Always* request a consultation if the first doctor tells you that "nothing can be done."

Is cancer surgery more difficult than other surgery?

Some is, most is not.

Should a good general surgeon perform cancer surgery?

Many cancer operations can be done by a well-qualified, board-certified general surgeon, or a board-certified specialty surgeon. However, a few procedures require special training and experience in a major hospital treating cancer. Inexpert surgeons, surgeons who do the operation infrequently, or who are not familiar with the area of the body involved, should not perform the surgery.

Are there special techniques in cancer surgery?

Yes.

Can a malignant tumor be spread by improper surgery?

Yes, in certain procedures.

How can I be sure my surgeon is qualified to do the operation?

Ask your family doctor about the surgeon's training and experience and his hospital affiliations.

Find out whether he is board-certified by the American Board of Surgery or some other surgical board, and a Fellow of the American College of Surgeons (FACS). There are some 100,000 doctors who perform surgery in the United States; of these, 52,000 are board-certified and 38,700 are FACS.

Ask your surgeon how many operations he does a week. You

want a busy surgeon, not one who operates occasionally, but he should not be so busy that he cannot give you the attention you deserve.

Look him up in the *Directory of Medical Specialists*. If he teaches at a medical school, or is affiliated with a teaching hospital, it is an advantage.

If possible, inquire about him from ex-patients.

What should my surgeon discuss with me before the operation?

He should describe the operation, recovery room procedure, and the postoperative course. He should tell you the objective of the operation, outline the risks, discuss possible alternative treatments, and answer your questions.

Does it make a difference in which hospital my surgery is done?

Yes, it should be performed in a hospital accredited by the Joint Commission on Accreditation of Hospitals (875 No. Michigan Ave., Chicago, IL 60611) because hospitals are not equally proficient. A congressional committee investigating surgical practices found that in the Boston area three hospitals where open heart surgery was performed had death rates from that operation of 49, 22, and 10 percent, respectively. A 1979 study by Stanford University and the University of California confirmed that complicated surgery is far riskier when done in hospitals where physicians seldom perform it. If a hospital is a teaching institution affiliated with a medical school, the standards of medical procedure, nursing support, patient care, and personnel training are apt to be high.

In the Preface to this book, I wrote that an informed public is a powerful weapon against cancer. It is my hope that these pages make a modest contribution to that goal.

The American Cancer Society estimates that about 131,000 men, women, and children with cancer—who might have been saved—will probably die in 1980—25,000 more people than fill the Rose Bowl every year. Add to this figure the cancers that can be prevented and you have half a million people who could be healthy and alive instead of sick or dying, an impressive number by any standard.

Sadly, we cannot cure everyone in spite of diligent medical care, but steady progress is being forged. Increasingly, our disappointments are balanced by the battles that the medical profession wins.

I can think of no more encouraging way to close this book than to share with you a letter written seven years ago to a physician at the Peter Bent Brigham Hospital in Boston. I am profoundly grateful to Mr. B. E. Spruill and Dr. Frederick Lane for their generous permission to include it in these pages.

Portsmouth, Va.
December 6, 1973

Frederick Carl Lane, M.D.
Peter Bent Brigham Hospital
721 Huntington Avenue
Boston, Mass. 02115

Dear Dr. Lane:

But for the grace of God and the expertise of you, Dr. William Hamilton, et al., there would be no Timothy at the Spruill household today. For this miracle you have my eternal gratitude. Though the eventual outcome for Timothy remains elusive, [it] would long have been concluded and Timothy just another Hodgkin's disease statistic except for you and your associates.

May the grace of God continue to direct and steady your hand so that the list of your Timothys may continue to grow. What greater honor, what finer treasure could be desired than the ability to extend life. My gratitude will fade in your memory with time, but the fact that because of you and your associates Timothy lives—this will never fade in my memory. . . . I gained an insight and knowledge of human character that I did not believe to exist.

I learned something beautiful, something I will treasure all my remaining days—people do care.

The Doctors Moore & Hamilton, Moloney & Hunter, Newman & Aberson, Frei & Lockich, Osteen & Kelly, and so many others not known by name; the nurses Austin & Chagnon, McCallum & Mackin, and so many, many more; the dieticians, laboratory technicians, X-ray technicians, inhalation therapists, the IV specialist, the housekeeping department . . . these and more make a great hospital.

Timothy* and Mrs. Spruill join me in thanking you and all

---

*Timothy Spruill, who had cancer of the lymphatic system, is now 22 years old, married, and a counselor at the New Life Youth Ranch, Winchester, Virginia.

the others on and behind the scenes in our weeks of ordeal. Peter Bent Brigham, Room B-20, and especially you, Dr. Lane, and Dr. Hamilton, are forever etched in our memories. May God keep and bless you and say, "Well done, my good and faithful servant."

Gratefully,
B. E. Spruill

In reading this moving letter once again, I thought of the words of Pablo Casals: "The capacity to care is the thing which gives life its deepest meaning and significance."

Reference Information

I

Life-Saving Information
About the Five Major Cancers

THE FIVE CANCERS COVERED in this section will account for 59 percent of the new cases, and 55 percent of the cancer deaths, in the United States in 1980. Being familiar with the basic facts about these diseases could well save your life, or the life of someone you love.

If every adult knew, and acted upon, the information in the few pages that follow, most of the 131,000 men, women, and children who will die of cancer *unnecessarily* in 1980 would have lived.

Unfortunately, this ideal situation cannot be achieved, but the attack in these pages upon the stubborn problems of apathy and ignorance is one more step toward the goal of prevention and cure. An informed public is truly one of the most powerful weapons against cancer. One physician even goes so far as to say that cancer is a curable disease if the patient does his part.

The facts that follow sum up data given elsewhere in this book as a convenient reference.

A word about the information that follows:

Cause   Where the cause is not known, the suspected cause is given; the cause or causes of about half of all cancers is not known.

Predisposing factors   These are the events that lead to the particular cancer, or are suspected of doing so.

Prevention   While some cancers can be prevented, others cannot. Where the cause is suspected but not known, the most logical preventive measures are listed.

Symptoms   The symptoms given may be caused by a number of conditions that are not cancer, but they should be investigated without delay by a physician.

Latent period   This is the time during which the tumor is growing in the body but is difficult or impossible to detect with our present knowledge.

Statistics   The statistics on cancer incidence are from the National Cancer Institute National Surveys, 1947 and 1969; those for mortality are from the National Center for Health Statistics, 1952–1977. The data on present and potential cure rates are from data published by the American

Cancer Society, medical journals, and the files of Memorial Sloan-Kettering Cancer Center, New York.

Cure rate A cancer is, in most cases, considered cured and the patient restored to health when five years pass with no evidence of disease; in certain cases, the period may be shorter or longer than five years; see Chapter 1.

Staging This refers to the extent of tumor spread, if any, at the time of diagnosis:

Stage I—early, localized tumor; no spread (metastasis).

Stage II—tumor has invaded underlying tissue but is still localized.

Stage III—cancer cells have metastasized (spread) to regional lymph nodes; termed "regional involvement."

Stage IV—cancer cells have spread to distant parts of the body; advanced cancer.

Stage I disease is the most curable, followed in order by the other stages.

Lung Cancer

Cause	80% caused by cigarette smoking; 10% occurs in nonsmokers, some of whom have occupational exposures to substances linked to lung cancer.
Predisposing factors	Increased risk from occupations involving inhalation of wood dust, radioactive dust, beryllium dust, nickel and chromium compounds, coal-tar fogs and fumes. Asbestos fibers promote lung cancer in smokers but do not cause it. Possible genetic factor.
Prevention	Do not smoke cigarettes. Safety precautions in hazardous industries.
Symptoms	Persistent cough; change in cough (longer, more persistent spells; more sputum); chest pain and blood in sputum usually not early symptoms. Difficult to diagnose in early stage.

Latent period	15–30 years.
How diagnosed	• Chest X ray (difficult to detect early tumors). • Examination of sputum for malignant cells. • Examination of trachea, bronchi and lungs with bronchoscope; examination of cells obtained by washing and brushing suspicious areas. • Bronchogram (special X-ray study); needle aspiration biopsy; exploratory surgery.
How treated	Surgical removal of diseased lobe or lung. Radiation therapy or chemotherapy used in some cases. Surgery not possible in about one-third of patients due to advanced stage of disease at diagnosis.
Number of new cases forecast for U.S. in 1980	117,000
Number of deaths forecast for U.S. in 1980	101,300
Comment	• 81,000 deaths in 1980 could have been prevented by not smoking cigarettes. • Present overall cure rate about 10%. Cure rate of over 60% probably achievable with early diagnosis, negative chest X ray, negative lymph nodes, positive sputum cytology. • Lung cancer is the #1 cancer killer of men and the #2 cancer killer of women. Deaths staying level in men, increasing rapidly in women. 200% increase in deaths in past 25 years. • Only 8% of men and 12% of women alive after 5 years with present diagnosis which is usually late. Tragedy is that this cancer is 80–90% preventable.

- Smoking also linked to cancers of mouth, pharynx, larynx, esophagus, kidney, bladder, and pancreas.
- Cigarette smoking often causes insomnia because nicotine is a well-known stimulant.
- (*Note to women:* smoking prematurely ages a woman's skin by reducing the amount of oxygen carried by the blood to nourish skin cells.)

Colon-Rectum Cancer

Cause	Not known. Excessive dietary intake of fat and insufficient bulk suspected. Intestinal bacteria may form carcinogens from dietary compounds or digestive secretions that remain in contact with bowel wall.
Predisposing factors	Family history of multiple intestinal polyps (familial polyposis); family history of cancers of colon, stomach, uterus; ulcerative colitis for 10 years or more.
Prevention	No sure prevention. Reducing amount of saturated fat and animal fat in diet and increasing amount of fiber bulk may help by altering composition of digestive secretions and decreasing stool transit time. Vitamins A and C may play a part in prevention.
Symptoms	Persistent diarrhea or constipation (more than 2 weeks); thin, small-diameter stools; blood in stool (red or black); cramping pains; excessive gas; abdominal fullness; weight loss. Nausea and vomiting if intestine is obstructed.

Latent period	1–3 years
How diagnosed	• Examination of rectum and lower bowel by physician's gloved finger (can detect about 15% of these lesions). • Chemical test (Guaiac) for blood in stool. • Examination of large bowel by physician using a proctoscope (small lighted tube); examination of large intestine with flexible colonoscope. • X-ray examination of colon and rectum using barium enema for contrast. • Certain blood tests (CEA) may be useful but at present are not 100% accurate. • Biopsy.
How treated	Removal of tumor and area lymph nodes by surgery. Radiation therapy and chemotherapy may be used after surgery in certain cases. The majority of patients who undergo surgery do not need a permanent colostomy (an opening in the abdomen through which wastes are eliminated).
Number of new cases forecast for U.S. in 1980	114,000
Number of deaths forecast for U.S. in 1980	53,000
Comment	• Present cure rate is 54% but this could be 75% with earlier diagnosis and treatment. When diagnosed in someone with no complaints, cure rate rises to 90%.

- The accuracy and relative simplicity of diagnostic tests makes colon-rectum cancer (sometimes called colorectal) a highly curable disease if the patient does his part.
- This is the most frequent cancer among males and females combined. Can occur before age 40 but not common. Incidence increases with advancing age.

Breast Cancer

Cause	Not known. Dietary fat suspected as facilitating factor. May be related to levels of female hormone estrogen and its fractions in the body; breast is responsive to hormone stimulation.
Predisposing factors	Family history of breast cancer. No pregnancy, or pregnancy after age 30; no lactation. Early menarche; late menopause. Possible increase with use of female hormone estrogen. Higher socioeconomic background. Occurs most often in women of middle age and older.
Prevention	None known. Possibly reduction of amount of fat in diet. Avoid excess weight. Early pregnancy and lactation.
Symptoms	None in early stage. Lump or thickening in breast (80% are not cancer); change in breast contour; lump in armpit. Nipple discharge, or retraction. Dimpling or puckering of breast skin. Enlargement of breast. Late case: pain; swollen glands in armpit.
Latent period	Probably 10–15 years.
How diagnosed	• Women over 35: monthly breast self-examination (BSE); see Chapter 10. Only 25–30% of women practice BSE. • Physician palpates breast lump; may

aspirate fluid from a cyst; checks for above symptoms.
- Mammogram (X ray) of breast (80% accurate if well done); see Chapter 10.
- Suspected cases of cancer need biopsy for diagnosis (microscopic examination of tissue).

How treated	Depends on stage of disease at diagnosis. In early cases, local excision of tumor plus radiation therapy is under investigation. In later cases, surgical excision of breast and tumor with examination of regional lymph nodes. Certain breast cancers are hormone-dependent; removal of adrenal and pituitary glands, and ovaries, to reduce hormone level is sometimes effective. Chemotherapy and radiation therapy may be used as adjuvant therapy.
Number of new cases forecast for U.S. in 1980	109,000
Number of deaths forecast for U.S. in 1980	36,000
Comment	• The most common way of detecting early Stage I disease is by breast self-examination (BSE) plus mammogram. These lesions have an 80% cure rate but fewer than half of all patients are diagnosed in Stage I. • The smallest breast tumors (¼″ to ⅜″ in diameter) are usually detected only by mammogram and are 95% curable. • In later stages, cure rate drops to 30–40%. • Overall cure rate is under 50% but should be much higher.

Prostate Cancer

Cause	Unknown. Hormone imbalance may play a role.

Predisposing factors	None known. History of prostate infections and venereal disease may be risk factors. Prostate cancer very common among older men.
Prevention	None known. Occurs more often among married men than among single, more frequent among blacks than whites.
Symptoms	None in very early cases (discovered at autopsy in 15–20% of men over age 50). Continuing urinary difficulties: weak or interrupted flow; need to urinate frequently (particularly at night); inability to urinate or trouble starting flow; flow not easily stopped; painful or burning urination; blood in urine. These symptoms frequently caused by BPH (benign prostatic hypertrophy—enlargement of prostate) which occurs in over half of males over age 50, or from inflammation, infection, or cysts. Advanced prostate cancer often causes pain in pelvis or lower back.
Latent period	Presumably many years.
How diagnosed	<ul><li>Physician palpates prostate gland with gloved finger in rectal examination.</li><li>Tests may include X ray, urine and blood analyses.</li><li>Needle biopsy under local or general anesthesia to obtain tissue for examination.</li></ul>
How treated	Depends on stage of disease, rate of tumor growth, age and general health of patient. Radiation therapy, internal or external. Surgical removal of prostate gland. In more advanced cases: hormone (estrogen) administration (risk of cardiovascular complications); castration.

Number of new cases forecast for U.S. in 1980	66,000

Number of deaths forecast for U.S. in 1980	21,500

Comment	• Annual rectal examination by physician can detect most early cases. • Most early cases can be controlled by radiation therapy. • The majority of cases occur in elderly males where the cause of death is not cancer of the prostate.

Uterus—Cancer of the Cervix (Invasive)

(Cancer *in situ* of the cervix (45,000 cases forecast for 1980), detected early by the Pap test, is so curable (95%) that it is not included here nor is it usually included in cancer statistics.)

Cause	Not known. Herpes virus B suspected.

Predisposing factors	Sexual intercourse before age 18; multiple sexual partners. Marriage at an early age. Poor male sex hygiene. Chronic irritation. More than 5 completed pregnancies. Vaginal infections; venereal disease.

Prevention	Good sex hygiene by male and female.

Symptoms	Vaginal discharge. Vaginal bleeding after sexual intercourse and after monthly periods (may not be cancer but should be investigated).

Latent period	Many years. A slow-growing malignant neoplasm.

How diagnosed	• Pap test (simple, painless, inexpensive) to detect atypical (abnormal) cells or malignant cells. • Pelvic examination. • Cervical biopsy (examination of tissue).

How treated	Carcinoma *in situ:* local excision.
	Stage I: radiation therapy or surgery (surgery preferred for younger women, radiotherapy for older women).
	More advanced cases: radiation therapy, or preoperative radiation plus surgery.

| Number of new cases forecast for U.S. in 1980 | 16,000 |

| Number of deaths forecast for U.S. in 1980 | 7,400 |

Comment	• Deaths from cancer of the cervix have decreased over 70% in the past 40 years due to early diagnosis by the Pap test and improved treatment. Cervical cancer in the early stage is very curable and can be largely prevented by good hygiene.
	• Annual Pap tests and pelvic examinations should start when sexual activity starts to detect any abnormality early when it is almost 100% curable.
	• Investigate *all* discharges and *all* irregular vaginal bleeding.

Uterus—Cancer of the Endometrium (Body of Uterus)

| Cause | Unknown. May be hormone related. |

| Predisposing factors | Completion of menopause. No pregnancy. Family history of endometrial cancer. Diabetes; hypertension; overweight. Estrogen prescribed for postmenopausal women. Occurs most often at, or after, menopause. |

Prevention	Not known. Frequent examination by physician if estrogen is prescribed.
Symptoms	Irregular menstrual cycle; vaginal bleeding; vaginal discharge especially if brownish (may not be cancer but should be investigated).
Latent period	Many years. A slow-growing cancer.
How diagnosed	• Pap test of vaginal secretions (accurate only about 40% of the time for endometrial cancer). • Aspiration of uterine secretions for analysis. • D & C (dilation and curettage).
How treated	Preoperative radiation therapy; hysterectomy (surgical removal of uterus).
Number of new cases forecast for U.S. in 1980	38,000
Number of deaths forecast for U.S. in 1980	3,200
Comment	• This is a very curable cancer. • Annual Pap test and pelvic examinations should start when sexual activity starts. • Investigate *all* discharges and *all* irregular vaginal bleeding.

CHECKUPS FOR EARLY CANCER DETECTION
RECOMMENDED BY AMERICAN CANCER SOCIETY
(For individuals with no symptoms and not at high risk)

Type of Cancer	Sex	Age	Test or Procedure	How Frequently?
All	M&F	over 20	Health counseling and cancer checkup[1]	every 3 years
	M&F	over 40	"	every year
Lung			See text below	
Colon-rectal	M&F	over 40	Digital rectal examination	every year
	M&F	over 50	Stool Guaiac slide test	every year
	M&F	over 50	Sigmoidoscopy	every 3–5 years[2]
Breast	F	over 20	Breast self-examination	every month
	F	20–40	Breast physical examination	every 3 years
		over 40	"	every year
	F	35–40	Mammography	once—base-line
		40–50	"	consult personal physician
		over 50	"	every year
Uterine	F	20–65[3]	Pap test	at least every 3 years[4]
	F	20–40	Pelvic examination	every 3 years
		over 40	"	every year
	F	at meno-pause	Endometrial tissue sample	at menopause[5]

1. To include examination for cancers of thyroid, testicles, prostate, ovaries, lymph nodes, oral region, and skin.

2. After two negative examinations a year apart.

3. Sexually active women under 20 should have a yearly Pap test.

4. After two negative Pap tests a year apart. High-risk women should have more frequent Pap tests.

5. High risk if history of infertility, obesity, failure of ovulation, abnormal uterine bleeding, estrogen therapy.

These recommendations by the American Cancer Society were released on March 21, 1980, in an effort to provide the same protection as earlier guidelines "with reduced cost, risk, and inconvenience" to the public. The society stated that these are general guidelines and that people should follow the advice of their own physicians. Unfortunately, many physicians disagreed with certain of the new recommendations, particularly in the area of lung cancer.

The new guidelines failed to recommend low-dose chest X rays and sputum examinations for heavy smokers and others at high risk for lung cancer, ignoring data from ongoing studies at Mayo Clinic, Johns Hopkins University, and Memorial Sloan-Kettering Cancer Center. These studies show that people with *early* lung lesions detected by X ray, sputum cytology (cell analysis), and bronchoscopic examination have a high projected five-year survival rate compared to the national average of less than 10 percent.

Until a new and better early warning test is developed, heavy smokers should have at least an annual low-dose chest X ray and sputum examination. The best and least costly solution, of course, is simply not to smoke cigarettes.

II

- *Comprehensive Cancer Centers*
- *Clinical Cancer Centers*
- *CANSCREEN Clinics*
- *Cancer Information Service*

COMPREHENSIVE CANCER CENTERS

Twenty-one large medical centers have been designated as Comprehensive Cancer Centers by the National Cancer Institute. These centers cooperate with local physicians, community hospitals, medical schools, and other medical centers in a nationwide system for the prevention, diagnosis, and treatment of cancer. In addition to treating patients, these centers offer consulting services to physicians and patients and provide the latest information about cancer to keep physicians abreast of research and clinical advances.

Treatment of certain rare or difficult types of cancer is best given at a Comprehensive Cancer Center, but once started it can frequently be carried on in a community hospital or medical center. Other hospitals and medical centers provide excellent cancer care and a number of them have been designated as Clinical Cancer Centers by NCI or approved by the Commission on Cancer of the American College of Surgeons.

Physicians may contact one of the cancer centers for consultation with the appropriate specialist or to arrange for a patient admission.

Alabama

Comprehensive Cancer Center
University of Alabama in Birmingham
University Station
Birmingham, AL 35294
Tel.: 205-934-5077

California

UCLA Jonsson Comprehensive
Cancer Center
924 Westwood Blvd., Suite 650
Los Angeles, CA 90024
Tel.: 213-825-1532
Tel.: 213-825-5268

University of Southern California
Comprehensive Cancer Center
2025 Zonal Ave.
Los Angeles, CA 90033
Tel.: 213-226-2008

Colorado

Colorado Regional Cancer Center
935 Colorado Blvd.
Denver, CO 80206
Tel.: 303-320-5921

Connecticut

Yale University
Comprehensive Cancer Center
333 Cedar St.
New Haven, CT 06510
Tel.: 203-432-4122
Tel.: 203-436-1736

District of Columbia

Georgetown University/Howard
University
Comprehensive Cancer Center

Cancer Research Center
Howard University Hospital
2400 Sixth St. NW
Washington, DC 20059
Tel.: 202-745-1406

Vincent T. Lombardi
Cancer Research Center
Georgetown University Medical
Center
3800 Reservoir Rd. NW
Washington, DC 20007
Tel.: 202-625-7066

Florida

Comprehensive Cancer Center
for the State of Florida
University of Miami School of
Medicine

Jackson Memorial Medical
Center
P.O.B. 520875, Biscayne Annex
Miami, FL 33152
Tel.: 305-547-6758

Illinois

Illinois Cancer Council
36 S. Wabash Ave., Suite 700
Chicago, IL 60603
Tel.: 312-346-9813

Northwestern University Cancer
Center
Ward Memorial Building
303 E. Chicago Ave.
Chicago, IL 60611
Tel.: 312-649-8674

University of Chicago
Cancer Research Center
905 East 59th St.
Chicago, IL 60637
Tel.: 312-947-6386

Maryland

Johns Hopkins Oncology Center
601 No. Broadway
Baltimore, MD 21205
Tel.: 301-955-8822

Massachusetts

Sidney Farber Cancer Institute
44 Binney St.
Boston, MA 02115
Tel.: 617-732-3555

Michigan

Comprehensive Cancer Center
of Metropolitan Detroit
110 E. Warren
Detroit, MI 48201
Tel.: 313-833-1088

Minnesota

Mayo Comprehensive Cancer
Center
200 First St. SW
Rochester, MN 55901
Tel.: 507-282-2511

New York

Columbia University Cancer
Research Center
College of Physicians & Surgeons
701 West 168th St.
New York, NY 10032
Tel.: 212-694-3807
Tel.: 212-694-4138

Memorial Sloan-Kettering Cancer
Center
1275 York Ave.
New York, NY 10021
Tel.: 212-794-7646

Roswell Park Memorial Institute
666 Elm St.
Buffalo, NY 14263
Tel.: 716-845-5770

North Carolina

Comprehensive Cancer Center
Duke University Medical Center
Durham, NC 27710
Tel.: 919-684-2282

Ohio

The Ohio State University
Comprehensive Cancer Center
357 McCampbell Hall
1580 Cannon Dr.
Columbus, OH 43210
Tel.: 614-422-5022

Pennsylvania

Fox Chase/University of
Pennsylvania
Comprehensive Cancer Center

The Fox Chase Cancer Center
7701 Burholme Ave.
Philadelphia, PA 19111
Tel.: 215-728-2717

University of Pennsylvania
Cancer Center
578 Maloney Building
3400 Spruce St.
Philadelphia, PA 19104
Tel.: 215-662-3910

Texas

The University of Texas Health
System Cancer Center
M.D. Anderson Hospital &
Tumor Institute
6723 Bertner Ave.
Houston, TX 77030
Tel.: 713-792-3000

Washington

Fred Hutchinson Cancer Research
Center
1124 Columbia St.
Seattle, WA 98104
Tel.: 206-292-2930

Wisconsin

The University of Wisconsin
Clinical Cancer Center
600 Highland Ave.
Madison, WI 53706
Tel.: 608-262-9703

CLINICAL CANCER CENTERS

Twenty-nine medical facilities which provide patient care and carry out clinical research have been designated as Clinical Cancer Centers by the National Cancer Institute. Among these institutions are hospitals, medical schools, and cancer treatment and research centers. These facilities provide excellent cancer care and consultation.

Arizona

University of Arizona Cancer
   Center
   University of Arizona
   College of Medicine
   Tucson, AZ 85724
   Tel.: 602-882-6372

California

Northern California
   Cancer Program
   1801 Page Mill Rd.
   Suite 200, Building B
   Palo Alto, CA 94304
   Tel.: 415-497-7431

University of California
   School of Medicine
   La Jolla, CA 92093
   Tel.: 714-452-3925
   Tel.: 714-452-3018

Georgia

Emory University Cancer Center
   Room 606F, Emory University
   Hospital
   Atlanta, GA 30322
   Tel.: 404-329-7016

Hawaii

Cancer Center of Hawaii
   University of Hawaii at Manoa
   1997 East-West Rd.
   Honolulu, HI 96822
   Tel.: 808-948-7173
   Tel.: 808-948-7246

Kansas

Mid-America Cancer Center
   Program
   The University of Kansas
   Medical Center
   College of Health Sciences &
   Hospital
   Rainbow Blvd. at 39th
   Kansas City, KS 66103
   Tel.: 913-588-5287

Kentucky

Ephraim McDowell Community
   Cancer Network, Inc.
   915 South Limestone St.
   Lexington, KY 40503
   Tel.: 607-233-6541

Massachusetts

Hubert H. Humphrey Cancer
   Research Center
   Boston University School of
   Medicine
   80 East Concord St.
   Boston, MA 02118
   Tel.: 617-247-6075

Tufts-New England Medical Center
   Box 842
   171 Harrison Ave.
   Boston, MA 02111
   Tel.: 617-956-5406

Missouri

Missouri Cancer Programs, Inc.
   115 Business Loop 70 W.
   Columbia, MO 65201
   Tel.: 314-449-3945

New Hampshire

Norris Cotton Cancer Center
Dartmouth-Hitchcock Medical
   Center
Hanover, NH 03755
Tel.: 603-643-4000, x 2535

New Mexico

Cancer Research and
   Treatment Center
University of New Mexico
900 Camino de Salude NE
Albuquerque, NM 87131
Tel.: 505-277-2151

New York

Cancer Center
   New York University Medical
   Center
550 First Ave.
New York, NY 10016
Tel.: 212-679-3200, x 2797

Cancer Research Center
   Albert Einstein College of
   Medicine
1300 Morris Park Ave.
Bronx, NY 10461
Tel.: 212-430-2302
Tel.: 212-792-2233

Department of Neoplastic Diseases
Mt. Sinai School of Medicine
Fifth Avenue at 100th St.
New York, NY 10029
Tel.: 212-650-6364

Research Institute for
   Skeletomuscular Diseases
Hospital for Joint Diseases and
   Medical Center
1919 Madison Ave.
New York, NY 10035
Tel.: 212-650-4119

University of Rochester
   Cancer Center
601 Elmwood Ave.
Rochester, NY 14642
Tel.: 716-275-4865

North Carolina

Cancer Research Center
University of North Carolina
Box 30, Clinical Science Building
   229
Chapel Hill, NC 27514
Tel.: 919-966-1183
Tel.: 919-966-3036

Oncology Research Center
   Bowman Gray School of
      Medicine
300 South Hawthorne Rd.
Winston-Salem, NC 27103
Tel.: 919-727-4464

Oklahoma

Oklahoma Cancer Center
   University of Oklahoma
   Health Sciences Center
P.O.B. 26901
Oklahoma City, OK 73190
Tel.: 405-271-4485

Puerto Rico

Puerto Rico Cancer Center
   University of Puerto Rico
   Medical Sciences Campus
G.P.O. Box 5067
San Juan, PR 00936
Tel.: 809-763-2443
Tel.: 809-765-2363

Rhode Island

Roger Williams General Hospital
825 Chalkstone Ave.
Providence, RI 02908
Tel.: 401-456-2070

Tennessee

Memphis Regional Cancer Center
800 Madison Ave.
Memphis, TN 38163
Tel.: 901-528-5739

St. Jude Children's Research
332 No. Lauderdale
Memphis, TN 38101
Tel.: 901-525-8381, x 271

Texas

Cancer Center
The University of Texas Medical
Branch Hospitals
Galveston, TX 77550
Tel.: 713-765-1902

Cancer Center
University of Texas Health
Science Center
5323 Harry Hines Blvd.
Dallas, TX 75235
Tel.: 214-688-2182

Vermont

Vermont Regional Cancer Center
University of Vermont
MCHV-Burgess Residence
Burlington, VT 05401
Tel.: 802-656-3743

Virginia

MCV/VCU Cancer Center
Box 37, MCV Station
Medical College of Virginia
Virginia Commonwealth
University
Richmond, VA 23298
Tel.: 804-770-7682
Tel.: 804-770-7476

Wisconsin

Milwaukee Children's Hospital
1700 W. Wisconsin Ave.
Milwaukee, WI 53233
Tel.: 414-931-4042

CANSCREEN CLINICS

CANSCREEN is a low-cost cancer detection and prevention program which is gradually being expanded throughout the country. While it is primarily aimed at those believed to be at increased risk, anyone can take advantage of the screening done by these clinics. Examination is by trained paramedical personnel—nurses and physicians' assistants—with a physician present in the clinic. CANSCREEN emphasizes early detection and prompt treatment, and counsels those examined on cancer prevention. The cost of this examination is presently between $40 and $60.

California

CANSCREEN Program
Daniel Freeman Hospital
Medical Center
333 N. Prairie Ave.
Inglewood, CA 90301
213-674-0050

Illinois

CANSCREEN Program
Evanston Hospital
2650 Ridge Ave.
Evanston, IL 60201
312-492-6860

Indiana

CANSCREEN Program
Northwestern Indiana Cancer
  Detection Center
8127 Merriville Rd.
Merriville, IN 46410
219-769-3579

Massachusetts

CANSCREEN Program
Health Association of
  Provincetown Inc.
P.O.B. 613
14 Center St.
Provincetown, MA 02657
617-487-9395

New York

CANSCREEN Program
Preventive Medicine
  Institute–Strang Clinic

55 East 34th St.
New York, NY 10016
212-683-0283

Pennsylvania

CANSCREEN Program
Fox Chase Cancer Center
Central and Shelmire Aves.
Philadelphia, PA 19111
215-742-1850

Wisconsin

CANSCREEN Program
Marshfield Medical Foundation
510 North St. Joseph Ave.
Marshfield, WI 54449
715-387-5242

CANCER INFORMATION SERVICE

The Cancer Information Service (CIS) is a toll-free telephone system under the sponsorship of a cancer center, often cosponsored by the American Cancer Society and other organizations, with funding from the National Cancer Institute. About 75 percent of the nation's population is now served by a regional CIS; the remainder of the United States is served by the CIS at the National Cancer Institute, Bethesda, Maryland. There is no charge for the calls or the information and the caller remains anonymous unless written material is to be sent by mail.

The goal of this service is to provide clear, accurate information about cancer to everyone who calls—the general public, cancer patients, families and friends of cancer patients, and health professionals including physicians. The trained CIS staffs answer questions about cancer causes, prevention, detection, diagnosis, treatment, and rehabilitation. Information is given about local medical facilities, patient referrals to physicians, physician consultations, and sources of financial aid. If the answers cannot be given in the first call, callbacks are made.

A major objective is to reduce the fear of cancer by helping the public understand and cope with the disease. Staff members also provide emotional support, and sometimes they just listen. CIS has handled more than 325,000 calls since it was started in 1976 and there are now nearly 9,000 calls a month.

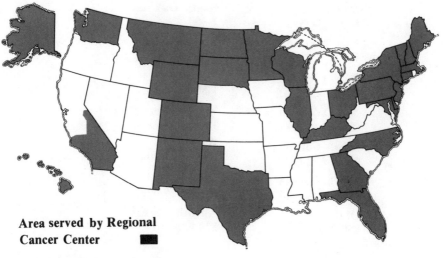

Area served by Regional Cancer Center ◼

Area served by National Line: 800-638-6694 ☐

Alaska
1-800-638-6070

California
From Area Codes
(213), (714), and (805):
1-800-252-9066

Colorado
1-800-332-1850

Connecticut
1-800-922-0824

Delaware
1-800-523-3586

District of Columbia
(Includes suburban
Maryland and
Northern Virginia)
(202)-636-5700

Florida
1-800-432-5953

Georgia
1-800-327-7332

Hawaii
Oahu: 524-1234
Neighbor Islands:
ask operator for
Enterprise 6702

Illinois
800-972-0586

Kentucky
800-432-9321

Maine
1-800-225-7034

Maryland
800-492-1444

Massachusetts
1-800-952-7420

Minnesota
1-800-582-5262

Montana
1-800-525-0231

New Hampshire
1-800-225-7034

New Jersey
800-523-3586

South Dakota
1-800-328-5188

New Mexico
1-800-525-0231

Texas
1-800-392-2040

New York State
1-800-462-7255

Vermont
1-800-225-7034

New York City
(212)-794-7982

Washington
1-800-552-7212

North Carolina
1-800-672-0943

Wisconsin
1-800-362-8038

North Dakota
1-800-328-5188

Wyoming
1-800-525-0231

Ohio
800-282-6522

All other areas:
800-638-6694

Pennsylvania
1-800-822-3963

If you need information about resources in a state other than your own, call the Cancer Information Service serving your area for proper referral.

"I cannot thank the Cancer Information Service enough for the genuine feeling of warmth, concern, and courtesy given me each time I call," wrote one woman. "Cancer is a frightening disease and most doctors do not have time just to chat about fears."

Physicians may arrange to speak with the appropriate clinician at a cancer center for medical consultation by calling a CIS number. If there is no local number, they may call the National Cancer Institute at either (800)-638-6694 or (301)-496-6600.

Most CIS telephone numbers are in the white pages of the telephone directories. If no number is listed, call the national CIS number, (800)-638-6694; in Maryland, call (800)-492-6600; in Alaska and Hawaii, 1-(800)-638-6070. In some areas, it may be necessary to dial "1" before the number.

Except for the New York City and Washington, D.C., areas, the CIS offices are reached by toll-free long-distance lines. In most offices, service is from 9 A.M to 4:30 P.M. with a recorded message referring callers to backup assistance after hours.

You and your physicians may also obtain information about cancer and cancer services directly from the National Cancer Institute by writing:

Office of Cancer Communications
National Cancer Institute
Building 31, Room 10A18
Bethesda, MD 20205
Tel.: 800-638-6694

III

• Hospitals with Cancer Programs Approved by the Commission on Cancer, American College of Surgeons • The American Board of Medical Specialties

The Commission on Cancer, a multidisciplinary group representing 19 lay and professional organizations, establishes standards for effective cancer programs in hospitals and medical centers. The goal is the best possible care for cancer patients. Upon invitation, the Committee on Approvals conducts on-site surveys and evaluates the cancer programs. The American College of Surgeons conducts this program, which is 25 years old in 1980, with funding from the American Cancer Society and the National Cancer Institute.

The basic approval requirements relate to professional education and patient care. The evaluation surveys include diagnostic and treatment facilities; staff training, including multidisciplinary cancer conferences; consultation and referral policies; tumor registry (diagnostic and treatment data); and research.

This is a voluntary program and hospitals that are not listed may still provide effective care; for one reason or another, they did not request that their cancer programs be evaluated.

ALABAMA
Birmingham
University of Alabama Hospitals
Veterans Administration Hospital
Mobile
University of South Alabama
Medical Center
Tuskegee
Veterans Administration Hospital

ALASKA
Anchorage
Alaska Hospital and Medical Center
Providence Hospital
USPHS Alaska Native Medical Center
Fairbanks
Fairbanks Memorial Hospital

ARIZONA
Mesa
Desert Samaritan Hospital and Health
Center
Mesa Lutheran Hospital
Phoenix
Good Samaritan Hospital
Maricopa County General Hospital
Memorial Hospital

Veterans Administration Medical
Center
Scottsdale
Scottsdale Memorial Hospital
Tucson
Tucson Medical Center
University Hospital
Veterans Administration Medical Center

ARKANSAS
Fayetteville
Washington Regional Medical Center
Little Rock
University Hospital
Veterans Administration Hospital
Texarkana
St. Michael Hospital

CALIFORNIA
Alhambra
Alhambra Community Hospital
Anaheim
Anaheim Memorial Hospital
Martin Luther Hospital Medical Center
Arcadia
Methodist Hospital of Southern
California

Bakersfield
 Kern Medical Center

Bellflower
 Bellwood General Hospital
 Kaiser Foundation Hospital

Berkeley
 Alta Bates Hospital
 Herrick Memorial Hospital

Burbank
 St. Joseph Medical Center

Canoga Park
 West Hills Medical Center

Concord
 Mount Diablo Hospital Medical Center

Covina
 Inter-Community Hospital

Culver City
 Dr. David Brotman Memorial Hospital

Duarte
 City of Hope National Medical Center

Fontana
 Kaiser Foundation Hospital

Fountain Valley
 Fountain Valley Community Hospital

Fresno
 Veterans Administration Medical Center

Glendale
 Glendale Adventist Medical Center
 Glendale Community Hospital

Granada Hills
 Granada Hills Community Hospital

Harbor City
 Kaiser Foundation Hospital

Imola
 Napa State Hospital

Inglewood
 Centinela Hospital Medical Center
 Daniel Freeman Memorial Hospital

La Jolla
 Green Hospital of Scripps Clinic
 Scripps Memorial Hospital

La Mesa
 Grossmont District Hospital

Livermore
 Veterans Administration Medical Center

Loma Linda
 Loma Linda University Medical Center

Long Beach
 Long Beach Community Hospital
 Los Altos Hospital
 Memorial Hospital Medical Center of
  Long Beach
 Naval Regional Medical Center
 St. Mary Medical Center - Bauer Hospital

Los Angeles
 California Hospital Medical Center
 Children's Hospital of Los Angeles

Hollywood Presbyterian Medical Center
Hospital of the Good Samaritan
Kaiser Foundation Hospital - Cadillac
Kaiser Foundation Hospital - Sunset
Los Angeles County, USC Medical
 Center
Martin Luther King, Jr. General Hospital
Orthopaedic Hospital
Queen of Angels Hospital
St. Vincent Medical Center
UCLA Hospital
White Memorial Medical Center

Lynwood
 St. Francis Medical Center

Montebello
 Beverly Hospital

Monterey Park
 Garfield Medical Center

Newport Beach
 Hoag Memorial Hospital - Presbyterian

Northridge
 Northridge Hospital Foundation

Oakland
 Naval Medical Center
 Samuel Merritt Hospital

Oceanside
 Tri-City Hospital

Orange
 St. Joseph Hospital
 University of California
  Irvine Medical Center

Oxnard
 St. John's Hospital

Palm Springs
 Desert Hospital

Panorama City
 Kaiser Foundation Hospital

Pasadena
 Huntington Memorial Hospital
 St. Luke Hospital of Pasadena

Pomona
 Pomona Valley Community Hospital

Redlands
 Redlands Community Hospital

Redondo Beach
 South Bay Hospital

Redwood City
 Sequoia Hospital

Riverside
 Parkview Community Hospital
 Riverside Community Hospital
 Riverside General Hospital —
  University Medical Center

Sacramento
 Mercy Hospital
 Sutter Community Hospitals of
  Sacramento
 University of California — Davis
  Medical Center

San Bernardino
St. Bernadine Hospital
San Bernardino County Medical Center

San Diego
Children's Hospital & Health Center
Donald Sharp Memorial Community
    Hospital
Kaiser Foundation Hospital
Mercy Hospital and Medical Center
Naval Regional Medical Center
University Hospital

San Dimas
Tri-Hospital Cancer Program
    Foothill Presbyterian Hospital,
        Glendora
    Glendora Community Hospital,
        Glendora
    San Dimas Community Hospital,
        San Dimas
    West Covina Hospital, *West Covina*

San Francisco
French Hospital/Medical Center
Letterman Army Medical Center
Mount Zion Hospital and Medical Center
St. Francis Memorial Hospital
St. Mary's Hospital and Medical Center
San Francisco General Hospital
    Medical Center
USPHS Hospital
University of California Hospitals and
    Clinics
Veterans Administration Medical Center

San Gabriel
Community Hospital of San Gabriel

San Jose
O'Connor Hospital
San Jose Hospital
Santa Clara Valley Medical Center

San Pablo
Brookside Hospital

San Pedro
San Pedro and Peninsula Hospital

Santa Ana
Santa Ana-Tustin Community Hospital

Santa Barbara
Santa Barbara Cottage Hospital

Santa Monica
St. John's Hospital and Health Center
The Santa Monica Hospital
    Medical Center

Thousand Oaks
Los Robles Regional Medical Center

Torrance
Los Angeles County Harbor —
    UCLA Medical Center
Torrance Memorial Hospital Medical
    Center

Travis AFB
David Grant USAF Medical Center

Van Nuys
Valley Presbyterian Hospital

Visalia
Kaweah Delta District Hospital

Walnut Creek
John Muir Memorial Hospital

Whittier
Presbyterian Intercommunity Hospital

COLORADO

Colorado Springs
Penrose Hospital

Denver
American Cancer Research Center
    and Hospital, *Lakewood*
Fitzsimons Army Medical Center
Porter/Swedish Cancer Program
    Porter Memorial Hospital
    Swedish Medical Center, *Englewood*
Presbyterian Medical Center
Rose Medical Center
St. Anthony Hospital Systems
Saint Joseph Hospital
St. Luke's Hospital
University of Colorado Medical Center —
    Colorado General Hospital
Veterans Administration Medical Center

Fort Carson
US Army Hospital

Fort Collins
Poudre Valley Memorial Hospital

Greeley
Weld County General Hospital

Longmont
Longmont United Hospital

Montrose
Montrose Memorial Hospital

Pueblo
St. Mary-Corwin Hospital

USAF Academy
USAF Academy Hospital

Wheat Ridge
Lutheran Medical Center

CONNECTICUT

Bridgeport
Bridgeport Hospital
Park City Hospital
St. Vincent's Medical Center

Danbury
Danbury Hospital

Derby
Griffin Hospital

Farmington
University of Connecticut Health Center-
    John Dempsey Hospital

Greenwich
Greenwich Hospital Association

Groton
Naval Submarine Medical Center

Hartford
Mount Sinai Hospital
St. Francis Hospital and Medical Center

Meriden
Meriden-Wallingford Hospital

New Haven
Hospital of St. Raphael
Yale-New Haven Hospital

Norwalk
Norwalk Hospital

Norwich
The William W. Backus Hospital

Stamford
St. Joseph Hospital

Torrington
Charlotte Hungerford Hospital

Waterbury
St. Mary's Hospital
Waterbury Hospital

DELAWARE

Lewes
Beebe Hospital of Sussex County

Wilmington
Veterans Administration Center
Wilmington Medical Center

DISTRICT OF COLUMBIA

Washington
Children's Hospital National Medical
Center
Georgetown University Hospital
Greater Southeast Community Hospital
Howard University Hospital
Walter Reed Army Medical Center

FLORIDA

Daytona Beach
Halifax Hospital Medical Center

Gainesville
Shands Teaching Hospital and Clinic

Jacksonville
Memorial Hospital of Jacksonville
Naval Regional Medical Center
St. Vincent's Medical Center
University Hospital of Jacksonville

Miami
James M. Jackson Memorial Hospital

Pensacola
Naval Aerospace and Regional Medical
Center
West Florida Hospital

Tallahassee
Tallahassee Memorial Hospital

Tampa
Tampa General Hospital

GEORGIA

Albany
Phoebe Putney Memorial Hospital

Americus
Americus and Sumter County Hospital

Atlanta
Crawford W. Long Memorial Hospital of
Emory University
Emory University Hospital
Georgia Baptist Medical Center
Grady Memorial Hospital
Piedmont Hospital
St. Joseph's Hospital
West Paces Ferry Hospital

Augusta
Eugene Talmadge Memorial Hospital
University Hospital

Columbus
Medical Center

Dalton
Hamilton Memorial Hospital

Decatur
De Kalb General Hospital
Veterans Administration Hospital,
Atlanta

East Point
South Fulton Hospital

Fort Benning
Martin Army Hospital

Fort Gordon
Dwight D. Eisenhower Army Medical
Center

Gainesville
Northeast Georgia Medical Center

La Grange
West Georgia Medical Center/Enoch
Callaway Cancer Clinic

Macon
Medical Center of Central Georgia

Savannah
Memorial Medical Center

Tifton
Tift General Hospital

HAWAII

Honolulu
Kaiser Foundation Hospital
Kapiolani Hospital
Kuakini Medical Center
Queen's Medical Center
St. Francis Hospital
Tripler Army Medical Center

IDAHO

Boise
St. Luke's Hospital & Mountain States
Tumor Institute

Lewiston
St. Joseph's Hospital
Nampa
Mercy Medical Center
Twin Falls
Magic Valley Memorial Hospital

ILLINOIS

Arlington Heights
Northwest Community Hospital
Aurora
Copley Memorial Hospital
Carbondale
Memorial Hospital of Carbondale
Chicago
Central Community Hospital
Children's Memorial Hospital
Columbus Hospital
Cook County Hospital
Franklin Boulevard Community Hospital
Holy Cross Hospital
Illinois Masonic Medical Center
Louis A. Weiss Memorial Hospital
Mercy Hospital and Medical Center
Mount Sinai Hospital Medical Center
Northwestern Memorial Hospital
Ravenswood Hospital Medical Center
Rush-Presbyterian-St. Luke's Medical
Center
St. Elizabeth's Hospital
St. Joseph Hospital
St. Mary of Nazareth Hospital Center
Swedish Covenant Hospital
University of Chicago Hospitals
and Clinics
University of Illinois Hospital
Veterans Administration West Side
Hospital
Chicago Heights
St. James Hospital
Danville
Lakeview Medical Center
St. Elizabeth Hospital
Decatur
Decatur Memorial Hospital
Effingham
St. Anthony's Memorial Hospital
Elgin
Saint Joseph Hospital
Elk Grove Village
Alexian Brothers Medical Center
Elmhurst
Memorial Hospital of DuPage County
Evanston
Evanston Hospital
St. Francis Hospital of Evanston
Great Lakes
Naval Regional Medical Center
Harvey

Ingalls Memorial Hospital
Hines
Veterans Administration Medical Center
Hinsdale
Hinsdale Sanitarium and Hospital
Kankakee
St. Mary's Hospital of Kankakee
Lake Forest
Lake Forest Hospital
McHenry
McHenry Hospital
Mendota
Mendota Community Hospital
Moline
Lutheran Hospital
Oak Lawn
Christ Hospital
Oak Park
West Suburban Hospital
Park Ridge
Lutheran General Hospital
Peoria
Methodist Medical Center of Illinois
St. Francis Hospital Medical Center
Quincy
Blessing Hospital
St. Mary Hospital
Rockford
Rockford Memorial Hospital
St. Anthony Hospital Medical Center
Swedish-American Hospital
Sterling
Community General Hospital
Streator
St. Mary's Hospital
Urbana
Carle Foundation Hospital

INDIANA

Bluffton
Caylor-Nickel Hospital
Evansville
Deaconess Hospital
Welborn Memorial Baptist Hospital
Gary
Methodist Hospital of Gary
Hammond
St. Margaret Hospital
Indianapolis
Community Hospital of Indianapolis
Methodist Hospital of Indiana
St. Vincent Hospital and Health Care
Center
Lafayette
St. Elizabeth Hospital Medical Center
Terre Haute
Terre Haute Regional Hospital
Union Hospital

Vincennes
Good Samaritan Hospital

IOWA

Des Moines
Iowa Methodist Medical Center
Mercy Hospital
Veterans Administration Hospital
Dubuque
Finley Hospital
Mercy Health Center - St. Joseph's Unit
Xavier Hospital
Iowa City
University of Iowa Hospitals and Clinics

KANSAS

Fort Riley
Irwin Army Hospital
Hays
Hadley Regional Medical Center
St. Anthony Hospital
Kansas City
Bethany Medical Center
University of Kansas Medical Center
Manhattan
Memorial/St. Mary Hospitals Cancer
Program
Memorial Hospital
The Saint Mary Hospital
Wichita
St. Francis Hospital
St. Joseph Medical Center
Veterans Administration Medical and
Regional Office Center
Wesley Medical Center

KENTUCKY

Fort Campbell
United States Army Hospital
Lexington
Good Samaritan Hospital
University Hospital
Louisville
Highlands Baptist Hospital
Louisville General Hospital
Norton Children's Hospitals
Children's Hospital Unit
Norton Memorial Infirmary Unit
Veterans Administration Medical Center
Madisonville
Hopkins County Hospital

LOUISIANA

Alexandria
Alexandria Tumor Registry Program
Rapides General Hospital
St. Frances Cabrini Hospital
Eunice
Moosa Memorial Hospital
Lake Charles

St. Patrick Hospital of Lake Charles
New Orleans
Charity Hospital of Louisiana at
New Orleans
Touro Infirmary
USPHS Hospital
Veterans Administration Hospital
Shreveport
Louisiana State University Hospital
Veterans Administration Medical Center

MAINE

Augusta
Augusta General Hospital
Bangor
Eastern Maine Medical Center
Lewiston
Central Maine General Hospital
St. Mary's General Hospital
Norway
Stephens Memorial Hospital
Portland
Maine Medical Center
Presque Isle
Arthur Gould Memorial Hospital
Rockland
Penobscot Bay Medical Center
Togus
Veterans Administration Medical Center
Waterville
Mid-Maine Medical Center

MARYLAND

Andrews A.F. Base
Malcolm Grow USAF Medical Center
Baltimore
Franklin Square Hospital
Greater Baltimore Medical Center
Johns Hopkins Hospital
St. Joseph Hospital
Sinai Hospital of Baltimore
South Baltimore General Hospital
USPHS Hospital
University of Maryland Hospital
Bethesda
National Naval Medical Center
Leonardtown
St. Mary's Hospital
Salisbury
Peninsula General Hospital
Towson
St. Joseph Hospital

MASSACHUSETTS

Boston
Beth Israel Hospital
Boston City Hospital
Faulkner Hospital, *Jamaica Plain*
Lahey Clinic Foundation

New England Deaconess Hospital
Peter Bent Brigham Hospital
St. Elizabeth's Hospital of Boston,
   Brighton
USPHS Hospital, *Brighton*
University Hospital
Veterans Administration Medical Center,
   Jamaica Plain
Brockton
   Brockton Hospital
   Cardinal Cushing General Hospital
Cambridge
   Mount Auburn Hospital
Chelsea
   Lawrence F. Quigley Memorial Hospital
   Soldier's Home in Massachusetts
Concord
   Emerson Hospital
Danvers
   Hunt Memorial Hospital
Framingham
   Framingham Union Hospital
Holyoke
   Holyoke Hospital
   Providence Hospital
Hyannis
   Cape Cod Hospital
Lynn
   Lynn Hospital
Medford
   Lawrence Memorial Hospital
Newton Lower Falls
   Newton-Wellesley Hospital
North Adams
   North Adams Regional Hospital
Northampton
   The Cooley Dickenson Hospital
Norwood
   Norwood Hospital
Pittsfield
   Berkshire Medical Center
Salem
   Salem Hospital
Springfield
   Baystate Medical Center
   Mercy Hospital
Stoughton
   Goddard Memorial Hospital
Walpole
   Pondville Hospital
Waltham
   Waltham Hospital
Winchester
   Winchester Hospital
Worcester
   St. Vincent Hospital
   The Memorial Hospital
   Worcester City Hospital

MICHIGAN
Allen Park
   Veterans Administration Hospital
Ann Arbor
   St. Joseph Mercy Hospital
   University Hospital
Battle Creek
   Calhoun County Medical Society Cancer
      Program
   Battle Creek Sanitarium Hospital
   Community Hospital Association
   Leila Y. Post Montgomery Hospital
Dearborn
   Oakwood Hospital
Detroit
   Detroit General Hospital
   Detroit-Macomb Hospitals Association
   Harper-Grace Hospitals
   Henry Ford Hospital
Flint
   Hurley Medical Center
Grand Rapids
   Blodgett Memorial Medical Center
   Butterworth Hospital
   Ferguson-Droste-Ferguson Hospital
   St. Mary's Hospital
Menominee
   Marinette, Wi - Menominee Cancer
      Program
   Menominee County-Lloyd Hospital
Muskegon
   Hackley Hospital and Medical Center
Rochester
   Crittenton Hospital
Royal Oak
   William Beaumont Hospital
Southfield
   Providence Hospital

MINNESOTA
Crookston
   Riverview Hospital Association
Fergus Falls
   Lake Region Hospital
Grand Rapids
   Itasca Memorial Hospital
Hibbing
   Hibbing General Hospital
Minneapolis
   Abbott-Northwestern Hospital
   Children's Health Center & Hospital
   Metropolitan Medical Center
   St. Mary's Hospital
   Veterans Administration Hospital
Moorhead
   St. Ansgar Hospital
Rochester
   Mayo Clinic
St. Louis Park
   Methodist Hospital

MISSISSIPPI

Biloxi
Howard Memorial Hospital
Veterans Administration Hospital

Hattiesburg
Forrest County General Hospital

Jackson
University Hospital
Veterans Administration Medical Center

Keesler
USAF Medical Center

Vicksburg
Mercy Regional Medical Center

MISSOURI

Cape Girardeau
St. Francis Medical Center
Southeast Missouri Hospital

Columbia
Ellis Fischel State Cancer Hospital

Kansas City
Baptist Memorial Hospital
St. Luke's Hospital
Trinity Lutheran Hospital
Truman Medical Center

St. Louis
Deaconess Hospital
Jewish Hospital of St. Louis
St. Anthony's Medical Center
St. Louis Children's Hospital
St. Mary's Health Center

Sikeston
Missouri Delta Community Hospital

MONTANA

Butte
St. James Community Hospital
Mary Swift Memorial Tumor Clinic

NEBRASKA

Lincoln
Lincoln General Hospital
Veterans Administration Medical Center

Omaha
Archbishop Bergan Mercy Hospital
Bishop Clarkson Memorial Hospital
Immanuel Medical Center
Nebraska Methodist Hospital
St. Joseph Hospital
University Hospital & Clinics
University of Nebraska

NEW HAMPSHIRE

Exeter
Exeter Hospital

Hanover
Mary Hitchcock Memorial Hospital

Keene
Cheshire Hospital

Manchester
Catholic Medical Center
Elliot Hospital

Portsmouth
Portsmouth Hospital

Rochester
Frisbie Memorial Hospital

NEW JERSEY

Atlantic City
Atlantic City Medical Center

Belleville
Clara Maass Memorial Hospital

Camden
West Jersey Hospital System

Denville
St. Clare's Hospital

East Orange
Veterans Administration Medical Center

Elizabeth
Elizabeth General Hospital and
Dispensary
Wuester Clinic

Englewood
Englewood Hospital

Green Brook
Raritan Valley Hospital

Hackensack
Hackensack Hospital

Hackettstown
Hackettstown Community Hospital

Livingston
St. Barnabas Medical Center

Montclair
The Mountainside Hospital

Morristown
Morristown Memorial Hospital

Mount Holly
Burlington County Memorial Hospital

Neptune
Jersey Shore Medical Center
Fitkin Hospital

Newark
Newark Beth Israel Medical Center

Newton
Newton Memorial Hospital

Orange
The Hospital Center at Orange

Passaic
Beth Israel Hospital

Paterson
St. Joseph's Hospital and Medical Center

Phillipsburg
Warren Hospital

Plainfield
Muhlenberg Hospital

Princeton
The Medical Center at Princeton

Somerville
Somerset Hospital Medical Center
Trenton
St. Francis Medical Center
Woodbury
Underwood-Memorial Hospital

NEW MEXICO

Albuquerque
Bernalillo County Medical Center
Lovelace Medical Center
St. Joseph Hospital
Veterans Administration Medical Center

NEW YORK

Albany
Veterans Administration Hospital
Amityville
Brunswick Hospital Center
Binghamton
Our Lady of Lourdes Memorial Hospital
Buffalo
Children's Hospital of Buffalo
Deaconess Hospital of Buffalo
Erie County Medical Center
Roswell Park Memorial Institute
Veterans Administration Medical Center
Castle Point
Veterans Administration Medical Center
Cobleskill
Community Hospital of Schoharie
County
Cooperstown
Mary Imogene Bassett Hospital
East Meadow
Nassau County Medical Center
Elmira
Arnot-Ogden Memorial Hospital
Glen Cove
Community Hospital at Glen Cove
Johnson City
Charles S. Wilson Memorial Hospital
Kenmore
Kenmore Mercy Hospital
Manhasset
North Shore University Hospital
Mineola
Nassau Hospital
Mount Kisco
Northern Westchester Hospital Center
Mount Vernon
Mount Vernon Hospital
New Hyde Park
Long Island Jewish Medical Center
New Rochelle
New Rochelle Hospital Medical Center
New York City
Bronx *(Mailing address: Bronx)*

Bronx-Lebanon Hospital Center
Misericordia Hospital Medical Center
Montefiore Hospital and Medical
Center
Veterans Administration Medical
Center
Brooklyn *(Mailing address: Brooklyn)*
Brooklyn-Cumberland Medical Center
Jewish Hospital & Medical Center of
Brooklyn
Long Island College Hospital
Lutheran Medical Center
St. John's Episcopal Hospital
State University of New York, Down-
state Medical Center and
Kings County Hospital Center
Wyckoff Heights Hospital
The Methodist Hospital

Manhattan *(Mailing address: New York)*
Beekman-Downtown Hospital
Bellevue Hospital Center
Beth Israel Medical Center
Cabrini Health Care Center
Harlem Hospital Center
Manhattan Eye, Ear and Throat
Hospital
Memorial Sloan-Kettering Cancer
Center
New York Infirmary
New York University Medical Center
University Hospital
St. Clare's Hospital and Health Center
St. Luke's Hospital Center
St. Vincent's Hospital and
Medical Center of New York
The New York Hospital
Veterans Administration Medical
Center

Queens *(Mailing addresses: Astoria,*
Edgemere, Elmhurst, Far Rockaway,
Flushing, Forest Hills, Glen Oaks,
Hollis, Jackson Heights, Jamaica,
Kew Gardens, Little Neck, Long
Island City, Queens Village, St.
Albans, and Whitestone)
Booth Memorial Medical Center,
Flushing
Flushing Hospital and Medical Center,
Flushing
LaGuardia Hospital, *Forest Hills*
Jamaica Hospital, *Jamaica*
Mary Immaculate Hospital, Division
of the Catholic Medical Center of
Brooklyn and Queens, *Jamaica*
Queens Hospital Center, *Jamaica*
St. John's Queens Hospital, Division
of the Catholic Medical Center of
Brooklyn and Queens, *Elmhurst*

Richmond *(Mailing address: Staten*
Island)

Doctors' Hospital of Staten Island
St. Vincent's Medical Center of
   Richmond
Staten Island Hospital
USPHS Hospital

Nyack
Nyack Hospital

Oceanside
South Nassau Communities Hospital

Plainview
Central General Hospital

Port Jefferson
John T. Mather Memorial Hospital and
   St. Charles Hospital

Port Jervis
St. Francis Hospital of Port Jervis

Poughkeepsie
Vassar Brothers Hospital

Rochester
Highland Hospital of Rochester
Park Ridge Hospital
Rochester St. Mary's Hospital of the
   Sisters of Charity

Rockville Centre
Mercy Hospital

Syracuse
St. Joseph's Hospital Health Center
University Hospital of Upstate Medical
   Center

Walton
Delaware Valley Hospital

NORTH CAROLINA

Asheville
Veterans Administration Hospital

Camp Le Jeune
Naval Regional Medical Center

Chapel Hill
North Carolina Memorial Hospital

Durham
Duke University Medical Center
Veterans Administration Medical Center

Shelby
Cleveland Memorial Hospital

Valdese
Valdese General Hospital

Winston-Salem
North Carolina Baptist Hospital

NORTH DAKOTA

Fargo
St. John's Hospital
St. Luke's Hospital - Fargo Clinic

Grand Forks
The United Hospital

Rugby
Good Samaritan Hospital Association

Williston
Mercy Hospital

OHIO

Akron
Akron City Hospital
Akron General Medical Center

Cincinnati
Children's Hospital Medical Center
University of Cincinnati Medical Center,
   Cincinnati General Hospital
Good Samaritan Hospital
Jewish Hospital of Cincinnati

Cleveland
Cleveland Clinic Hospital
Deaconess Hospital of Cleveland
Huron Road Hospital
Lutheran Medical Center
St. Alexis Hospital

Columbus
Children's Hospital
Ohio State University Hospitals
The Hawkes Hospital of Mount Carmel
   Mount Carmel Medical Center
   Mount Carmel East Hospital

Dayton
Good Samaritan Hospital and Health
   Center
Miami Valley Hospital
St. Elizabeth Medical Center
Veterans Administration Center

Dover
Union Hospital Association

Kettering
Kettering Medical Center

Mayfield Heights
Hillcrest Hospital

Sandusky
Good Samaritan Hospital

Springfield
Springfield-Urbana Cancer Program
   Community Hospital/Springfield and
   Clark County
   Mercy Medical Center
   Mercy Memorial Hospital, *Urbana*

Sylvania
Flower Hospital

Toledo
Medical College of Ohio Hospital
Toledo Hospital

Wright-Patterson AFB
USAF Medical Center

Youngstown
Youngstown Hospital Association

OKLAHOMA

Ada
Valley View Hospital

Ardmore
Memorial Hospital of Southern Oklahoma

Bartlesville
Jane Phillips Episcopal Memorial
   Medical Center

Chickasha
Grady Memorial Hospital

Oklahoma City
Baptist Medical Center of Oklahoma
Mercy Health Center
Oklahoma Children's Memorial Hospital
Presbyterian Hospital
St. Anthony Hospital
University Hospital & Clinics

Okmulgee
Okmulgee Memorial Hospital Authority

Shattuck
Newman Memorial Hospital

Shawnee
Shawnee Medical Center Hospital

Tulsa
Hillcrest Medical Center
Saint Francis Hospital
St. John's Medical Center

OREGON

Bend
St. Charles Medical Center

Coos Bay
Bay Area Hospital

Corvallis
Good Samaritan Hospital

Eugene
Sacred Heart General Hospital

Grants Pass
Josephine General Hospital

Medford
Medford Tumor Clinic Cancer Program
Providence Hospital
Rogue Valley Memorial Hospital

Oregon City
Willamette Falls Community Hospital

Pendleton
St. Anthony Hospital

Portland
Emanuel Hospital
Good Samaritan Hospital and Medical
Center
Kaiser Foundation Hospitals,
Oregon Region
Physicians and Surgeons Hospital
Portland Adventist Medical Center
Providence Medical Center
St. Vincent Hospital and Medical Center
University of Oregon Health Sciences
Center Hospital & Clinics
Veterans Administration Hospital

Roseburg
Veterans Administration Medical Center

Salem
Salem Hospital

Tualatin
Meridian Park Hospital

PENNSYLVANIA

Allentown
Allentown Hospital Association
Allentown and Sacred Heart Hospital
Center
Sacred Heart Hospital

Altoona
Altoona Hospital
Mercy Hospital

Bethlehem
St. Luke's Hospital

Bryn Mawr
Bryn Mawr Hospital

Dansville
Geisinger Medical Center

Easton
Easton Hospital

Erie
Hamot Medical Center

Greensburg
Westmoreland Hospital Association

Johnstown
Conemaugh Valley Memorial Hospital

Lancaster
Lancaster General Hospital
St. Joseph Hospital

Latrobe
Latrobe Area Hospital

Lewiston
Lewistown Hospital

McKeesport
McKeesport Hospital

Natrona Heights
Allegheny Valley Hospital

Norristown
Montgomery Hospital
Sacred Heart Hospital

Paoli
Paoli Memorial Hospital

Philadelphia
Albert Einstein Medical Center —
Northern Division
Fox Chase Medical Center
American Oncologic Hospital
Jeanes Hospital
Children's Hospital of Philadelphia
Episcopal Hospital
Graduate Hospital of the University of
Pennsylvania
Hahnemann Medical College and
Hospital
Hospital of the University of
Pennsylvania
Lankenau Hospital
Medical College of Pennsylvania and
Hospital
Mercy Catholic Medical Center
Naval Regional Medical Center
Presbyterian-University of Pennsylvania

Medical Center
Temple University Hospital
Thomas Jefferson University Hospital

Pittsburgh
Allegheny General Hospital
Children's Hospital of Pittsburgh
Magee-Women's Hospital
Mercy Hospital of Pittsburgh
St. Francis General Hospital
St. Margaret Memorial Hospital

Pottsville
Pottsville Hospital and Warne Clinic

Reading
Community General Hospital
The Reading Hospital and Medical Center

Sayre
Robert Packer Hospital

Scranton
Mercy Hospital

Sellersville
Grandview Hospital

State College
Centre Community Hospital

West Chester
Chester County Hospital

Wilkes-Barre
Veterans Administration Hospital
Wilkes-Barre General Hospital

York
York Hospital

RHODE ISLAND
Newport
Naval Regional Medical Center

SOUTH CAROLINA
Anderson
Anderson Memorial Hospital

Beaufort
Naval Hospital

Charleston
Medical University of
South Carolina Hospital

Columbia
Richland Memorial Hospital
South Carolina Baptist Hospital
Veterans Administration Medical Center

Florence
McLeod Memorial Hospital

Fort Jackson
Moncrief Army Hospital

Greenwood
Self Memorial Hospital

Spartanburg
Spartanburg General Hospital

SOUTH DAKOTA
Aberdeen
St. Luke's Hospital

Watertown
Memorial Medical Center

Yankton
Sacred Heart Hospital

TENNESSEE
Bristol
Bristol Memorial Hospital

Johnson City
Memorial Hospital
Veterans Administration Center

Memphis
Baptist Memorial Hospital
Methodist Hospital
St. Jude Children's Research Hospital
University of Tennessee/
City of Memphis Hospitals

Millington
Naval Regional Medical Center Memphis

Nashville
George W. Hubbard Hospital of
Meharry Medical College
Nashville Metropolitan General Hospital
Vanderbilt University Hospital

TEXAS
Amarillo
Panhandle Regional Tumor Clinic and
Registry
High Plains Baptist Hospital
Northwest Texas Hospital
St. Anthony's Hospital
Deaf Smith General Hospital, *Hereford*

Big Spring
Malone-Hogan Hospital
Veterans Administration Hospital

Corpus Christi
Memorial Medical Center
Naval Regional Medical Center
Spohn Hospital

Dallas
Baylor University Medical Center
Methodist Hospitals of Dallas
Parkland Memorial Hospital
St. Paul Hospital
Veterans Administration Medical Center

El Paso
R. E. Thomason General Hospital
William Beaumont Army Medical Center

Fort Sam Houston
Brooke Army Medical Center

Fort Worth
John Peter Smith Hospital
St. Joseph's Hospital

Galveston
University of Texas Medical
Branch Hospitals

Houston
Ben Taub General Hospital
Park Plaza Hospital
Rosewood General Hospital

St. Elizabeth Hospital
St. Joseph Hospital
Texas Children's Hospital
The University of Texas, M.D. Anderson
 Hospital and Tumor Institute
Jacksonville
 Nan Travis Memorial Hospital
Kerrville
 Veterans Administration Hospital
Lubbock
 Highland Hospital
 Methodist Hospital
Plainview
 Central Plains General Hospital
San Antonio
 Bexar County Hospital District
 Santa Rosa Medical Center
Stephenville
 Stephenville Hospital
Temple
 King's Daughters Hospital
 Scott and White Memorial Hospital
 Veterans Administration Center
Texarkana
 St. Michael Hospital
Waco
 Hillcrest Baptist Hospital
 Providence Hospital
Wharton
 Gulf Coast Medical Center

UTAH
Salt Lake City
 Holy Cross Hospital
 Latter-Day Saints Hospital
 University of Utah Medical Center
 Veterans Administration Hospital

VERMONT
Burlington
 Medical Center Hospital of Vermont
Randolph
 Gifford Memorial Hospital

VIRGINIA
Big Stone Gap
 Lonesome Pine Hospital
Charlottesville
 University of Virginia Hospitals
Clifton Forge
 Emmett Memorial Hospital
Danville
 The Memorial Hospital
Falls Church
 Fairfax Hospital
Hampton
 Veterans Administration Medical Center
Harrisonburg
 Rockingham Memorial Hospital

Leesburg
 Loudoun Memorial Hospital
Lynchburg
 Lynchburg General-Marshall Lodge
 Hospitals
 Virginia Baptist Hospital
Norfolk
 DePaul Hospital
 Norfolk General Hospital
Portsmouth
 Naval Regional Medical Center
Richmond
 Medical College of Virginia Hospitals
 St. Luke's Hospital
 St. Mary's Hospital
Roanoke
 Community Hospital of Roanoke Valley
 Roanoke Memorial Hospital
Salem
 Lewis-Gale Hospital
 Veterans Administration Hospital
Winchester
 Winchester Memorial Hospital

WASHINGTON
Aberdeen
 Aberdeen Cancer Program
  Grays Harbor Community Hospital
  St. Joseph Hospital
Bellevue
 Overlake Memorial Hospital
Bellingham
 St. Joseph Hospital
 St. Luke's General Hospital
Bremerton
 Naval Regional Medical Center
Everett
 General Hospital of Everett and
  Providence Hospital
Kirkland
 Evergreen General Hospital
Mount Vernon
 Skagit Valley Hospital
Olympia
 St. Peter Hospital
Seattle
 Children's Orthopedic Hospital &
  Medical Center
 Doctors Hospital
 Group Health Hospital of Puget Sound
 Northwest Hospital
 Providence Medical Center
 Swedish Hospital Medical Center
 University Hospital
 Virginia Mason Hospital
Sedro Woolley
 United General Hospital
Spokane
 Deaconess Hospital
 Sacred Heart Medical Center

Tacoma
   Madigan Army Medical Center
   Tacoma General Hospital
Walla Walla
   St. Mary Community Hospital
Wenatchee
   Wenatchee Valley Clinic

WEST VIRGINIA

Beckley
   Appalachian Regional Hospital
   Beckley Hospital
Charleston
   Charleston Area Medical Center
Clarksburg
   Veterans Administration Hospital
Elkins
   Davis Memorial Hospital
   Memorial General Hospital Association
Huntington
   Cabell Huntington Hospital
   St. Mary's Hospital
   Veterans Administration Medical Center
Kingwood
   Preston Memorial Hospital
Man
   Man Appalachian Regional Hospital
Montgomery
   Montgomery General Hospital
Morgantown
   West Virginia University Hospital
Philippi
   Broaddus Hospital
Wheeling
   Ohio Valley Medical Center

WISCONSIN

Appleton
   St. Elizabeth Hospital
Cudahy
   Trinity Memorial Hospital
Eau Claire
   Luther Hospital
   Sacred Heart Hospital
Fond du Lac
   St. Agnes Hospital
Green Bay
   St. Vincent Hospital
Janesville
   Mercy Hospital of Janesville

La Crosse
   La Crosse Lutheran Hospital
   St. Francis Hospital
Madison
   Madison General Hospital
   Methodist Hospital
   St. Mary's Hospital Medical Center
   University of Wisconsin Hospitals
Manitowoc
   Holy Family Hospital
Marinette
   Marinette-Menominee, MI Cancer
      Program
   Marinette General Hospital
Marshfield
   Marshfield Clinic
Milwaukee
   Columbia Hospital
   Deaconess Hospital
   Milwaukee County General Hospital
   Mount Sinai Medical Center
   St. Francis Hospital
   St. Joseph's Hospital
   St. Luke's Hospital
   St. Mary's Hospital
Oshkosh
   Mercy Medical Center
Watertown
   Watertown Memorial Hospital
Wausau
   Wausau Hospital Center
Wood
   Veterans Administration Center

WYOMING

Cheyenne
   De Paul Hospital
   Memorial Hospital of Laramie County

PUERTO RICO

Ponce
   Clinica Oncologica Andres Grilasca
   Hospital De Damas
San German
   Hospital De La Concepcion
San Juan
   I. Gonzales Martinez Oncologic Hospital
   University District Hospital
   Veterans Administration Center &
      Hospital

THE AMERICAN BOARD OF MEDICAL SPECIALTIES

The American Board of Medical Specialties is a nonprofit organization that represents 23 specialty boards. The primary function of each board is to determine the competence of physicians in its field who appear voluntarily for examination and to certify as diplomates those who are qualified. Specialty boards determine if candidates have received adequate educational preparation; provide comprehensive examinations to determine the competence of candidates; and certify to the competence of those physicians who satisfy the requirements. Certain boards require periodic reexamination. Each board is composed of specialists qualified in the field represented by that board.

The American Board of Medical Specialties is actively concerned with the establishment, maintenance, and elevation of the standards for the education and qualifications of physicians recognized as specialists.

American Board of Allergy and
Immunology
University City Science Center
3624 Market St.
Philadelphia, PA 19104

American Board of Anesthesiology
100 Constitution Plaza
Hartford, CT 06103

American Board of Colon and
Rectal Surgery
615 Griswold, Suite 516
Detroit, MI 48226

American Board of Dermatology
Henry Ford Hospital
Detroit, MI 48202

American Board of Emergency
Medicine
Capital Commerce Building
Suite 8
3900 Capital City Blvd.
Lansing, MI 48906

American Board of Family Practice
2228 Young Drive
Lexington, KY 40505

American Board of Internal
Medicine
University City Science Center
3624 Market St.
Philadelphia, PA 19104

American Board of Neurological
Surgery
LSU Medical Center
1542 Tulane Ave.
New Orleans, LA 70112

American Board of Nuclear
Medicine
211 East 43rd St.
New York, NY 10017

American Board of Obstetrics and
Gynecology
711 Stanton L. Young Blvd.
Oklahoma City, OK 73104

American Board of Ophthalmology
8870 Towanda St.
Philadelphia, PA 19118

American Board of Orthopedic
Surgery
444 North Michigan Ave.
Suite 2970
Chicago, IL 60611

American Board of Otolaryngology
220 Collingwood-Suite 130
Ann Arbor, MI 48103

American Board of Pathology
112 Lincoln Center
5401 West Kennedy Blvd.
P.O.B. 24695
Tampa, FL 33623

American Board of Pediatrics
Suite 402, NCNB Plaza
136 East Rosemary St.
Chapel Hill, NC 27514

American Board of Physical
  Medicine and Rehabilitation
Suite J. 1A Kahler East
Rochester, MN 55901

American Board of Plastic Surgery
1617 John F. Kennedy Blvd.
Philadelphia, PA 19103

American Board of Preventive
  Medicine
Graduate School of Public Health
University of Pittsburgh
Pittsburgh, PA 15261

American Board of Psychiatry and
  Neurology
1 American Plaza, Suite 808
Evanston, IL 60201

American Board of Radiology
Kahler East
Rochester, MN 55901

American Board of Surgery
1617 John F. Kennedy Blvd.
Philadelphia, PA 19103

American Board of Thoracic
  Surgery
14640 E. Seven Mile Rd.
Detroit, MI 48205

American Board of Urology
4121 West 83rd St.
Prairie Village, KS 66208

IV

Cancer Clinical Cooperative Groups

THE CANCER CLINICAL COOPERATIVE GROUPS are made up of more than 2,000 physicians at some 400 institutions funded by the National Cancer Institute. Each group specializes in particular types of cancer and conducts controlled studies to determine the best treatment for patients with those diseases.

When research determines that a new treatment may be more effective than standard therapy, the new treatment is administered and evaluated by Cooperative Group physicians. These studies cover surgery, radiation, chemotherapy, and various combinations of these and other modalities. The medical facilities in these groups treat over 20,000 patients a year many of whom receive part of their care without cost.

Physicians may contact these groups to obtain information about the most effective treatment methods or to inquire about having a patient admitted to a study.

1. Brain Tumor Study Group

Michael D. Walker, M.D., Chairman
Building 31, Room 4B32
National Cancer Institute, NIH
Bethesda, MD 20205
301-496-6361

2. Cancer and Leukemia Group B

James F. Holland, M.D., Chairman
Department of Neoplastic Disease
Mt. Sinai School of Medicine
100th St. and Fifth Ave.
New York, NY 10029
212-650-6364

3. Children's Cancer Study Group

Denman Hammond, M.D., Chairman
University of Southern California
2025 Zonal Ave.
Keith Administration Building
Room #509
Los Angeles, CA 90033
213-226-2008

4. Eastern Cooperative Oncology Group

Paul Carbone, M.D., Chairman
Wisconsin Clinical Center
Room #K4-614
600 Highland Ave.
Madison, WI 53792
608-263-8610

5. Gastrointestinal Tumor Study Group

Douglas Holyoke, M.D., Chairman
Roswell Park Memorial Institute
666 Elm St.
Buffalo, NY 14263
716-845-3243

Philip Schein, M.D., Co-Chairman
Georgetown University Medical Center
3800 Reservoir Rd. NW
Washington, DC 20007
202-625-7081

6. Gynecologic Oncology Group

George C. Lewis, Jr., M.D., Chairman
Gynecologic Group Headquarters
P.O.B. 60
Philadelphia, PA 19105
215-928-6030

7. Head and Neck Contracts Program

Gregory Wolf, M D., Project Officer
Landow Building, Room 8C04
National Cancer Institute, NIH
Bethesda, MD 20205
301-496-2522

8. Lung Cancer Study Group

Joseph Allegra, M.D., Project Officer
Landow Building, Room 8C04
National Cancer Institute, NIH
Bethesda, MD 20205
301-496-2522

9. National Surgical Adjuvant Project for Breast and Bowel Cancers

Bernard Fisher, M.D., Chairman
914 Scaife Hall
3550 Terrace St.
Pittsburgh, PA 15261
412-624-2671

10. National Wilm's Tumor Study Group

Giulio D'Angio, M.D, Chairman
Children's Cancer Research Center
34th & Civic Center Blvd.
Philadelphia, PA 19104
215-387-5518

11. Northern California Oncology Group

Stephen K. Carter, M.D., Chairman
1801 Page Mill Rd.
Building B, Suite #200
Palo Alto, CA 94304
415-497-7431

12. Ovarian Cancer Study Group

Daniel Haller, M.D., Project Officer
Landow Building, Room 8C04
National Cancer Institute, NIH
Bethesda, MD 20205
301-496-2522

13. Polycythemia Vera Study Group

Louis R. Wasserman, M.D., Chairman
Department of Hematology
Mt. Sinai Hospital
11 E. 100th St.
New York, NY 10029
212-876-2734

14. Radiation Therapy Oncology Group

Simon Kramer, M.D., Chairman
Thomas Jefferson University Hospital
1025 Walnut St.
Philadelphia, PA 19107
215-928-6700

15. Southeastern Cancer Study Group

John R. Durant, M.D., Chairman
Comprehensive Cancer Center
University of Alabama
Tumor Institute, Room 214
Birmingham, AL 35294
205-934-5077

16. Southwest Oncology Group

Barth Hoogstraten, M.D., Chairman
University of Kansas Medical Center
Kansas City, KS 66103
913-588-5996

17. Uro-oncology Research Group

David F. Paulson, M.D., Chairman
P.O.B. 2977
Duke University Medical Center
Durham, NC 27710
919-684-5057

18. Veterans Administration Surgical Oncology Group

George A. Higgins, M.D., Chairman
Chief, Surgical Service
VA Hospital
50 Irving St. NW
Washington, DC 20422
202-389-7266

Types of Cancers Studied by the Clinical Cooperative Groups

(Numbers refer to the 18 clinical cooperative groups)

Type of Cancer	Clinical Cooperative Groups
Bladder	3, 4, 11, 14, 15, 16, 17
Brain and spinal cord	1, 3, 4, 11, 14, 16
Breast	2, 4, 9, 11, 15, 16
Cervical	6, 11, 14, 15, 16
Colon-rectum	2, 4, 9, 14, 15, 16, 18
Esophagus	4, 11, 14, 15, 16, 18
Ewing's sarcoma (bone marrow)	2, 3, 16
Head and neck	2, 4, 7, 11, 14, 15, 16, 18
Hematologic tumors (myeloma, histiocytosis, polycythemia vera, mycosis fungoides)	2, 3, 4, 13, 15, 16
Hepatoma (primary liver)	3, 4, 5, 11, 14, 15, 16
Histiocytosis	(see Hematologic tumors)
Hodgin's disease (and non-Hodgkin's lymphoma)	2, 3, 4, 15, 16
Kidney	4, 15, 16
Leukemia (adults)	2, 4, 11, 15, 16
Leukemia (children)	3, 16
Lung (small cell)	2, 4, 11, 14, 15, 16
Lung (other)	2, 4, 8, 11, 14, 15, 16, 18
Lymphoma	(see Hodgkin's disease)
Melanoma	4, 11, 14, 15, 16
Mycosis fungoides	(see Hematologic tumors)
Myeloma	(see Hematologic tumors)
Neuroblastoma (nerve tumor)	2, 3, 16
Osteosarcoma (primary bone)	2, 3, 4, 16
Ovary	3, 4, 6, 11, 14, 15, 16
Pancreas	4, 5, 11, 14, 16, 18
Polycythemia vera	(see Hematologic tumors)
Prostate	11, 14, 15, 16, 17
Retinoblastoma (eye)	3, 16
Rhabdomyosarcoma (muscle)	2, 3, 16
Sarcoma (soft tissue)	2, 4, 14, 15, 16
Stomach	2, 4, 5, 11, 16, 18
Testes	4, 11, 15, 16
Ureter	16
Uterus	4, 6
Vulva-vagina	6
Wilm's tumor (kidney in children)	2, 3, 10, 16

V
The Hospice Movement

THE HOSPICE MOVEMENT treats death as an inevitable part of life and believes that the dying need close contact with loved ones, emotional and physical comfort, and effective relief from pain if it is present. A bright, pleasant atmosphere "full of plants and families including young children"—and favorite pets—removes the loneliness that so often characterizes dying in an institution.

When pain is present, a special mixture of drugs (Brompton's mixture) is given not in response to pain but to "maintain the patient on a plateau of comfort." Only about half of dying patients experience any pain.

While the principal emphasis is on helping the family care for the patient at home—where most people want to die—about 10 hospices with inpatient beds will exist in the United States by 1981. By that date, there will be some 120 hospice organizations in this country. The National Hospice Organization, with 1,600 members, is developing standards and an accreditation program for U.S. hospices.

The goals of the hospice health care program as stated by Connecticut Hospice, Inc., New Haven, Connecticut, the first hospice in this country, are:

1. To help the patient to live as fully as possible.

2. To support the family as the unit of care.

3. To keep the patient at home as long as appropriate.

4. To educate health professionals and lay people.

5. To supplement, not duplicate, existing services.

6. To keep costs down.

Hospice home care is suitable only where the family can function as the primary unit of care with the effective, compassionate support of the hospice team. Hospice staff members visit patients regularly and are on call 24 hours a day, seven days a week. Care is provided by teams of physicians, nurses, social workers, clergymen, and trained volunteers. The hospice philosophy includes aiding the family during bereavement.

At this writing, most hospices provide care for terminally ill cancer patients since the program is partially funded by the National Cancer Institute, although some hospices care for patients with other illnesses. This provision will undoubtedly be expanded in the future.

The hospice program reduces substantially the private and public cost of caring for the dying, although this is not a primary objective. Most patients are with the home care program about three months at a cost of perhaps $1,000 to $1,500; the cost of hospitalization would be many times greater.

Although physicians generally approve of the hospice movement, they share one concern which is expressed by Dr. Irwin Krakoff of the Vermont Regional Cancer Center: "In seeking 'death with dignity' we may overlook treatable disease and provide patients with the indignity of premature death. . . . Our efforts should be aimed not only at easing patients out of the world but also, when appropriate, at restoring them to an active role in it."

Dr. Krakoff cites the difficulty of accurate diagnosis in certain cases and points out that some "terminal" patients are, in fact, not terminal and can be restored to healthy life.

His point is, of course, well taken and physicians are aware of this potential problem. The answer hinges on the accuracy of diagnosis, the knowledge and experience of the attending physician, and the fact that hospice patients are not removed from the mainstream of medicine.

In an editorial in the *New England Journal of Medicine,* Dr. Arnold S. Relman wrote: "Every experienced physician knows that there is a time to treat aggressively and a time merely to comfort—a time to resist disease and a time to recognize that further resistance would be inhumane as well as futile."

A thorough account of the hospice philosophy, including its origin in Great Britain under Dr. Cicely Saunders, is contained in the book *The Hospice Movement: A Better Way of Caring for the Dying,* by Sandol Stoddard, Stein & Day Publishers, New York. It is also available in paperback from Vintage Books, a division of Random House, New York.

To obtain more information on the hospice program in the United States, including the nearest hospice, write or call:

National Hospice Organization
301 Maple Ave. W
Tower Suite 506
Vienna, VA 22180
Tel.: 703-938-4449

VI

The American Cancer Society
The Canadian Cancer Society

THE AMERICAN CANCER SOCIETY is a national organization fighting cancer through scientific research, public and professional education, patient services, and rehabilitation programs. These activities account for 78 percent of the ACS annual budget; 22 percent is spent for fund raising, management, and office services. The funds contributed to the American Cancer Society in one year are expended during the following year; only such reserve funds as are necessary to ensure continuing support for major programs and continuity of organization are retained.

The basic ACS service and rehabilitation programs in most areas include: information and counseling; loan, supply, and transportation services; hospitalization assistance; social services; home health care programs; blood procurement; childhood cancer programs; and services for patients with financial hardship.

The ACS is organized into a national society with 58 chartered divisions and 3,035 local units; more than 73,000 community leaders direct the programs at the local level. To obtain information and assistance, contact your state-chartered division or a local unit listed in the telephone directory under "American Cancer Society" or in some areas, "Cancer."

National headquarters:
The American Cancer Society
777 Third Ave.
New York, NY 10017
Tel.: 212-371-2900

Chartered Divisions of the American Cancer Society

Alabama Division
2926 Central Ave.
Birmingham, AL 35209
205-879-2242

Alaska Division
1343 G St.
Anchorage, AK 99501
907-277-8696

Arizona Division
634 W. Indian School Rd.
P.O.B. 33187
Phoenix, AZ 85067
602-264-5861

Arkansas Division
5520 W. Markham St.
P.O.B. 3822
Little Rock, AR 72203
501-664-3480-1-2

California Division
731 Market St.
San Francisco, CA 94103
415-777-1800

Colorado Division
1809 East 18th Ave.
P.O.B. 18268
Denver, CO 80218
303-321-2464

Connecticut Division
Barnes Park So.
14 Village Lane
P.O.B. 410
Wallingford, CT 06492
203-265-7161

Delaware Division
Academy of Medicine Bldg.
1925 Lovering Ave.
Wilmington, DE 19806
302-654-6267

District of Columbia Division
Universal Building, So.
1825 Connecticut Ave., NW
Washington, DC 20009
202-483-2600

Florida Division
1001 South MacDill Ave.
Tampa, FL 33609
813-253-0541

Georgia Division
1422 W. Peachtree St. NW
Atlanta, GA 30309
404-892-0026

Hawaii Division
Community Services Center Building
200 North Vineyard Blvd.
Honolulu, HI 96817
808-531-1662-3-4-5

Idaho Division
1609 Abbs St.
P.O.Box 5386
Boise, ID 83705
208-343-4609

Illinois Division
37 So. Wabash Ave.
Chicago, IL 60603
312-372-0472

Indiana Division
4755 Kingsway Dr., Suite 100
Indianapolis, IN 46205
317-257-5326

Iowa Division
Highway #18 West
P.O.B. 980
Mason City, IA 50401
515-423-0712

Kansas Division
3003 Van Buren St.
Topeka, KS 66611
913-267-0131

Kentucky Division
Medical Arts Building
1169 Eastern Parkway
Louisville, KY 40217
502-459-1867

Louisiana Division
Masonic Temple Building, Room 810
333 St. Charles Ave.
New Orleans, LA 70130
504-523-2029

The unhappy U

Maine Division
Federal and Green Sts.
Brunswick, ME 04011
207-729-3339

Maryland Division
200 East Joppa Rd.
Towson, MD 21204
301-828-8890

Massachusetts Division
247 Commonwealth Ave.
Boston, MA 02116
617-267-2650

Michigan Division
1205 East Saginaw St.
Lansing, MI 48906
517-371-2920

Minnesota Division
2750 Park Ave.
Minneapolis, MN 55407
612-871-2111

Mississippi Division
345 North Mart Plaza
Jackson, MS 39206
601-362-8874

Missouri Division
715 Jefferson St.
P.O.B. 1066
Jefferson City, MO 65101
314-636-3195

Montana Division
2820 First Ave. So.
Billings, MT 59101
406-252-7111

Nebraska Division
Overland Wolfe Centre
6910 Pacific St., Suite 210
Omaha, NB 68106
402-551-2422

Nevada Division
953-35B East Sahara
Suite 101 ST&P Building
Las Vegas, NV 89104
702-733-7272

New Hampshire Division
22 Bridge St.
Manchester, NH 03101
603-669-3270

New Jersey Division
2700 Route 22, P.O.B. 1220
Union, NJ 07083
201-687-2100

New Mexico Division
525 San Pedro, NE
Albuquerque, NM 87108
505-262-1727

New York State Division
6725 Lyons St.
P.O.B. 7
East Syracuse, NY 13057
315-437-7025

Long Island Division
535 Broad Hollow Rd.
(Route 110)
Melville, NY 11747
516-420-1111

New York City Division
19 West 56th St.
New York, NY 10019
212-586-8700

Queens Division
111-15 Queens Blvd.
Forest Hills, NY 11375
212-263-2224

Westchester Division
246 North Central Ave.
Hartsdale, NY 10530
914-949-4800

North Carolina Division
222 North Person St.
P.O.B. 27624
Raleigh, NC 27611
919-834-8463

North Dakota Division
Hotel Graver Annex Building
115 Roberts St.
P.O.B. 426
Fargo, ND 58102
701-232-1385

Ohio Division
453 Lincoln Building
1367 East Sixth St.
Cleveland, OH 44114
216-771-6700

Oklahoma Division
1312 NW 24th St.
Oklahoma City, OK 73106
405-525-3515

Oregon Division
910 NE Union Ave.
Portland, OR 97232
503-231-5100

Pennsylvania Division
Route 422 & Sipe Ave.
P.O.B. 416
Hershey, PA 17033
717-533-6144

Philadelphia Division
21 South 12th St.
Philadelphia, PA 19107
215-665-2900

Puerto Rico Division
(Avenue Domenech 273
Hato Rey, P.R.)
GPO Box 6004
San Juan, PR 00936
809-764-2295

Rhode Island Division
345 Blackstone Blvd.
Providence, RI 02906
401-831-6970

South Carolina Division
2442 Devine St.
Columbia, SC 29205
803-787-5623

South Dakota Division
1025 North Minnesota Ave.
Hillcrest Plaza
Sioux Falls, SD 57104
605-336-0897

Tennessee Division
2519 White Ave.
Nashville, TN 37204
615-383-1710

Texas Division
3834 Spicewood Springs Rd.
P O.B. 9863
Austin, TX 78766
512-345-4560

Utah Division
610 East South Temple
Salt Lake City, UT 84102
801-322-0431

Vermont Division
13 Loomis Street, Drawer C
Montpelier, VT 05602
802-223-2348

Virginia Division
3218 West Cary St.
P.O.B. 7288
Richmond, VA 23221
804-359-0208

Washington Division
2120 First Ave. No.
Seattle, WA 98109
206-283-1152

West Virginia Division
Suite 100
240 Capital St.
Charleston, WV 25301
304-344-3611

Wisconsin Division
611 North Sherman Ave.
P.O.B. 1626
Madison, WI 53701
608-249-0487

Milwaukee Division
6401 W. Capitol Dr.
Milwaukee, WI 53216
414-461-1100

Wyoming Division
Indian Hills Center
506 Shoshoni
Cheyenne, WY 82001
307-638-3331

Affiliate of the
American Cancer Society
Canal Zone Cancer Committee
Drawer A
Balboa Heights, Canal Zone

Canadian Cancer Society—Provincial Divisions

Alberta

Canadian Cancer Society
1134 8th Ave. SW
Calgary, Alta. T2P 1J5
403-263-3120

British Columbia & Yukon

Canadian Cancer Society
955 W. Broadway St.
Vancouver, B.C. V5Z 3X8
604-736-1211

Manitoba

Canadian Cancer Society
202-960 Portage Ave.
Winnipeg, Man. R3G ØR4
204-775-4449

New Brunswick

Canadian Cancer Society
61 Union St., E2L 1A3
P.O.B. 2089
Saint John, N.B. E2L 3T5
506-652-7600

Newfoundland

Canadian Cancer Society
Pippy Pl.
P.O.B. 8921
St. John's, Nfld. A1B 3R9
709-753-6520

Nova Scotia

Canadian Cancer Society
1485 So. Park St.
Halifax, N.S. B3J 2L1
902-423-6550

Ontario

Canadian Cancer Society
185 Bloor St. E.
Toronto, Ont. M4W 3G5
416-923-7474

Canadian Cancer Society
Administrative Office
77 Bloor St. W., Suite 401
Toronto, Ont. M5S 2V7
416-961-7223

Prince Edward Island

Canadian Cancer Society
51 University Ave.
P.O.B. 115
Charlottetown, P.E.I. C1A 7K2
902-894-9675

Quebec

Canadian Cancer Society
1118 St. Catherine St. W.
Montreal, Que. H3B 1H5
514-866-2613

Saskatchewan

Canadian Cancer Society
4219 Dewdney Ave.
Regina, Sask. S4T 1A9
306-522-6320

VII

Rehabilitation Assistance

THE AMERICAN CANCER SOCIETY provides supportive emotional and physiological assistance for cancer patients who have undergone certain surgical procedures necessary to save their lives. With the approval of the attending physician, trained volunteers who have had similar operations work on a one-to-one basis with the new ex-cancer patient. Seeing and talking with men and women who have adapted well to the same surgery restores confidence and belief in the future.

The major rehabilitation programs are for people who have had a breast removed, a larynx removed, and for "ostomy" patients who have a new small opening in the abdominal wall. Over 90,000 patients were assisted in 1979; there are no charges for these services.

Breast Cancer The Reach to Recovery program aids women after breast surgery. Thousands of volunteers who once had breast cancer surgery work with new mastectomy patients to help them make a successful adjustment to normal life. Contact the local unit or state division of the American Cancer Society.

Cancer of the Larynx Men and women who have had a laryngectomy (removal of the larynx or voice box) need to learn esophageal speech and care of the stoma (the small opening in the throat). Speech therapy and encouragement are particularly important in these cases because once mastered, esophageal speech can be very effective.

The national organization, sponsored by the American Cancer Society, is:

International Association of Laryngectomees
American Cancer Society
777 Third Ave.
New York, NY 10017
Tel.: (212)-371-2900

The training of esophageal speech therapists is sponsored by the IAL and a list of certified teachers is available from ACS units or divisions and from the various member clubs—Lost Chord, Anamilo, and New Voice. While some esophageal speech therapists volunteer their services, these are professional people and, like other professionals, customarily charge for their services.

In 1979 there were 277 affiliated clubs in 48 states and 16 foreign countries registered with the IAL. Contact the local unit or state division of the American Cancer Society for assistance.

Colon-rectal (Colorectal) and Bladder Cancer   In surgery for bladder or colon-rectal cancer it is sometimes necessary to create a new body opening—an "ostomy"—in the abdominal wall through which the body's wastes are voided (a urinary ostomy or a colostomy). After an initial adjustment period, people with an ostomy live normal lives. The Ostomy Rehabilitation Program of the ACS provides emotional support and aids in adjustment.

A number of American Cancer Society divisions are helping to train enterostomal therapists (ETs), health professionals skilled in assisting people with stomas. More than 1,000 ETs have been trained since 1970 and over half were taught through the support of the ACS. Contact the local unit or state division of the American Cancer Society, or:

United Ostomy Association
2001 West Beverly Blvd.
Los Angeles, CA 90057

Other Service Programs   Additional national programs, staffed by volunteers including ex-patients, are:

I Can Cope, to help patients understand cancer, learn proper nutrition and exercise, and handle problems of stress and self-image.

Cancer Adjustment Programs, in which patients and/or their families meet to discuss mutual problems and concerns. The primary benefits result from the interaction among the members.

Contact the local unit or state division of the American Cancer Society.

VIII

How to Stop Smoking

IN AN EFFORT TO SELECT the most qualified men and women for positions in industry, psychologists devised elaborate tests to measure knowledge and personal attributes. Psychological testing is helpful but falls short of expectations because it cannot measure the one personal attribute which is more crucial than any other in predicting job success: *motivation.*

Employers find that many individuals who achieve average test scores actually are more successful in their work than those who score at the top because they are more highly motivated to do an outstanding job.

It is not surprising to learn that the single most important factor that determines a person's success or failure in quitting cigarettes is also *personal motivation.* The man or woman who is highly motivated to stop smoking—for whatever reason—will be successful while those with weak or moderate motivation often do not succeed. Personal motivation also determines whether a smoker who has quit will backslide into smoking again.

Seven Examples of High Motivation

Strong motivation to stop smoking is illustrated by the following:

• Patients who have experienced a myocardial infarction (heart attack) and are counseled by their physicians to stop smoking are able to quit cigarettes with 60 percent or higher long-term success.

• Smokers who suffer from emphysema or other serious, disabling respiratory disease give up smoking when breathing becomes frightening.

• Pregnant women who want to avoid labor complications and give birth to a healthy baby with the best chance of a normal, healthy life stop smoking.

• Teenagers who see that the captain of the football team, or the president of the student body, does not smoke tend to follow their examples and not smoke.

• The middle-aged executive promoted up the corporate ladder quits because he feels better, works better, and knows that most successful businessmen, with the highest incomes, do not smoke.

• Loving, conscientious mothers and fathers stop smoking in order to set a good example for their children (twice as many high school students smoke if their parents smoke).

• Many people who give up smoking when they have the flu, a heavy cold, or other illness find this is the ideal time to quit permanently—they simply do not go back to smoking when they regain their health.

There are other examples of strong motivation which enables people to stop smoking without too much difficulty. The reasons are highly personal and what motivates one person may not motivate another.

What Motivates Teenagers?

Unlike an older individual, a teenager does not fear cancer or other illness which may strike him in 20 to 30 years but he does fear being "uncool," not knowing how to handle a cigarette, and not being an "in" member of his social group.

The implication of cigarette advertising that to be beautiful, vigorous, and sexually attractive one must smoke is particularly pernicious where teenagers are concerned. Banning misleading advertising which implies that smoking increases self-esteem would seem in the public interest.

Experiments show that peer pressure is effective in convincing teenagers not to smoke. In one junior high school, student leaders were taught the dangers of smoking and, in turn, led discussion groups and made video tapes explaining why they did not smoke and suggesting tactful ways to refuse a cigarette. The program was successful.

In New Hampshire, biofeedback was used to demonstrate the immediate physiological changes produced by smoking. Monitoring instruments measured the carbon monoxide level in exhaled breath, hand tremor, pulse rate, and skin temperature. Students were surprised to see that just one cigarette produces an increase in carbon monoxide, heart rate, and hand tremors, and a drop in skin temperature. The results of this biofeedback demonstration were impressive and Connecticut instituted a similar program late in 1979.

The Reasons Why Adults Quit

Research by SmokEnders disclosed that people stop smoking for these reasons:

1. "Mastery over my own life."

2. "Disease prevention" and "Setting an example for my children" tied for second place.

The Kaiser Foundation in California found that men who stopped smoking were more satisfied with their lives, their work, and their relations with women, and had less anxiety and illness. Nonsmokers are better planners and believe they are in control of their lives while smokers tend to think that what happens to them results from fate or bad luck.

Interesting Facts About Quitters

• 9 out of 10 smokers either have tried to quit or would if there were an "easy way" to quit.

• Experts believe that half of the 54 to 60 million smokers in the United States can stop smoking without too much difficulty; these are the light and moderate smokers.

• Of the 30 to 33 million men and women who have stopped smoking, about 90 percent did it on their own. Half quit "cold turkey" and half tapered off gradually.

• A Gallup poll found that 33 percent of smokers were interested in attending a smoke cessation clinic.

• Light smokers, and those deeply concerned about health, are the most successful in giving up cigarettes.

• For some reason which is "poorly understood," women find it more difficult than men to stop smoking. As business success is achieved, men smoke less but women smoke more (a good research project for NOW and other women's groups).

Cigarette smoking is learned behavior which involves physiological dependence on nicotine and psychological dependence on social satisfactions. But more than 30 million men and women in the United States have quit cigarettes (including 100,000 doctors) and, with very few exceptions, the remaining 54 to 60 million smokers also can quit this pervasive threat. Perhaps the following suggestions will be helpful.

CLEANING THE AIR
A GUIDE TO QUITTING SMOKING

(Reprinted courtesy of U.S. Department of Health, Education, and Welfare, Public Health Service, National Institutes of Health. Prepared by: Office of Cancer Communications, National Cancer Institute, Bethesda, MD 20014; DHEW Publication No. NIH 79-1647)

INTRODUCTION

In this booklet you'll find a variety of tips and helpful hints on kicking your smoking habit. These methods can make your own personal efforts a little easier.

Take a few moments to look at each suggestion carefully. Pick those you feel comfortable with. And decide today that you're going to use them to quit.

It may take a while to find the combination that's right for you. But you *can* quit.

Many smokers have quit "cold turkey," without first cutting down, planning a special program, or seeking professional help. But many others have successfully given up cigarettes by replacing them with new habits or by using some gimmick.

The following approaches include those most popular with ex-smokers. Remember that sucessful methods are as different as the people who use them. What may seem silly to others may be just what you need to quit— so don't be embarrassed to try something new.

Pick the ideas that make sense to you. And then follow through—you'll have a much better chance of success.

WHEN THINKING ABOUT QUITTING . . .

- List all the reasons why you want to quit. Every night before going to bed, repeat one of the reasons 10 times.
- Decide positively that you want to quit. Try to avoid negative thoughts about how difficult it might be.
- Develop strong personal reasons in addition to your health and obligations to others. For example, think of all the time you waste taking cigarette breaks, rushing out to buy a pack, hunting a light, etc.
- Set a target date for quitting—perhaps a special day like your birthday, your anniversary, a holiday. If you smoke heavily at work, quit during your vacation. Make the date sacred, and don't let anything change it.
- Begin to condition yourself physically: start a modest exercise regimen; drink more fluids; get plenty of rest and avoid fatigue.

INVOLVE SOMEONE ELSE . . .

- Bet a friend you can quit on your target date. Put your cigarette money aside every day, and forfeit it if you smoke.
- Ask your spouse or a friend to quit with you.

SWITCH BRANDS . . .

- Switch to a brand you find distasteful.
- Change to a brand that's low in tar and nicotine a couple of weeks before your target date. This will help lessen your physical dependence on cigarettes.

CUT DOWN THE NUMBER OF CIGARETTES YOU SMOKE . . .

- Smoke only half of each cigarette.
- Each day, postpone lighting your first cigarette one hour.
- Decide you will smoke only during odd or even hours of the day.
- Decide beforehand how many cigarettes you'll smoke during the day. For each additional smoke, give a dollar to your favorite charity.
- Don't smoke when you first experience a craving. Wait several minutes; and during this time, change your activity or talk to someone.
- Stop buying cigarettes by the carton. Wait until one pack is empty before buying another.
- Stop carrying cigarettes with you at home and at work. Make them difficult to get to.
- Smoke only under circumstances which are not especially pleasurable for you. If you like to smoke with others, smoke alone.
- Make yourself aware of each cigarette by using the opposite hand, or putting cigarettes in an unfamiliar location or different pocket to break the automatic reach.
- If you light up many times during the day without even thinking about it, try to look in a mirror each time you put a match to your cigarette—you may decide you don't need it.
- Don't smoke "automatically." Smoke only those you *really* want.
- Reward yourself in some way other than smoking.
- Reach for a glass of juice instead of a cigarette for a "pick-me-up."
- Change your eating habits to aid in cutting down. For example, drink milk, which is frequently considered incompatible with smoking. End meals or snacks with something which won't lead to a cigarette.
- Don't empty your ashtrays. This will not only remind you of how many cigarettes you have smoked each day, the sight and smell of stale butts will be very unpleasant.

JUST BEFORE QUITTING . . .

- Smoke more heavily than usual so the experience becomes distasteful.

- Collect all your cigarette butts in one large glass container as a visual reminder of the filth smoking represents.
- Practice going without cigarettes. Don't think of *never* smoking again. Think of quitting in terms of one day at a time. Tell yourself you won't smoke today and then don't.

ON THE DAY YOU QUIT . . .

- Throw away all cigarettes and matches. Hide lighters and ashtrays.
- Visit the dentist, and have your teeth cleaned to get rid of tobacco stains. Notice how nice they look, and resolve to keep them that way.
- Make a list of things you'd like to buy yourself or someone else. Estimate the cost in terms of packs of cigarettes, and put the money aside to buy these presents.
- Keep very busy on the big day. Go to the movies, exercise, take long walks, go bike riding.
- Buy yourself a treat, or do something special to celebrate.

IMMEDIATELY AFTER QUITTING . . .

- The first few days after you quit, spend as much free time as possible in places where smoking is prohibited, e.g. libraries, museums, theaters, department stores, churches, etc.
- Drink large quantities of water and fruit juice.
- Try to avoid alcohol, coffee, and other beverages with which you associate cigarette smoking.
- Strike up a conversation with someone instead of a match for a cigarette.
- If you miss the sensation of having a cigarette in your hand, play with something else—a pencil, a paper clip, a marble.
- If you miss having something in your mouth, try toothpicks or a fake cigarette.

AVOID TEMPTATION . . .

- Instead of smoking after meals, get up from the table and brush your teeth or go for a walk.
- If you always smoke while driving, take public transportation for a while.
- Temporarily avoid situations you strongly associate with the pleasurable aspects of smoking, e.g., watching your favorite TV program, sitting in your favorite chair, having a cocktail before dinner, etc.
- Develop a clean, fresh non-smoking environment around yourself—at work and at home.

- Until you are confident of your ability to stay off cigarettes, limit your socializing to healthful, outdoor activities or situations where smoking is prohibited.
- If you must be in a situation where you'll be tempted to smoke (such as a cocktail or dinner party), try to associate with the non-smokers there.
- Look at cigarette ads more critically to better understand the attempts to make individual brands appealing.

FIND NEW HABITS . . .

- Change your habits to make smoking difficult, impossible, or unnecessary. Try activities such as swimming, jogging, tennis or handball. Wash your hands or the dishes when the desire for a cigarette is intense.
- Do things to maintain a clean mouth taste, such as brushing your teeth frequently, and using a mouthwash.
- Do things that require you to use your hands. Try crossword puzzles, needlework, gardening, or household chores. Go bike riding; take the dog for a walk; give yourself a manicure; write letters; try new recipes.
- Stretch a lot.
- Get plenty of rest.
- Pay attention to your appearance. Look and feel sharp.
- Absorb yourself with activities which are the most meaningful, satisfying and important to you.
- Add more spontaneity and excitement to your daily routine.

WHEN YOU GET THE "CRAZIES" . . .

- Keep oral substitutes handy—things like carrots, pickles, sun-flower seeds, apples, celery, raisins, sugarless gum, and so on.
- Take 10 deep breaths, and hold the last one while lighting a match. Exhale slowly, and blow out the match. Pretend it is a cigarette, and crush it out in an ashtray.
- Take a shower or bath if possible.
- Learn to relax quickly and deeply. Make yourself limp, visualize a soothing, pleasing situation, and get away from it all for a moment. Concentrate on that peaceful image and nothing else.
- Light incense or a candle, instead of a cigarette.
- Never allow yourself to think that "one won't hurt"—it will.

MARKING PROGRESS . . .

- Each month, on the anniversary of your quit date, plan a special celebration.

- Periodically, write down new reasons why you are glad you quit, and post these reasons where you'll be sure to see them.
- Make up a calendar for the first 90 days. Cross off each day and indicate the money saved by not smoking.
- Set other intermediate target dates, and do something special with the money you've saved.

ABOUT GAINING WEIGHT

Many people who are considering quitting are very concerned about gaining weight. If you are one of those, there are two things you should keep in mind:

1) Most of those who quit don't gain weight. About one-third do gain; one-third stay about the same weight, and another third actually lose weight, often the result of a combined exercise and/or diet program.
2) Giving up cigarettes is far healthier for you than adding on a few extra pounds. It would take the addition of more than 75 pounds to offset the health benefits which a normal smoker gains by quitting.

If you are terribly concerned about putting on extra pounds, you may want to consider the following:

- Start a diet program while you are preparing to quit.
- Don't set a target date for a holiday when the temptation of high calorie food and drinks may be too hard to resist.
- Weigh yourself daily.
- Plan menus carefully and count calories.
- Have low calorie foods on hand for nibbling.
- Take time for daily exercise, or join an organized exercise group.

SNACK CALORIES   *Calories*

BEVERAGES

Carbonated (per 8-ounce glass)
Cola-type 95
Fruit flavors (10-13% sugar) 115
Ginger ale 75

Fruit drinks (per ½ cup)
Apricot nectar 70
Cranberry juice 80
Grape drink 70
Lemonade (frozen) 55

Fruit juices (per ½ cup)
Apple juice, canned 60
Grape, bottled 85
Grapefruit, canned, unsweetened 50
Orange, canned, unsweetened 60
Pinapple, canned, unsweetened 70
Prune, canned 100

Vegetable juices (per ½ cup)
Tomato juice 25
Vegetable juice cocktail 20

BEVERAGES   *Calories*
Coffee/Tea
Coffee, black 3-5
w/1 tsp. sugar 18-20
w/1 tsp. cream 13-15
Tea, plain 0-1
w/1 tsp. sugar 10

CANDY/CHIPS/PRETZELS
Candy (per ounce)
Hard candy 110
Jelly beans 105
Marshmallows 90
Gumdrops 100

Chips (per cup)
Corn chips 230
Potato chips 115
Popcorn 40

Pretzels
Dutch, 1 twisted 60
Stick, 5 regular 10

CHEESE (per ounce)
American, process 105
Cottage, creamed 30
    uncreamed 20
Swiss, natural 105

CRACKERS
Butter, 2-inch in diameter 15
Graham, 2, 2½-inches square 55
Matzoh, 6-inch in diameter 80
Rye 45
Saltine 50

FRUITS (raw)
Apple, 2¾-inch in diameter 80
Banana, 6-7 inches (about ⅓ pound) 85
Blueberries, ½ cup 45
Strawberries, ½ cup 30
Cantaloupe, ½ of a 5-inch melon 80
Cherries (per ½ cup) sour 30
Sweet 40
Grapefruit, ½ of 3¾ inch fruit 45
Honeydew melon, 2 x 7-inch wedge 50
Orange, 2⅝-inch 65
Peach, 2½-inch 40
Pear 3½ x 2½ inch 100
Plums, 5 1-inch plums 35
Raisins, ½ cup, packed 240
Tangerine, 2⅜-inch 40
Watermelon, 2-pound wedge 110

NUTS (per 2 tablespoons)
Almonds 105
Brazil nuts 115
Cashews 100
Peanuts 105
Pecans, halves 95

VEGETABLES (raw)
Carrots, 7½ x 1⅛ inch 30
½ cup grated 25
Celery, three 5-inch stalks 10
Pickle, 1 15-20

Source: Calories and Weight, the USDA Pocket Guide, U.S. Department of Agriculture, Agriculture Research Service.

ONE POPULAR FOUR-WEEK PROGRAM

These self-help suggestions can be combined into a variety of programs to meet your needs. One popular four-week quitting program is outlined below.

First week: List the positive reasons you want to quit smoking, and read the list daily. Wrap your cigarette pack with paper and rubber bands. Each time you smoke, write down the time of day, what you are doing, how you are feeling, and how important that cigarette is to you on a scale from 1 to 5. Then rewrap the pack.

Second week: Keep reading your list of reasons, and add to it if possible. Don't carry matches, and keep your cigarettes some distance away. Each day, try to smoke fewer cigarettes, eliminating those least or most important (whichever works best).

Third week: Continue with the second week's instructions. Don't buy a new pack until you finish the one you're smoking and never buy a carton. Change brands twice during the week, each time choosing a brand lower in tar and nicotine. Try to stop smoking for 48 hours sometime during the week.

Fourth week: Continue the above. Increase your physical activity. Avoid situations you must closely associate with smoking. Find a substitute for cigarettes. Do deep breathing exercises whenever you get the urge to smoke.

SEEKING PROFESSIONAL HELP

An increasing number of formal programs using group therapy or individual counseling are being offered for smokers who want to quit. Various success rates are claimed, but it is rather difficult to compare them. In general, 20% to 40% of participants find formal programs effective. Shown here are brief descriptions of the more widely available programs. This information is intended to provide you only with a better understanding of the more formal help available, and the approximate costs involved. It does not represent an endorsement or recommendation by us to use any of these methods.

FORMAL PROGRAMS

Programs	Brief Description	Duration	Cost
Group Therapy American Cancer Society (ACS) American Heart Assoc. (AHA) American Lung Assoc. (ALA)	Physicians, psychiatrists and ex-smokers provide volunteer services. Positive reinforcement and group interaction are stressed. Participants number 8-18.	ACS groups meet approx. two hours, twice a week, for four weeks. ALA groups meet for 1½ hrs., twice a month, for an indefinite period of time.	No fee or minimal fee.
smokEnders	Programs are offered in approximately 30 cities. The moderator is an ex-smoker and smokEnder graduate. The course features a gradual reduction in smoking over the first five weeks, followed by four weeks of reinforcement after the quit date.	SmokEnder participants attend nine weekly meetings of two hours each. Reunions and other reinforcement contact is provided after the last meeting.	Average cost $175 per program
Five Day Plans Seventh Day Adventist Church	Programs usually include lectures, inspirational messages, films, and group interaction. Some use scare tactics and aversion therapy. Participants are urged to keep personal records, force	1½ to 2 hours for five consecutive days.	$3 to $10

Programs	Brief Description	Duration	Cost
	fluids, stay in frequent contact with "buddies," avoid alcohol, caffeine, other smokers, and tension-causing situations. Special diets and exercise programs are often recommended.		
Five Day Plans Schick Laboratories	Programs are available at 22 cessation centers. Aversion therapy is stressed which includes methods such as over-exposure to smoke, rapid smoking and electric shock applied to the participant's arm.	One hour for five consecutive days.	$450 with a money-back guarantee.
Five Day Live-In Program Seventh Day Adventist	At St. Helena Hospital and Health Center in Deer Park, Calif. Individual and group counselling, lectures, films, physical therapy and exercise.	One week.	$395 which covers room and board, tests, etc.
Graduated Filters Venturi Five-Week Stop Smoking System	Consists of four reusable filters which are reported to reduce tar and nicotine by 95% in the fourth filter.	Each filter is used for one week.	$4.00
Waterpik One Step At A Time	Consists of 4 reusable filters: reported to reduce tar & nicotine by 90%.	Filters are used for two weeks.	$10.00
Nu-Life Stop Smoking Kit	Consists of 44 disposable filters which are reported to gradually remove up to 96% of cigarette tar and 88% of nicotine.	One filter is to be used each day.	$10.00
Aqua-Filter	Unlike the other filters, Aqua-Filter makes no claim that its product will assist in gradual smoking withdrawal. The filters are sold 10 to a package and are supposed to eliminate all but an average of 3.15 mg. of tar and .22mg. of nicotine from each cigarette.	Each filter is to be used for 20 cigarettes.	$1.00

WHAT HAPPENS AFTER YOU QUIT SMOKING

a. Immediate rewards

Within 12 hours after you have your last cigarette, your body will begin to heal itself. The levels of carbon monoxide and nicotine in your system will decline rapidly, and your heart and lungs will begin to repair the damage caused by cigarette smoke.

Within a few days, you will begin to notice some remarkable changes in your body. Your sense of smell and taste will return. Your smoker's hack will disappear. Your digestive system will return to normal.

Most important of all, you feel really *alive*—clear-headed, full of energy and strength. You're breathing easier. You can climb a hill or a flight of stairs without becoming winded or dizzy. And you will be free from the mess, smell, inconvenience, expense and dependence of cigarette smoking.

b. Long-range benefits

Now that you've quit, you've added a number of healthy productive days to each year of your life. Most important, you've greatly improved your chances for a longer life. You've significantly reduced your risk of death from heart disease, stroke, chronic bronchitis, emphysema, and cancer.

c. Recovery symptoms

As your body begins to repair itself, instead of feeling better, you may feel worse. These "withdrawal pangs" are really symptoms of *recovery*. Immediately after quitting, many ex-smokers experience "symptoms of recovery" such as temporary weight gain caused by fluid retention, irregularity and sore gums or tongue. You may also feel edgy and more short-tempered than usual.

It is important to understand that the unpleasant aftereffects of quitting are only temporary and signal the beginning of a healthier life.

WHEN YOU CALL IT QUITS

When you call it quits, you will feel a great deal of personal satisfaction. You will have accomplished a very difficult task. And you will be rewarded in more ways than you had imagined. But, because it is a difficult challenge, you must anticipate the problems, and avoid self-pity or compromises.

The information collected in this booklet can only give you a good start. Now it's up to you. With a strong commitment, and with the support of your friends, YOU CAN QUIT SMOKING!

OTHER SOURCES OF INFORMATION ON QUITTING

American Cancer Society*
777 3rd Avenue ·
New York, New York 10017
(212) 371-2900

American Heart Association*
7320 Greenville Avenue
Dallas, Texas 75231
(214) 750-5300

American Lung Association*
1740 Broadway
New York, New York 10019
(212) 245-8000

General Headquarters
5 Day Plan To Stop Smoking
Seventh Day Adventist Church*
Narcotics Education Division
6840 Eastern Avenue, N.W.
Washington, D.C. 20012
(202) 723-0800

Office on Smoking and Health
U.S. Department of Health, Education &
  Welfare
200 Independence Avenue, S.W,
Room 622E
Washington, D.C. 20201
(202) 472-4357

National Interagency Council on Smoking and
  Health
419 Park Avenue South, Suite 1301
New York, New York 10016
(212) 532-6035

Schick Laboratories
1901 Avenue of the Stars, Suite 1530
Los Angeles, CA 90067
(212) 553-9771

smokEnders
Memorial Parkway
Phillipsburg, New Jersey 08864
(201) 454-HELP

Office of Cancer Communications
National Cancer Institute
National Institutes of Health
Bethesda, Maryland 20014
800-638-6694

*Consult your local telephone directory for listings of local chapters.

Good luck!

Aflatoxins Cancer-producing chemicals made by a natural mold.
Antibody Specific substance produced by the body as a reaction to an antigen.
Anticarcinogen An agent that offers protection against a carcinogen.
Antigen A substance that incites the formation of antibodies or an immune response.
Atypical Not typical; abnormal, as in "atypical cell."
Benign Not malignant.
Biopsy The removal and microscopic examination of tissue from the body for the purpose of diagnosis.
Cancer The general term for the disease characterized by uncontrolled cell growth.
Carcinogen A cancer-causing agent.
Carcinoma Cancers of the epithelial cells which make up the skin and line the surfaces of body organs.
Chemotherapy Treatment of cancer by chemicals (drugs).
Chromosome Small, rod-shaped bodies in the nucleus of a cell.
Cocarcinogen An agent which acts with another to cause cancer.
Cytologist A pathologist who specializes in cell identification.
DNA (deoxyribonucleic acid) One of two kinds of nucleic acid found in all cells (RNA is the other); these control life processes.
Enzyme Complex organic compounds (proteins) produced within an organism to accelerate a chemical reaction; a catalyst.
Estrogen A female sex hormone.
Gene A segment of a chromosome which contains a unit of genetic information.
Hodgkin's disease Cancer of the lymphatic system.
Hormone A chemical substance produced in one part of the body which is transported in body fluids to another part where it exerts a specific effect.
Iatrogenic An illness produced by a physician or by medication.
Immunity The power of a living organism to resist infection.

Immunotherapy   Treatment of cancer by increasing the response of the body's immune system.

Interferon   Special proteins made by cells to fight virus infection.

Ionizing radiation   Radiation which separates molecules into charged particles (ions), such as X ray; causes physical and genetic damage to the body when administered in excessive amounts.

Lesion   A localized, abnormal structure in the body.

Leukemia   Cancer of the blood-forming organs such as bone marrow, characterized by a marked increase in the number of white blood cells (leukocytes) in the blood.

Lymph   An almost colorless liquid composed of tissue fluid, proteins, and some blood cells found in the lymphatic vessels of the body.

Lymphoma   Cancer of the lymph tissue, which is part of the body's immune system.

Malignant   Life-threatening; applies to any serious disease; "malignant hypertension" is life-threatening high blood pressure.

Melanoma   A serious skin tumor usually containing dark pigment.

Metastasis (pronounced me-TAS-ta-sis)   The transfer of disease from one part of the body to another; in cancer, the spread of malignant cells which starts a new growth of the same type as the original tumor.

Neoplasm   Any abnormal formation or growth, either benign or malignant.

Nitrosamines   Natural chemicals which cause cancer in animals and probably in man.

Oncologist   A physician specializing in tumors; a cancer specialist.

Pap smear   A technique developed by Dr. George N. Papanicolaou for detection of atypical and malignant cells through microscopic examination of cells collected from the vagina, cervix, and uterus; now used to examine cells from any part of the body.

Polyp   A mass of swollen tissue projecting into a body cavity.

Radiation therapy   The use of X rays, electrons, neutrons, gamma rays, etc., to destroy malignant tumors.

RNA (ribonucleic acid)   One of two kinds of nucleic acid found in the body (see DNA).

Sarcoma   Cancer of the supporting structures of the body such as bone, cartilage, and muscle.

Tumor   An abnormal mass of tissue; may be benign or malignant.

Tumor promoter   A substance that promotes the growth of a tumor.

Bibliography

Alexander, J. W., and Good, R. A. *Immunobiology for Surgeons.* Philadelphia: W. B. Saunders Company, 1970.

American Cancer Society. *Cancer Facts & Figures, 1980.* New York, 1979.

American Cancer Society Symposium. "Nutrition in the Causation of Cancer." In *Cancer Research,* vol. 35, no. 11, pt. II, November 1975.

American Cancer Society. Report of the National Commission on Smoking and Public Policy. *A National Dilemma: Cigarette Smoking or the Health of Americans.* New York, 1978.

Beattie, Edward J., Jr., ed. *The Surgical Clinics of North America,* vol. 54, no. 4, Philadelphia: W. B. Saunders Company, 1974.

Bok, Sissela. *Lying: Moral Choice in Public and Private Life.* New York: Pantheon Books, 1978.

Borberg, H., Oettgen, H. F., Choudry, K., and Beattie, E. J., Jr. "Inhibition of Established Transplants of Chemically Induced Sarcomas in Syngeneic Mice by Lymphocytes From Immunized Donors." *International Journal of Cancer,* 1972.

Department of Public Health, Tohoku University School of Medicine, Sendai, Japan: *Cancer Mortality for Selected Sites in 24 Countries,* no. 5, 1969.

Foley, K. M. "The Management of Pain of Malignant Origin." In H. R. Tyler and D. M. Dawson, eds., *Current Neurology,* vol. 2. Boston: Houghton Mifflin Company, 1979.

Foley, K. M. "Pain Syndromes in Patients with Cancer." In J. J. Bonica and V. Ventafridda, eds., *Advances in Pain Research and Therapy,* vol. 2. New York: Raven Press, 1979.

Good, R. A., Fernandes, G., and West, M. A. "Nutrition, Immunity, and Cancer—a Review. Pt. I: Influence of Protein or Protein-Calorie Malnutrition and Zinc Deficiency on Immunity." *Clinical Bulletin,* vol. 9, no. 1. New York: Memorial Sloan-Kettering Cancer Center, 1979.

Houde, R. W. "Cancer Pain in the Head and Heck: Role of Analgesics and Related Drugs." In J. J. Bonica and V. Ventafridda, eds., *Advances in Pain Research and Therapy,* vol. 2. New York: Raven Press, 1979, pp. 533–35.

———. "Systemic Analgesics and Related Drugs. Narcotic Analgesics. *Ibid.,* pp. 263–73.

———. "Visceral and Perineal pain: Role of Analgesics and Related Drugs." *Ibid.,* pp. 593–95.

Laws, Priscilla. *Medical and Dental X-rays.* Washington, D.C.: Health Research Group, 1974.

Mason, T. J., et al. *Atlas of Cancer Mortality for U.S. Counties, 1950–1969.* U.S. Dept. of Health, Education and Welfare, DHEW Pub. No. NIH 75-780, 1975.

Miller, Elizabeth C. *Some Current Perspectives on Chemical Carcinogenesis in Humans and Experimental Animals.* Address given before American Association for Cancer Research, Denver, Colo., 1977.

National Advisory Cancer Council. *Progress Against Cancer.* Washington, D.C.: Department of Health, Education and Welfare (Public Health Service), 1970.

President's Biomedical Research Panel. *The Place of Biomedical Science in Medicine.* Washington, D.C., 1976.

Schloen, L. H., et al. "Nutrition, Immunity, and Cancer—a Review. Pt. II: Zinc, Immune Function and Cancer." *Clinical Bulletin,* vol. 9, no. 2. New York: Memorial Sloan-Kettering Cancer Center, 1979.

Schottenfeld, David. *Cancer Epidemiology and Prevention.* Springfield, Ill.: Charles C. Thomas, Publisher, 1975.

———, and Haas, J. F. "The Workplace As a Cause of Cancer—pt. I." *Clinical Bulletin,* vol. 8, no. 2. New York: Memorial Sloan-Kettering Cancer Center, 1978.

———. "The Workplace As a Cause of Cancer—Part II." *Ibid.,* vol. 8, no. 3, 1978.

Seydel, H. G., Chait, A., and Gmelich, J. T. *Cancer of the Lung.* New York: John Wiley & Sons, 1975.

Stoddard, Sandol. *The Hospice Movement: A Better Way of Caring for the Dying.* New York: Vintage Books, a division of Random House. 1978.

Thomas, Lewis. *The Lives of a Cell.* New York: The Viking Press, 1974.

———. *The Medusa and the Snail.* New York: The Viking Press, 1979.

The Tobacco Institute. *The Smoking Controversy.* Washington, D.C., 1978.

Toxic Substances Strategy Committee. *Report to the President.* Draft. Washington, D.C., 1979.

U.S. Department of Health, Education and Welfare. *Cancer Patient Survival.* Report no. 5, DHEW Pub. No. NIH 77-992.

Wynder, Ernst L. "Environmental Carcinogenesis." *Clinical Bulletin,* vol. 8, no. 1. New York: Memorial Sloan-Kettering Cancer Center, 1978.

———, and Hoffman, Dietrich. *Tobacco and Tobacco Smoke.* New York: Academic Press, 1967.

———, and Stellman, S. D. "Impact of Long-term Filter Cigarette Usage on Lung and Larynx Cancer Risk. A Case-Control Study." *Journal of National Cancer Institute,* vol. 62, no. 3, March 1979, pp. 471–77.